Cultivating Congress

STUDIES IN GOVERNMENT
AND PUBLIC POLICY

Cultivating Congress
Constituents, Issues, and Interests in Agricultural Policymaking

William P. Browne

 University Press of Kansas

© 1995 by the University Press of Kansas
All rights reserved

Published by the University Press of Kansas (Lawrence, Kansas 66049), which was organized by the Kansas Board of Regents and is operated and funded by Emporia State University, Fort Hays State University, Kansas State University, Pittsburg State University, the University of Kansas, and Wichita State University

Library of Congress Cataloging-in-Publication Data

Browne, William Paul, 1945–
    Cultivating Congress : constituents, issues, interests, and
agricultural policy / William P. Browne.
        p.   cm.—(Studies in government and public policy)
    Includes index.
    ISBN 0-7006-0700-5 (cloth)—ISBN 0-7006-0701-3 (pbk.)
    1. Agriculture and state—United States.   2. Agriculture and
politics—United States.   I. Title.   II. Series.
HD1761.B728   1995
338.1'873—dc20   94-40790

British Library Cataloguing in Publication Data is available.

Printed in the United States of America

10 9 8 7 6 5 4 3 2 1

CONTENTS

FIGURES AND TABLES

PREFACE

This book is about interest politics but not about organized groups. It focuses on how members of Congress and their staffs pursue their own interests in making policy, merging their interests with those of constituents. Most significantly, it shows how members use information and sources of information as they engage in the tasks of representing people, places, groups, and various levels of policy ideas. The theme is that Congress is a reactive institution, organized and bounded by public policies and rules that limit its members' choices, and the emphasis of the theme, as it develops throughout the book, is on reacting to constituents as one among many groups who cultivate Congress. A secondary concern is to explain the limits members face in their own highly individualistic decision making.

The book borrows from but does not entirely agree with two perspectives on Congress: the primacy of reelection and the importance of member discretion. Both views are integrated into the text throughout, but I also emphasize how members use their limited policy discretion to represent those with whom they are most familiar and dependent. Even members of Congress who are preparing to leave that institution tend to think of home first.

There are significant questions about how Congress operates in the 1990s. As Kenneth Shepsle notes, our textbook notions of the way policy is handled within Congress are changing,[1] and institutionally, Congress is indeed different today than it has been in the past. Individual members face an institutional uncertainty that gives them an unprecedented ability to make highly personal choices on the basis of distinct interests. I will explore how Congress has changed in its policy responsiveness because of increased individualism and a more opportunity-laden policy environment.

The idea is well accepted that interactive networks made up of regular participants from Congress, the administration, organized interests, and assorted other nooks and crannies of a complex Washington environment matter collectively in policymaking. Most of that acceptance is premised on the assumption that routine meetings produce policy results because getting together matters. These results, presumably, reflect the exclusivity of the networks and the specialized expertise and authority of their participants. To a great extent, this book adds to the network—or, as some say, the "iron triangle" or subgovernment—literature because it deals with the involvement and influence of very nonspecialized players in core issues of different policy networks. In particular, I suggest changes in how contemporary networks operate and affect the Congress without their prior specialization and influence. Much of the analysis in the following chapters leads to the conclusion that members of Congress respond first to their districts and to specific and familiar informants in or from those geographic places.[2] In the sense that Congress is changing, the shifts are attributed largely to factors of place, or district, as they are served more forcefully under modern structural arrangements than they appear to have been in the past, and it is these dynamics that undermine the exclusivity and specialization of congressional network participation.

The context for my analysis of congressional involvement is to consider agricultural policy a domain of public decision making, which includes rural policies. The domain idea is very simple, yet theoretically in need of further development. Basically, the policies and issues of a domain are considered as a single entity, which is bounded by the prevailing institutional order of congressional committee and administrative agency jurisdictions as well as the integrating mechanisms of the budget process. Yet, unlike networks, no one set of players routinely meets in an attempt to bring order. Thus, domains reflect institutional configurations of rules while networks are organized around specific behaviors.

In a practical sense, domain policies are what congressional participants treat as a holistic, though certainly not coordinated, package. Numerous policy networks are active in any domain, and in this book, particularly in the last chapters, I show that the failure to develop meaningful rural policies is a problem inherent in domain politics. A rural policy network has basically not evolved because certain farm issues, with a collectively defined domain purpose, historically have crowded other rural initiatives off the policy agenda. Little in the way of a policy base exists to sustain rural network activity, and in part, the crowding out of rural advocates explains continued long-term congressional neglect of things labeled rural.

The more contemporary part of the problem of rural neglect is that constituents in rural places seldom organize around generic rural issues, preferring instead to deal with more location-specific problems of their own home places. This behavior, however, is linked to the previous patterns of policy neglect. Specifically, if there were a more extensive base of programs, they could be modified to achieve a more rewarding place-specific distribution, and rural residents, then, would be more inclined to express their feelings and concerns about rural problems to their members of Congress.

Obviously, the treatment of all of these topics must be interdependent. To attempt to understand the reactions of Congress without emphasizing who it is that members and staff react to and what they react about is largely futile. This book, even with its theoretical focus, attempts to be very specific. My intent is to remove the abstractions that are so inherent in many studies of congressional institutions and behavior, without resorting to a case study, and an extensive range of systematically collected data is used in the explanation and analysis of how Congress operates in its management of the agricultural policy domain.

In no small part, this book is a sequel, or at least a second-stage study of political interests, to an earlier book on interest groups as suppliers of information.[3] That earlier work leaves open the questions, How do the users respond? and Why are organized interests so careful about what information they provide to Congress and other policymakers? Agricultural lobbyists and activists are selective about more than just the spin, or biasing, they give their information. They avoid a considerable number of seemingly relevant arguments, types of information, issues, and entire public policy decisions, and even when one group takes a public stand on an issue or a pending decision, there may well be no lobbying follow-up or any acknowledgment to public officials that the statement matters at all. Indeed, interest representatives often acknowledge their posturing on such occasions and candidly note—from behind closed doors—that they really don't care a great deal for what they expressed publicly. As in election campaigns, such statements appear to be like thirty-second sound bites whose life span ends as soon as they are broadcast.

In my earlier book, I showed that a lobby's selective use of information and selective attention to issues and policy decisions result from strategic considerations. In particular, a successfully organized interest lobbies from an issue niche, a well-considered range of issues that it feels compelled to address for reasons of its own political legitimacy and credibility.[4] Other issues are routinely excluded, partly because the organized interest's resources are limited but also because addressing them might mean the organization would lose credibility in the eyes of policy-makers.

What this behavior suggests is obvious. Apparently there are many things that members and the staffs of Congress simply do not want to hear from any particular interest group that they use as an information source. To put the matter another way, otherwise reactive congressional members will listen and respond to only some things. What are these messages? Why do they get attention? How does this fact affect public policy deliberations? And, of course, what else preempts some issues and policies? These are the questions that emanated from my previous study of interest groups to be dealt with in this book. It is also the importance of those questions that makes this book of interest to more than just a variety of political scientists, even though the political science audience is still the major one. No one has explained the relationship between policy networks and the structural changes that have taken place in the era of a postreform Congress, and I hope that this book will fill a theoretical and empirical void in both the policy network and the literature dealing with Congress.

Two other audiences, the analytical agricultural-policy audience and the rural-policy-advocacy audience, get nearly equal treatment. Both face applied problems because of limited and inadequate information about Congress, about what its members listen to, and why. To an extent, the two audiences overlap. Agricultural-policy specialists include agricultural economists, rural sociologists, some natural scientists, and numerous administrators and staff professionals of assorted background within government, from universities, and from the private sector. As part of a functional agricultural establishment, these policy players address an incredibly wide array of policies and issues, from farm price supports to environmental degradation. They do theoretical analysis, applied research, education, outreach, and policy implementation. Some are influential, some serve merely to justify the politically desirable positions of others. Congress matters, however, to their collective work, and they need to understand better the set of congressional institutions.

The agricultural-policy audience tends to rely exceptionally on old truths and myths often misapplied in understanding Congress and public policymaking.[5] Traditionalists tend to see policymaking as driven primarily by the force of electoral numbers.[6] Thus, with a shrinking farm population, traditionalists seek urgently to expand the services provided by their establishment. Others, particularly economists who hold a narrow view of public-choice analysis, see the policy process as driven by mischievous and monolithic interest groups—conceptualized by these scholars as extractive rent-seekers—that promote inefficiencies and a lack of economy in public programs. They are, therefore, the recognizable villains in whatever policy failures the processes of government create.[7] Policy reformers, though not unanimous in affixing blame for policy failures, tend to agree with that view.[8] As readers will see, I indirectly refute each of these positions, concluding instead that Congress produces very much what the interested public wants. If agricultural policies are uncoordinated and often fail to realize the claims rhetorically made for them, these results occur because the grassroots public that uses these many programs is diverse and splintered by place and sector. Moreover, within that changing public, the old farm clientele of Congress retains a great deal of very legitimate influence.

Rural-policy advocates are mostly outside the agricultural-policy audience, often from non-land grant universities and from nonagricultural government agencies. But, because they work largely within the policies of the agricultural domain, their commitment to rural rather than to farm issues keeps them peripheral participants in the policy process. Within the current expansion of agricultural establishment services, rural advocates and their issues are taking on useful if quite restricted importance. They offer another new approach to providing relevant services through the agricultural establishment. As a result, a much smaller but equally wide-ranging band of rural advocates are networking with considerable difficulty alongside other issue advocates in agriculture.[9] Although many in Congress and the administration have encouraged them to interact and plan, rural advocates have been faintly rewarded. Often their initiatives have been brutally rejected. In no small part I intend to demonstrate here to these advocates why their policy rewards are so few. Understanding the reasons for their limited success and realizing more about the importance of particular rather than generic local places will, I hope, lead them to strategies and tactics better than merely networking among the experts.

Careful readers will note that the three audiences and the structure of this book are quite compatible. There is no need to assemble a patchwork quilt of ideas to satisfy the needs of each audience; quite the contrary. The focus on network interactions and domain consequences brings the topics of academic concern directly to bear on the problems of the book's second and third audiences, with two caveats. First, my perspective is primarily that of political science, the discipline wherein much of my theoretical basis lies. However, I also borrow heavily from economics, a discipline that has long given considerable attention to agriculture and its policies.

Second, given my emphasis on nondisciplinary problems, I often provide what may seem to many to be simple and unnecessary clarifications; such processes as log rolling, vote trading, and coalition building are not always understood by everyone to have the same meaning, even among those actively engaged in them. An elaboration on agricultural policy implications may seem too long for political scientists. Other readers, I trust, will excuse what may seem for them to be a few wasted elaborations.

ACKNOWLEDGMENTS

No book can be completed by just the author, and many people and a few organizations contributed to this one. First among the contributors were those who provided background information and insights: nearly 150 members of Congress, legislative staff, agency personnel, and interest group representatives as this study was organized and designed and another 115 individuals after the project began. In addition, the members and their staffs in 113 congressional enterprises—i.e., personal offices—cooperated with formal and very structured interviews, and when the book was well under way, 54 members and 133 staff members from respondent offices discussed a long list of questions. In addition, several other staff members of House and Senate leaders patiently answered questions and offered constructive comments. Almost all of these respondents were courteous, generous, and candid.

I owe a special obligation to the entire House Agriculture Committee, but especially then-chairman Kika de la Garza and ranking member Pat Roberts. They put up with me during a three-day committee retreat when my insights to them were a hardly sufficient return for their insights to me. Although the conversations there were all in confidence and off-the-record, what was said there was a vital testing ground for my ideas. I also owe thanks to a few members who reacted to what I was writing in more direct fashion as I posed ideas to them before and after the retreat. Former Secretary of Agriculture Mike Espy and his senior policy staff get the same thanks, as many of their ideas added to the final version of my manuscript.

Thanks are also due to the people who helped give credibility to the project by intervening with the respondents. Former Secretaries of Agriculture Bob Bergland and Richard Lyng each wrote personal letters to members of Congress to encourage their cooperation. George "Ed" Rossmiller, then Director of the National Center for Food and Agriculture Policy (NCFAP), did the same thing. Susan Sechler and her staff at the Aspen Institute made numerous calls to arrange background meetings.

Both Susan and Ed listened carefully to ideas that I bounced off them during the field research, as did John Lee, former administrator of the Economic Research Service (ERS).

Susan, Ed, and John were also key patrons of this project. ERS, as the policy-analysis branch of the U.S. Department of Agriculture, nurtured the entire effort through three slow years of development grants. This support enabled the Ford Foundation, through the Rural Economic Policy Program of Aspen, to undertake major funding for field research. That funding allowed me to spend most of 1991 in Washington, D.C. NCFAP and Resources for the Future generously provided office facilities. NCFAP also allowed use of its staff and equipment. The Everett M. Dirksen Congressional Leadership Research Center provided additional funds to look at the intervention of congressional leadership. Central Michigan University allowed released time for parts of the project. In addition to CMU's support of a sabbatical leave for writing, that university's Research Professor Program and its Institute for Social and Behavioral Studies also provided released time for, respectively, data collection and grant preparation.

Several people at CMU deserve special thanks for getting this project completed. Debra Ervin, in particular, made it work by carefully preparing the manuscript and then getting a final draft. Rosemary Thelen helped as well, as did Beth, Brian, Holly, Melissa, Shelly, Ruth, Teri, and Theresa as slaves of the typing pool. Won K. Paik served as methodological brewmaster and co-authored three papers from the survey data set. Noelle Schiffer, now with the Engineering Society of Detroit, did initial data entry and managed logistics on-campus. Dennis Pompilius arranged graphics, Douglas Spathelf managed grants, and Delbert J. Ringquist ran interference effectively as chair of the Department of Political Science. Del's work has always been particularly instrumental to my research by keeping my life otherwise simplified through his excellent administration.

A group of scholars deserve profound thanks. James T. Bonnen, David Rohde, and Robert H. Salisbury assisted in construction of the survey questionnaire. All commented on and critiqued parts of manuscripts from the project. Jim commented on every line. Frank Baumgartner, Burdett A. Loomis, and Eric M. Uslaner helped greatly, cleaning up my obscurities. Other valued manuscript comments were offered by David G. Abler, Jeffrey M. Berry, Allan J. Cigler, Willard W. Cochrane, Richard F. Fenno, Jr., Don F. Hadwiger, Dale Hathaway, John R. Hibbing, Kenneth J. Meier, David C. Nixon, David B. Schweikhardt, Jerry R. Skees,

Louis E. Swanson, and David J. Webber. Kristen Allen helped with interviews and, along with Schweikhardt, in putting together a related essay.

One academic contributor stands out: David Hadwiger, now of the University of New Mexico, who served as full-time scheduler for most of this project. Sitting at NFCAP, and trying to write a dissertation, he played telephone tag, opened doors, argued for entry, scheduled and rescheduled meetings, and always got the interviewer to the right place at the right time.

Institutional support of the usual and unusual variety needs final acknowledgment. Fred Woodward and his staff at the University Press of Kansas gave both support and suggestions on making this a much better book. Such assistance is indeed usual for them, and the reason I wanted to publish another book with that press. Unusual support came from the medical staff of the University of Texas M.D. Anderson Hospital, particularly Moshe Talpaz, who kept me up and well so I could finish this project—and get on with new ones.

A GUIDE TO KEY TERMS

Bentley's Theory of Groups. Arthur F. Bentley saw politics as being conducted by groupings of those who share a collective interest in whatever decision is at hand. Thus, the group as an ad hoc network must be understood in terms of its interest. Bentley's theory suggests that policy players do not network, or form groups, just because they are organized or in a formal position to be involved. Even when organized, individuals or groups may not be interested in a policy or issue, so they may fail to network when expected.

Congressional or Member Enterprises. The individual office of each member and his or her personal staff, organized to promote rank-and-file entrepreneurism and other personalized tasks, are congressional or member enterprises. Enterprises are often compared to "small businesses."

Entrepreneurial Congressional Members. Those who seize the opportunities provided by postreform rules and become proponents and advocates of particular public policies or parts of them are entrepreneurial congressional members.

Home-Style Work. The efforts of congressional enterprises, from maintaining caseworkers to attending local events, that go into creating a favorable member image in the home district or state, are home-style work.

The Individualistic Congress. The postreform Congress is noted for being member driven. With influence more widely shared under postreform procedures, rank-and-file members have become more comfortable in challenging one another and various legislative authorities.

Institutional Rules. The procedures of Congress, which govern behavior and allocate House and Senate resources (including influence), are institutional rules.

The Iron Triangle (Subgovernment) Metaphor. The "Iron Triangle" is an analogy for the three-part policy network that "everyone knows to be true." Over time, the assumption of social scientists has been that only a few policy players, including congressional committee members, key lobbyists, and the agency officials who implement programs, dominate any single public policy. Others have been seen as largely excluded from these specialized, tripartite networks.

Issue Initiatives. These initiatives are the actions of a congressional enterprise taken to advance an issue within a policy vehicle; they are taken to create public policy (substantive rules) one piece at a time.

Issues. Issues are the exact substantive topics of political interest for any network or any policy player; or, what someone wants in law. Any public policy will be composed of numerous issues, often not well coordinated with one another.

Maintenance Initiatives. Initiatives that are taken to build on or protect existing public policies, thus preserving previous policy directions, are maintenance initiatives.

Networking. Networking is the interactive behavior of those who are trying to influence public policy; being involved with the other players. Those interested in the same policy move in the same networks.

Norms. Norms are informally agreed-on procedural rules that, by congressional consensus, govern member behavior and prescribe appropriate behavior. Norms are supplemental to institutional rules and appear to be less important in the postreform Congress than in the days of strong committees.

Originating Initiatives. Initiatives that seek to change, or reform, some part or parts of public policy within a domain are originating initiatives. Originating issues lead to new policy directions.

Policy Domains. A domain is a policy area of government with its own substantive focus. Although the policy community is defined by potential policy players, domains are defined by a common set of issues, policies, and institutions that are treated as a single entity by government. Agricultural policy is a domain of interest bounded by the prevailing institutional order of congressional committee and administrative agency jurisdictions as well as by the integrative mechanisms of the budgetary process. Domains, because they reflect institutional rules, are not networks in that no single set of players routinely need meet to order their policy decisions. Domains are maintained by rules, whereas networks are maintained by players.

Policy Games. Policy games are ongoing contests over well-defined and commonly understood issues by competing policy players within or even between policy domains. Policy games exist only when interests are clearly understood as central to the continued allocation of at least some of the domain's public policy benefits.

Policy Players. Those whose interests are served by influencing public policy, and who take an active role in the policy process as a result, are policy players.

Policy Vehicles. A policy vehicle is the substantive mechanism by which issues become law or institutional rule. Bills, legislative oversight, appropriations, and administrative and regulatory decisions are all but vehicles through which public policies are made.

The Postreform Congress. This term refers to Congress after the procedural reforms of the 1970s, which (1) weakened committee autonomy, (2) vested more influence in individual members, (3) turned over much policy control to subcommittees, and (4) strengthened party leaders. Congressional influence, in consequence, is widely shared.

Specialization, Division of Labor, Expertise, and Reciprocity. These terms refer to norms of Congress that once ensured considerable committee autonomy by promoting adherence to committee jurisdictions over distinct types of policy. Members of Congress specialized in policy areas and respected the opinions and conclusions of others who did the same on other issues. These norms have been in particular eclipse in the postreform Congress, opening the way to greater rank-and-file influence over a wider range of policy.

The Washington Policy Community. This community is the collection of agencies, interest groups, congressional and executive personnel, and foundations and consultants who tend to network regularly on different areas of public policy.

Washington Work. The efforts of congressional enterprises that go into policymaking and congressional leadership, largely centered on committee and party caucus responsibilities, are Washington work.

PART ONE
The Politics of a Postreform Era

This is a new Congress. Old centers of power exist, but those who hold them do so through clever negotiation, juggling a little bit for everyone. The capacity to make another member do something is gone. They listen to their districts.
            —A senior Appropriations Committee staff member commenting on
            the biggest change in Congress.

1

Congress and Policy Networks in a Postreform Era

I had a job in college. It was cleaning plates from the dining room. My job in Congress is a lot like that—shovel, rinse, and get on with the next one. I'm the only one who can decide how to select and handle what needs to be done, along with my staff, of course.
—A junior member of Congress, discussing the frequency and diversity of issues of personal importance, the many sources of demands on those issues, and the impersonal way they need be considered even while playing a lead role on them.

Congressmen Steve Gunderson (R-Wis.) and Kweisi Mfume (D-Md.) appear to be congressional opposites. The collegial Scandinavian served as one of his party's chief deputy whips and played an important policy role within the House Republican Conference. Mfume, with his Black Power past, took over as chair of the Congressional Black Caucus in 1992 and diversified its issue interests. But in addition to both being leaders in Washington politics, Gunderson and Mfume are both skilled players in converting the problems of their district constituents into public policy. Gunderson, from the nation's number-one dairy district, worked successfully to create more equity for his local farmers by changing the milk marketing order pricing formula. Reversal of the Eau Claire basing point, as a single issue in a larger bill, won new fans in the district. Mfume, without benefit of Gunderson's House Agriculture Committee seat, became a player in agricultural policy—and did so for his constituents. In Mfume's case, he initiated a General Accounting Office report criticizing the Maryland-based Agricultural Research Service Center of the U.S. Department of Agriculture (USDA) for not hiring African Americans.

Like Gunderson's, Mfume's aim was to put more dollars in the pockets of his constituents.

But better dairy prices in Wisconsin or more African-American jobs in Maryland are not unusual policy goals for agriculture or in Congress. Some agricultural programs are even more plentiful cornucopias for those back home. For instance, new agricultural trade programs that will involve subsidies for commodities and products create a rush whenever Congress or USDA considers their enactment, as members of Congress flock to deliver federal dollars to support marketing assistance for designated crops and brandnames that are important in their districts and states.

All of these congressional efforts have an important impact on public policy. The bits and pieces become the whole, as building blocks of evolving programs. The net result is that most members constantly shuffle myriad issues, just as the congressman above once rapidly moved through his college dishes. The Gundersons and Mfumes are the rule, not the exception. Changes in the modern Congress have made it easier for members to listen to local constituents and ignore such traditionally influential players as interest groups and government agencies. But Congress has not been solely responsible for this change in emphasis. Because members of Congress only structure the proposals that others bring them, changes in the House and Senate only reflect a more general evolution in politics.[1]

Members of Congress do their considerable business under uncertain circumstances. What Richard F. Fenno, Jr., describes as "home-style" politics has been practiced on Capitol Hill more widely than in the past because members are extraordinarily unsure as to who in the Washington policy community most helps them.[2] The reason for that uncertainty is quite simple: members live and work in both the district and Washington, in nearly equal amounts of time and throughout the year. Accordingly, they network extensively in both places. The expectations of district constituents, committee chairs, subcommittee members, and the leadership prevail on them in both places.[3] So, too, do the actions of other policy players: interest groups, research institutes, public agencies, and administration officials. The interplay of forces is intense, affecting both campaigns and policymaking.

Members of the modern Congress resolve their uncertainties by seeking safety in the home district, by keeping selected home folks happy with the local effects of national public policymaking. As one member said, "in case of disagreement, choose your local voter." Changes in

Congress and changes in the broader policy community explain this choice.

THE CHANGING CONGRESS: AN INDIVIDUAL PERSPECTIVE

Congress in the 1990s is tailored to meeting its individual members' interests, but without radically altering institutions of earlier eras. It still makes sense to think of campaigning and governing as two separate processes that drive individual senators and representatives.[4] The sequence of campaigning and governing recur repeatedly to shape congressional behavior. The cumulative effects of Washington and the district are mutually reinforcing, blurring the impact of two competing congressional worlds. Members therefore adjust to a single identity and wear it. For example, Robert K. Dornan (R-Calif.) wears the nickname "B-1 Bob" because he supports both aerospace industries back home and hawkish national defense stands in Washington; Gunderson maintains intense policy interests; and Mfume stays directed to expanding issues on behalf of African Americans. Thus, no clear distinction exists between the perpetual campaign for reelection and the processes of governing. Fenno, in discussing governing processes, finds congressional committees integrating members into highly functional units with shared policy values.[5] Yet, he also discovers that (1) not all committees are well integrated and that (2) successful integration depends on the degree to which individualized member goals are satisfied through cooperation.[6]

This discovery indicates that, within committees, members react to more than just institutional rules and expectations that promote cohesive and deliberative governance. They react as well to a highly individualized agenda that emphasizes good constituent relations. To further constituent relations, members help write procedural rules that "are devised to accommodate personal goals to the constraints of the environment."[7] Merging home and Washington is far from an impossible dream.

Changing Rules in the House

District-inspired behavior has become easier as procedures have changed. Institutional rules in the House of Representatives at the time of Fenno's studies allowed committee chairs far more power to limit members than they do today. Claiming their seats via seniority into the early 1970s, chairs were able to propose legislation, set committee agendas, and refuse any member or proposal they wished. They had central control, which discouraged following the most blatant of constituent interests. A strong chair could put forth a coordinated set of national policy goals, even if those reflected the needs of his own region. But committees and their chairs no longer constrain the entrepreneurial tendencies of individuals in either the House or the Senate.[8]

The postreform congressional era began modestly in 1971. Both evolving procedural reforms and the accommodation of informal norms to contemporary member needs followed, and the House changed.[9] The reforms of 1971–1977, which are best known for the "subcommittee bill of rights," were an idiosyncratic chain of single-party events[10] in response to tensions in the Democratic party between younger liberals and traditional partisans, who included a vastly disproportionate number of conservative committee chairs from the South. The result changed much of the calculus for pursuing individual congressional goals.

Changes made for two differences from the prereform Congress that many observers mistakenly still see in existence. The first difference furthers rank-and-file member influence at the expense of that of committee chairs. Legislation now goes to the subcommittees, which have authority over hearings and markup procedures, and adequate staff and budgets for their own review. The entire committee caucus has authority over subcommittee jurisdictions and numbers, with election of committee chairs by secret ballot without regard to seniority. This democratizes the processes of the committee, makes chairs dependent on member goodwill rather than the reverse, creates far more chairs because there are so many subcommittees, and, thus, dissipates chair influence. Authority over increasingly narrow parts of policy are also institutionalized at a more decentralized and even fragmented level. Partisanship increases on more issues, too, as chairs lose the capacity to squelch conflicts in behalf of committee unity.[11]

Related reforms open the floor process to more amendments and threats of them, by both lessening the likelihood of unrecorded votes and restraining the Rules Committee. This openness makes it easier for individuals to offer proposals successfully. More rank-and-file members raise more issues to produce more decisions than ever. They also introduce their issues earlier in the process,[12] making any bill less manageable and its content less predictable. With the legislative process open ended throughout, modern subcommittees are more responsive to members' concerns than prereform committees. There are fewer opportunities for an offended chair to be punitive, and members can threaten to form floor coalitions that can now do more than merely challenge a final floor vote or a restricted number of amendments.

The second postreform difference changes leadership rules. The Speaker of the House gains greater influence, particularly with regard to managing legislative workload and determining who gets assignments. When jurisdictional questions arise, generally because of issue overlap, the leadership can have the bill referred to more than one committee.[13] Also, the Speaker can assign task forces to supplement committees of jurisdiction.[14] Both options give the leadership the ability to expand coverage of any problem or policy. Referrals to two or more committees, either concurrently or in sequence, are particularly important to the leadership. As with structuring of votes by the House Rules Committee, multiple referrals help congressional leaders control the flow of legislation. Such referrals also add something else: they allow more members the occasion to get involved in their own committees on atypical issues. This increased involvement enhances individualism, as fostered by the leadership, and it creates greater committee responsiveness to the general values of the House membership. For example, hearings held on pesticides in other committees prompted the agriculture committee to address the problem more seriously.

As this example suggests, leadership influences are balanced by that of the rank and file under postreform rules. Current party leaders are more accountable to the Democratic Caucus, which further enhances the potential policy influence of the rank and file as well as that of the party: caucus majorities now elect subcommittee chairs of the Appropriations Committee; a minority of caucus members can request meetings on any policy or procedural question; and, finally, the caucus gains greater influence over who holds committee seats with the transfer of assigning them from Democratic Ways and Means Committee members to a steering committee. The Speaker shares influence by acquiring appointment and removal powers covering a majority of the new Steering and Policy Committee positions.[15] Committee operations are not much different for Republicans.

Each of these institutional changes in the House contributes to the complexity of the individual representative's Washington world—where more people matter to one's career. Yet each one matters less than did strong committee chairs of an earlier era. These changes intensify the importance for each member of making satisfying choices. No longer is it always useful to follow the once-accepted norms of specialized attention to committee assignments, development of policy expertise, and deference to the actions of other members. The norms supporting such behavior fell along with the old rules for strong committees. Because these norms set many of the conditions for congressional behavior, the sense of obligation to the House is less.

Changing Norms in the Senate

The Senate changed significantly as well as the House, but without reform as the catalyst. In the 1950s, only a few members carried considerable personal influence in the Senate. The behavior of all senators was quite constrained in, as Barbara Sinclair puts it, a "committee-centered, member-expertise dependent" and closed world. By the 1980s, however, "decision making (took) place in multiple arenas," providing considerable latitude for members to act on behalf of a great variety of forces from outside the Senate.[16]

Change in the Senate was less by formal rules than was that in the House because the upper chamber has never been as internally rule-bound. Rigidly enforced norms long governed Senate behavior in ways that the far larger House could never duplicate. But Senate norms are also largely gone because the ones that enhanced specialization, division of labor, recognition of expertise, and reciprocity are simply outmoded by circumstances. Deferring to others no longer meets the needs of members who find it necessary to service a variety of interests. Following norms made members forfeit opportunities, and so these norms eroded. Changes in rules then followed that were much like those in the House.[17] New procedural rules provide seats on the most prominent committees to nearly all members, expand the number and influence of subcommittee chairs, restrict the powers of committee chairs, open committee deliberations, and reduce the importance of seniority. Some committee seats rotate to give more members a temporary chance to best advance their agendas. Like the House changes, Senate rule-changes advance individualism by accommodating rank-and-file members.

Staff and the Congressional Enterprise

Despite the importance to the development of congressional individualism of changes in rules and norms, increased staffing appears to be even more important to congressional change. Long before reforms were institutionalized, structural change allowed members to acquire far greater personal independence through the expansion of their individual offices into 535 "small businesses" of Congress, or what Salisbury and Shepsle call "member enterprises."[18] Although members once discussed the importance of legislative events mostly with one another, the professionalization of the member enterprise allows far greater information flow from many more sources. On average, House members have seventeen office staff employees and senators, thirty-seven.[19] Some have many more. Staff can be used to represent the member's interest in whatever comes up.

Today's modern Congress only expands the individual use of staff employees that were added in large numbers in the 1960s. Although numbers of staff have not grown rapidly in recent years, their allocation or use is different. Traditionally, some of a member's staff were given committee assignments while others were assigned to work with district or state constituents. Usually, staff attentions were restricted to their assigned world, either home or Washington.

But with committee-centered governance giving way and specialization less important, responsibilities shifted. Staff in most offices are now assigned to cover the entire range of congressional policy areas and to be involved in related constituent work as well. Staff expertise in an assigned policy area ranges from modest to extensive. The average House enterprise keeps six of its personal staff in the district, whereas senators average thirteen staff assigned to multiple offices in the state. Most staff both collect policy information and work on constituent complaints. This joint responsibility gives a greater sense of collective purpose to the office enterprise, even though policy expertise is divided among several legislative assistants.

This purposiveness means members have at least limited resources available to intervene on nearly any type of issue within any type of policy, both in the Congress and in executive branch agencies. Members can also respond to any interest group or type of constituent. In addition, staff have incentives to find projects that produce payoffs for their enterprise, for success means employees keep their at-will positions or move on to more attractive jobs as they make their reputations. Moreover, with the reallocation of committee staff to subcommittee chairs and to ranking members, available staff resources of many member enterprises are greater than office budgets indicate. The addition of associate staff to the enterprises of all senators and to those of House members on the three prestige committees—Rules, Appropriations, and Ways and Means—has the same impact. Daily assignments of extra staff are made by enterprises, tying that staff more to the members' purposes than to coordinated public policy.

Thus, increased staffing, procedural reforms, and the relaxation of norms of specialization and deference only enhance the likelihood of merging district and Washington work. Members have greater capacity to influence more policies than they did in a prereform era. As Fenno explains, creating a favorable home-style image entails allocating resources such as staff to local problems, being seen as compatible with the district voters, and explaining what goes on in Washington to them.[20] The most difficult aspect, however, is communicating to them the complexities of Washington policymaking in concrete ways because informing them about the generalities, and even many of the specifics of policymaking, is a problem.[21] The national media are useful but, for most members, carry few messages home.[22] Local media, in contrast, carry far more stories that the enterprise generates through press releases and guest columns than through diligent reporting. These stories, though, seldom grab headlines.

This cultivation of home-style image brings up the modern congressional dilemma. On the one hand, it seems inconceivable that members will not use their capacity to provide for home places. Lacking parties that will win their elections, and reliant upon independent campaigns organized to explain their actions, members find that having some accomplishment to show their constituents takes on greater importance now than it did in the 1950s and 1960s.[23] On the other hand, what can they do for the home folks that actually shows them something? Credit claiming, even without doing much, is one option.[24]

Another strategy better resolves member uncertainty, however. Members also work their attentive publics, as Gunderson and Mfume do. They do so one public at a time until the cumulative effects of serving multiple district interests pay off. They use their extensive staffs and the individually accommodative postreform rules to move from one policy domain to another in pursuit of handfuls of issues. Each issue is pursued on behalf of its own beneficiaries, who are select sets of useful or troublesome district constituents. As a member explained, "I had to study my district and then determine who I had to work with to maintain popularity."

THE CHANGING CONTEXT OF THE WASHINGTON
POLICY COMMUNITY

Congress alone has not changed in providing its members broader opportunities and in directing the enterprise to the district. Barbara Sinclair sees congressional changes rooted in a no-less-altered Washington policy community.[25] Like turn-of-the-century Tammany Hall's George Washington Plunkitt, members have to see opportunities somewhere in order to take advantage of them.[26] Some observers argue that those improved chances exist because of an "advocacy explosion" in which there are more interest groups to satisfy.[27] That argument, however, tells only part of the story and neglects home-style motives for change.

Purging Iron Triangles

To better see opportunities for members in their districts, we need to understand one myth for its tradition and convenience as well as for its decided lack of reality.[28] It focuses too much attention on the ease of conducting Washington politics. The metaphor of the iron triangle, or the subgovernment or closed policy network, has become the formula for oversimplifying the complexities of politics. A generation of network scholars has used the metaphor to account for and categorize all the institutional pieces of American politics, explaining that some pieces routinely matter and that others do not, except for exceptional circumstances.[29] Scholars look for triangles, as does the popular press.[30] These hopelessly reductionist arrangements are, as Salisbury and colleagues suspiciously note, the story that everyone knows—revealing in its bare-bones essentials.[31]

The triangle metaphor for the governing process portrays committees of Congress, executive agencies, and interest groups as the routine players, mutually dependent sets of highly autonomous decisionmakers.[32] No matter how expansive each set of players, all the players must get along with one another. Players in one policy area seldom confront or challenge those in another, even when policies overlap. Recurring problems give the different policy triangles permanence. The White House, parties, congressional leaders, and others matter to policymaking only under exceptional circumstances. They can be effective if, as Schattschneider suggests, a fight breaks out and public attention converts low-salience policy problems to ones of high salience.[33] This shift, when it happens, merges the interests of the routine and the exceptional policy players.

But government has much to do, the public is seldom attentive, and fights, then, seldom occur. Avoiding fights keeps the triangle players cozy and cooperative among themselves.[34] Little uncertainty exists for those who fall back on this metaphor or its extensions. Institutional responsibilities, the story goes, will eventually lead to cooperation and the completion of policymaking tasks. Forget the complexities of factors that limit government's responsiveness. Among a few players, everyone wins:[35] Congress gains from the resulting public support of policy beneficiaries; interest groups win because of the distribution of policy rewards to their members; and agencies benefit through stable or growing programs and budgets. This institutionally structured explanation is so nice that a new generation of scholars tinkers with it endlessly, reshaping triangles into hexagons and even transitory clouds.[36]

Oversimplification disregards the effects of rules in ways that limit understanding politics. Constitutional complexities, such as checks and balances, and their ensuing games are trivialized by the triangle metaphor and its extensions, as is changing congressional rules. With its emphasis on ongoing and institutionally stable relationships, the metaphor makes it hard to conceive of members of Congress pursuing issues and opportunities in ad hoc fashion in either a prereform or a postreform setting. Yet there is plenty of evidence of ad hoc pursuit.

Issue Fragmentation

Understanding the possibility of ad hoc member behavior means reinterpreting a common assumption about the lack of issue overlap in American politics. The most persistent reason for clinging to the triangle metaphor is the continuing need to explain why no core of central players attend to the many issues of American politics. Two early studies of issues find that numerous organized interests exercise great influence in American politics, but none of these groups ever seem to share concerns over identical issues and policies.[37] Research in the 1980s found the same pattern, even when the unit of analysis changes from government as a whole to a single policy domain, such as agriculture, or a network of participants within it, such as farm price-support proponents. Each participating interest seems to have its own issues. No central players in a domain or a network, not even a peak interest association of relatively diverse affiliates, integrate these narrow interests by providing comprehensive policy attention to otherwise disparate positions. Balkanization of issue attention is pervasive, and inconsistencies are allowed to persist into law. A hollow core rather than an inner circle characterizes the uncoordinated processes of governing.[38]

The absence of an integrative structural mechanism and the resulting lack of central attention to issues and policies do not, however, confirm the existence of institutionally induced triangles or any other shapes. Between the observation of a hollow core and the claim that the absence of centralization substantiates such elegantly simple networks is a large gap, and there is no bridge. Empirical research, using extensive data sets about who meets with whom, fails to find core triangles except in the most isolated of instances.[39]

But there is evidence to support the idea of ad hoc alliances in resolving public policies. Hugh Heclo notes a systematic ebb and flow of players in what were still principally closed political networks;[40] there were more agencies and more congressional committees involved. Later analysts, continuing this perspective on accommodation, find irregular and shifting clusters of interest groups and agency players in networks.[41] Forced strategies of entry were then found, showing unwanted interests who gain entry to network deliberations and forestall them.[42] Other studies demonstrate how public officials meet with and yield to new interests as well as old insiders.[43]

The issue-niche behavior of groups explains the expanding influence of interests within networks that are more than just friendly and compatible. From their self-selected niche, even potentially competitive groups pursue a limited range of issues with as little conflict from other players as possible.[44]

Potential competitors understand that Washington politics is not easy. Accordingly, a growing number of interest groups crowd new networks but do not necessarily forestall compromise. Instead, they adjust their issue preferences and demands to take tactical and strategic advantage of the governing processes' exceedingly hollow core. No one insists on comprehensiveness or coordinated public policy, just on politically acceptable results. Interests also use other players to facilitate their own narrow emphases. Some players are instrumental in networks, not because of their substantive policy expertise, but because they represent unique and important partisan positions or have ties, for example, to the White House or congressional leadership.[45] Private- and public-sector consultants are hired in the short-term for those contacts or for their skills in the ad hocracy of putting a network or its plans together.[46] This resort to networks makes the governing process resplendent with contests but, through accommodation, does much to mute the effects of disagreement.

Policy networking in the 1990s is not about institutional structure but rather about the answers to two questions: Who can contribute as a player? Who becomes willing and capable of playing?

Interest Group Changes

The most obvious change in breaking routines is the number of interest groups active in Washington politics. There was as much as a 700 percent increase in groups between 1947 and 1984.[47] Between 30 and 40 percent of groups active after 1960 are new.[48] Groups are not only greater in number but are also now more diverse than in the 1960s.[49] More kinds of business, trade association, and mass-membership groups have arisen as new types of industries and civic-use interests have emerged. These organizations also engage in a wider range of activities, centered on providing information to policymakers but also mobilizing the grassroots, litigating, and carrying their campaigns to the media. Even farm groups grew in number from 1977 to 1985, with new ones emphasizing grassroots lobbying and protest rather than Washington work.

Far more of the new groups are organized around broad public issues of the environment, world peace, opposition to taxes, civil rights, and assorted causes. For example, several agroenvironmental groups organized in the 1980s, challenging farm groups. Still other interests are organized to represent the disadvantaged: the poor, the handicapped, or the emotionally impaired. Much of the organizational momentum behind the proliferation of groups has come from the financial patronage of philanthropists and other organizations that contributed when masses of members fail to join. Patrons support not only liberal causes but conservative ones, especially when existing organized interests feel restrained from lobbying on some sensitive or, for them, peripheral issue.[50]

One other change, which again brings up issue niches, has created much of the fluidity of ad hoc networking. Increasingly, new groups, which often have very limited finances anyway, have taken on narrower and more selectively defined identities. Some of these groups are regional. In most instances, these narrowly interested organizations follow only parts of policy debates, pursuing the small number of issues around which the group organizes from one domain or event to another.

With the proliferation of narrow interests, older and more diffusely interested peak associations have become less relevant to policymaking when they speak on behalf of an entire occupation, profession, or segment of the economy. In comparison with more typical interests, peak associations want too much and know too little about their wide-ranging demands to be effective. Consequently, most peak associations restrict their own attention to those issues where they can maintain credibility. Or, they reduce their involvement to that of coalition builders, who wait for the right networking circumstances and engage only the most prominent issues.[51] The American Farm Bureau Federation and the American Medical Association, for example, are more media and public relations spokesgroups than they are representatives of specific solutions to farm or health care problems. Certainly neither can negotiate all interest group views— even allied ones—within the networks they enter.[52] As a congressional member stated: "The Farm Bureau . . . is a vague collection of unrelated sentiments." Why should policymakers try to resolve much with them?

Changes in Administration

Agencies elicit the same response from policymakers that peak associations do because it is unlikely that a modern public agency will become either the sole architect or service delivery operative for a policy network. Agencies also suffer another problem. To an important extent, contemporary politics between the White House and Congress strip agencies of their once cordial network relations. The changes of the past three decades bring less agency cooperation and more political control from both the White House and the Congress.[53]

Changes can be traced, in part, to greater budget and expenditure concerns of the administration. These concerns create an emphasis on the importance of organization and structure at a time when networking is more fluid. Through the Council of Economic Advisors, more administrative attention is directed to specific policy areas. In addition, the greater involvement of the President's Office of Management and Budget— which, in turn, generates more centralized congressional budget attention—brings more contentious policy involvement over specific issues than the triangle metaphor implies.[54]

Money alone is not responsible for these changes. Running parallel with congressional budget reforms begun in 1972 are shifts that create more shared agency jurisdictions over policy. New federal responsibilities for issues in the broad public interest, from consumer protection to environmental protection, mean that new offices exist throughout the federal government.[55] These offices operate as units within numerous departments and also as central agencies that coordinate or at least prompt action in several other departments.

The addition to agencies of separate units for policy analysis similarly fragments bureaucratic authority.[56] Without analysis well integrated into agency and department business, too few administrators understand the rationale and logic of ongoing or future policy. Although designed to accommodate cooperation and planning across shared policy boundaries, separate policy analysis also brings narrower and less agency-inclusive responsibilities to a wide range of administrative offices. As a result, efforts at performing new tasks fail to integrate public agencies. Narrow tasks and fewer shared purposes make problems of external and internal agency politics more severe. These problems inevitably spill over into conflicts between the White House and Congress as agency personnel try to cooperate with whoever best serves their interests.

Executive-legislative conflict matters a great deal because it creates still other conditions for procedural changes in congressional policymaking. Far more than just recent reorganizations shape the networking of administrators. Beginning with the Nixon administration, presidents of both parties and their expanded staffs have railed against the permanent government. Hostility to the bureaucracy becomes synonymous with presidential strategies for control of those who contribute to political decisions made outside the White House.[57] The increasingly ideological and partisan tone set by the Reagan administration only escalated the linkage between White House anger and the limits imposed on administrative discretion. Congress has the same effect when its members pass and fund programs that agency administrators find unnecessary or even destructive of their organizations' existing purposes.

Therefore, the assumptions about bureaucratic behavior made in the triangle metaphor are not entirely accurate. To paraphrase John Erlichman, the opportunities for career administrators to marry the other natives within the Washington policy community are now considerably fewer.[58] Political appointees find White House staff checking their performance; career appointees are limited in their ability to share expertise on issues, policies, and problems with either Congress or interest groups; they may not be allowed to participate in some forums and with certain individuals. Some networking chances are missed as a result. Nor can agency officials always speak freely when they are allowed to network.

In this hostile atmosphere more often than not, legislative liaison offices within the agencies limit and approve what agencies present and discuss. Reports are subject to increased scrutiny as are requests to do research and release the results.[59] The combined effect produces extraordinarily circumspect networking by administrators. Like members of Congress, agency officials get whipsawed by uncertainty because of competing centers of power.[60] Unlike congressional members, however, administrators squeezed by tightening rules are limited by what they can contribute as network players as well as by whether they can play. Without the stability of agency participation, networking is even more ad hoc than it otherwise appears.

Networking Consequences

To continue to think of policy networks in terms of stable triangles or even expansive but well-structured networks is unrealistic. The same is true in conceiving of networking as exclusionary and specialized. There seems to be very little chance for modern network participants to exclude all but the most iconoclastic and resourceless activists, which certainly means few members of Congress. Issue expertise, whether derived from a position of authority or from knowledge, seems an unenforceable criterion for limiting network participation. Indeed, all the experts may not even be included.

Easily reconciled policy solutions to pending problems seem unlikely results of modern policy networking. Results are more likely to be problematic. Contrary to the implications of the triangle metaphor, few public-policy steamrollers that can roll unhaltingly through the Congress are built within contemporary networks. Instead of heavily institutionalized relationships, what seem to exist are exceptionally ad hoc networks where those who participate look less for long-term alliances on recurring issues than for short-term gains on what may or may not prove to be pending government decisions. Policy players win where they can. Modern policy networks, then, appear quite to be complementary forums for the active participation of members of an individualistic and less committee-bound Congress that looks increasingly to home for the sources of its members' policy answers.

These members, moreover, are used to two circumstances in Washington that give rise to easy inclusion of constituent preferences in policymaking. First, the process is more accommodative to narrow than to broad interests, and specific constituent interests in a district, of course, are the most narrow and most easily serviced of policy claimants. Second, members of Congress seem to have adjusted well to a Washington policy community where public-agency analysis is at least somewhat removed from policy choices; often they disregard analysis. In either instance, turning to the district resolves one more aspect of congressional uncertainty over likely policy effects. Gunderson and Mfume knew that, from their efforts, selected constituents gained good policy treatment.

DEVELOPING A THEORY OF
CONGRESSIONAL NETWORKING

In a changing Congress and a changing Washington policy community those with an interest do group together. That remains the lesson from Bentley's classic, but often vague, explanation of how governing works.[61] More current analysis also suggests that grouping, or networking, is inevitable in the governing process. Networking brings together the expertise needed to build or reconstruct policy. Networks also facilitate collective action, functional differentiation, knowledge about the formulation of plans, an expanded scope of government, private and public sector cooperation, and international interdependence in addressing common problems.[62] As a consequence, it would be unwise to think that members of Congress fail to network. Extensions of the iron-triangle metaphor are inappropriate, however, for understanding their networking under current congressional rules and contextual circumstances.

Rather, a competing theory of contemporary congressional networking is necessary. Within networks, according to this theory, those in Congress commit themselves less to ad hoc configurations of players than to iron triangles. In choosing to enter a network's area of expertise, congressional players are not necessarily acknowledging any recurring personal interest in what goes on there. Congressional entrepreneurs simply push their way in the network's door, bringing with them no norms about common or collective purpose. The explanation for that reduction of network commitment lies with three factors: large numbers of players, increasingly narrow issues of interest to each of them, and common attention only to the policy vehicle in which they all want to include their issues. Networks focus mostly on getting the vehicle, such as a bill or an administrative ruling, included as part of the base of existing public policy. Finding the appropriate vehicle, if large and accommodating enough, advances the issues of each player.[63]

The result of networking under those conditions is less stability than even those who see networks as institutionally expansive would expect. There exists, obviously, considerable coming and going of players. Those who come and go do so because they know or care more about their own issues and the rationale for them than anyone else within the network.

What generally interests them are their own issues, not the whole of the policy to which issues belong. Moreover, at any one time, not all the issues of all the players may prove to be germane to the policy vehicle eventually pursued by those who continue networking. Players who do not see their issues being addressed in one policy network look elsewhere for yet another network and another policy vehicle.

Congress, of course, is central to this theory, but it hardly stands alone as the key to policymaking. Within free-flowing but otherwise orderly networks, members of Congress and their staffs come and go at will. Their individual goals, based on member enterprises, are no more narrow than the goals set by other players. The only real difference is that attention of the congressional enterprise to the issue that brings that enterprise to the network may be, in a comprehensive policy sense, less long-term and less knowledge based than that of other players. Within the network it makes no difference why and for whom the member is participating.[64] Motivation may have origins within a committee, a sub-committee, the leadership, the party, an interest group, the district, or whatever. For the most part, however, members pursue issues for their places back home, or for selected district constituents.

In summary, the networking member of Congress has numerous choices to make—what issues to address, to whom to respond in addressing them, to whom to look for help, where to attach the issues so they win, and, perhaps most important, what to avoid in pursuing issues. The effect of the member's choices on the policy network, however, is ambiguous. In a negative sense the new congressional participant becomes one more intensely interested member of Congress to satisfy. Yet, in a positive sense, this new player is also one additional congressional supporter for the desired policy vehicle, as long as the issue of interest to the member is included.

Why are constituents so important? For both voting decisions and committee actions, constituents are known to be only one of several information sources that set member agendas.[65] The difference with issue initiation is clear. Members vote on many vehicles; in committee they cover considerable material that their constituents care little about; but when they initiate issues their actions are targeted to their own small portion of the entire congressional agenda.

Accordingly, in the following chapters, member enterprises will be seen following a common strategy: looking for home-style opportunities in whatever policy vehicles provide them the most open entry, selecting issues that can most easily be affixed to existing policy or timely policy debates, following a pattern of district interests in their selection, and resolving uncertainty by discussing likely issues with whomever they see as particularly useful constituents.[66] After that, member relationships with the postreform committee system will be discussed. The emphasis is on the iterative nature of policymaking in Congress, which moves back and forth to reconcile member issues with collective committee preferences.

Several other factors are addressed that make it possible for members to turn to their districts in selecting issues: the suspicions of interest groups, the disregard for agency analysis when it disagrees with the ideas of district interests, and the accommodative emphasis of contemporary committees. Members are seen to be only somewhat restrained by institutions associated with the iron-triangle metaphor, particularly in finding winnable issues. As the next chapter emphasizes, these restraints are exercised primarily through the base of public policies that networking players recognize as a loosely structured yet bounded political arena, the policy domain.

CONCLUSION

The modern Congress is more likely to be driven by individual member concerns than by those of the institutional House of Representatives, the Senate, or of committees within either chamber. Rules and norms that once constrained individualism no longer exercise the same influence. What exists within both chambers of Congress is a far greater capacity for single member enterprises to act on their own strategic choices. The uncertainty over who exercises authority—leadership, caucus, committee, or subcommittee—enhances the importance of enterprises making those choices carefully and largely without clear guidance.[67]

Not only congressional changes are responsible for such behavior, however. The Washington policy community, as a series of nonencompassing policy networks, is as changed as Congress and no doubt responsible for much of what goes on within congressional institutions. Changes among the players in traditional policy networks affect how individual members can successfully pursue their own strategic choices, which, it seems, are the product of keeping a diverse array of local interests content and, not incidently, future electoral options secure. Networking appears to be less cordial, routine, and recurring, as the iron-triangle metaphor would describe relations among policy players, than it is unstable, flexible, and ad hoc. Thus, in policy networks, as compared to iron triangles, interest group players are more numerous and collectively hold more contradictory positions; agency players are less the experts who can comprehensively plan and point to effective implementation of proposed solutions; and administrators are less able to participate fully and are more burdened by their own problems of administrative politics. The combined results, open congressional networking suggests, lessen the commitment of modern members of Congress to the Washington policy community and to a comprehensive national public policy in any domain. In consequence, Washington work of the early 1990s appears to be less about producing mutually agreed-upon and coordinated public policy.

Little pressure from congressional authorities for comprehensive policy exists. Nor are there a core group of well-defined network players who, without interference, develop such policies. Under those circumstances, the pursuit of issues for purely district, or back-home reasons looks increasingly easy, probable, and rewarding for member enterprises— especially since, as this book reveals, those in congressional districts emerge as significant and reliable information sources in their own right.

2

Agriculture as a Policy Domain

What you have to understand is that the agriculture committees are the most parochial in Congress, except maybe for those that deal with interior and public lands policy. Everything about agriculture lends itself to home-turf politics, from what you wear in a parade in the district to what you fight for in committee.
—A leading congressional party strategist, known for ably representing his own district's interests through bipartisan cooperation.

The community context in which congressional members initiate issues is a single policy domain, although its policies overlap with those of other domains. The domain selected for analysis is agriculture, whose emphasis has grown to include numerous policies for nonfarmers. These nonfarm policies range widely from nutrition and health concerns to food assistance programs and rural economic development. Agriculture historically makes up 15 to 20 percent of the gross national product,[1] and its presence is felt in areas considered largely urban, such as southern Florida's Dade County. After Hurricane Andrew and federal base closures, the Florida congressional delegation's fight to keep Homestead Air Force Base alive was well understood, yet the area impact of its 9,000 jobs was only $500 million annually. Farms and agribusinesses, before Andrew, contributed $900 million to the same region each year. These factors, which emphasize diversity of interests, make for a good test of the way a policy domain works.

Both size and diversity can be seen in federal agricultural budgets, where considerable policy adjustments have allowed plenty of room for congressional intervention.[2] In 1992, total expenditures were $61,794

22

million, up from $9,722 million in 1975 and $5,684 million in 1960. This increase was 56 percent in real dollars, controlling for inflation. Farm-income programs made up 30 percent of these total dollars in 1960, only 7 percent in 1975, and 19 percent in 1992. Real growth in farm-income programs was 35 percent from 1960 to 1992. As a percentage of all budget outlays, agriculture was 6.2 in 1960 while farm programs were 1.8. By 1975, those figures were 2.9 and 0.2, respectively. By 1992, they were 4.3 and 0.6, respectively. Thus, agricultural policy represents a comparatively large and somewhat variable budget outlay, primarily for nonfarm-income policies. But even farm expenditures continue to grow.

The agricultural policy domain also provides an excellent context for studying congressional networking because of uncertain relationships in its own policy community. The historic linkage between members of Congress who make policy and those for whom they make it is subject to two views. The prevailing view of agriculture is that closed networks exercised control without conflict among the insiders. The arguments are all familiar from Chapter 1: the lack of presidential and partisan influence are criticized;[3] iron triangles are the rule; farmers get whatever they want because "a basic political principle established before the turn of the century" keeps all relevant policymaking inside agriculture;[4] the domain represents "the new feudalism," where public officials work for interest groups.[5]

A competing view, far more compatible with what we see of politics in Chapter 1, argues that the absence of conflict is vastly overstated. Agriculture's expansive policies result from the demands of always diverse interests, even in the farm sector. John Mark Hansen's analysis of agricultural policymaking in Congress shows member uncertainty owing to major splits within the farm lobby that have existed since its inception in the 1920s. Extended conflict between the American Farm Bureau Federation (AFBF) and party leaders followed after AFBF emerged as the major farm organization. Important partisan and ideological differences also divided AFBF and the National Farmers Union (NFU) as they competed for national prominence in the late 1940s and early 1950s.[6] Farm-commodity groups later kept the general farm groups, notably AFBF and NFU, from presenting coordinated legislation for price support programs.[7] But it has been the introduction of nonfarm interests that has most changed agriculture. "New agenda" issues such as food stamps and environmental quality had particularly disruptive effects within the U.S. Department of Agriculture (USDA) and Congress.[8]

According to this second view of agricultural policy, two things are evident about its governance. First, there has long been a lack of consensus among its policy beneficiaries. Second, there have been remarkable adjustment processes—that is, accommodation—within its policymaking structures. The players and the rules, or the games they play, both change with some regularity. For example, nonfarm policies, or the "new agenda," eventually gained domain legitimacy that rivaled that of farm programs.[9] Also, farm price programs survived several political disruptions without being severely altered, as general farm groups lost out to commodity groups and again as nonfarm interests gathered influence.[10] No one should be much surprised, then, if networking members of Congress bring numerous of their district interests into agriculture. Because agricultural policy is not just farm policy, and because even farm policy serves multiple interests, many members have reasons to play agricultural policy games. Neither iron triangles nor any other policy networks seem likely to keep them out.

USING A HAMMER IF YOU HAVE IT:
OR, STUCK ON THE TRIANGLE METAPHOR

Before an explanation of agriculture as a policy domain can be elaborated, more needs to be said about the problems of perpetuating an iron-triangle myth in explaining network behavior. At present, and despite Hansen's work, agricultural policy observers still see the triangle metaphor as *their* paradigm in explaining *their* politics, having missed the point about changes and accommodation. As it was popularized over thirty years ago, AFBF, USDA, and the chair of the House Agriculture Committee ruled the paradigm's roost.[11] Influence passed to commodity groups only from AFBF. New issue types, such as nutrition, gained their own triangles.[12] The Extension Service advised of the need to use triangles in gaining power.[13] Economists implied that vote trading between triangles was the reason for policy failure.[14] This oversimplified story of politics causes two problems. First, most observers seem surprised at any adaptiveness in agricultural policy and, then, when they see it, seem certain that such change constitutes a revolution. Second, because of this rigidity observers see few opportunities for most members of Congress to influence policies within this domain except to try to dismantle them. What develops is a sector-under-siege mentality, as if only agriculture is subject to policy conflict. To my mind, nothing seems further from true for any of these points.

Conflict and the Policy Game

Falling back on any form of the triangle metaphor brings too great a cost in understanding the complexities of agricultural policy and its politics. Historic and contemporary conflicts within agriculture are ignored. The coming and going of networking players in a changing Washington policy community is unexplained, even by those such as Heclo who see expanded jurisdictional overlap. Indeed, most changes in the Washington policy community associated with a postreform congressional era are ignored except as they fragment policy.[15] One might get the impression that conflicts within agriculture are only anomalies in a stable governing process threatened by outsiders.

John Mark Hansen, by focusing on the primacy of issues rather than on the networks, shows why agriculture is dynamic and rooted in conflict.[16] From 1919 to 1932, one network of players was created around highly specific farm-price issues that were recurring at the grassroots and, therefore, in Washington. After a period of network maintenance that benefited from crucial USDA leadership, cooperative network relationships began to break down in the late 1940s.[17] USDA was frequently ignored and its plans were defeated at key junctures during the next two decades. The defeat of the Brannan Plan and its direct farm payments, with its support by the Secretary of Agriculture and its opposition by Congress and the Farm Bureau, is the most visible example. The rocky road that ensured the survival of farm-price policy during the following years of network erosion was maintained by grassroots-motivated and opportunistic members of Congress. Interest groups never drove that process of survival because of their splits. Congress refused to listen to any of the groups unless they first agreed among themselves, which they could not do at the time. In a postreform setting with an even more fragmented Washington policy community than that of the prereform era, why would not members of Congress still be most attentive to their local districts and farmers on price problems? They still understand that farm-policy issues will persist as long as sectorwide economic problems continue and that no other competing interests provide lawmakers with better sources of information. As Hansen concludes, farmers are "in it for the long haul."[18]

The important point for members of Congress and the opportunities to realize the policies they seek is obvious: there exists far more to policy success than simply networking in Washington. A network occurs because a policy game already exists as a mutually understood contest over scarce resources.[19] Moreover, the continued existence of the policies on which the game depends relies on grassroots support from multiple congressional districts and states. Those who determine agricultural policy relevance, or viability within districts, include far more members than just those of congressional agriculture committees and far more farmers than only a few interest group leaders. As a consequence, modern agricultural policy networks and the expansive farm and nonfarm games on which they rest are inherently unstable. Exit of players, at any point, will be permanent if there are no competitive reasons, or opportunities, for staying.

Opportunities, Trades, and Omnibus Bills

How widespread are the opportunities to score political success in the district for members of a postreform Congress by passing agricultural policies? Why does attending to agriculture help with reelection for those from nonfarm districts? The answers lie in the extensive expansion of agricultural policy issues, interests, and policy vehicles since 1960.[20] Agricultural policy games on which networks depend go on as two concurrently staged events. First, networking among those with farm constituencies goes on to maintain farm policy. Second, reaching out beyond traditional agricultural policy supporters to assemble voting majorities on the floor of the House and Senate means going to those who have other constituent interests tied to food and fiber. By no means is this a smooth or even a sequential process.

After 1960 this process initially began with vote trading and congressional coalition building.[21] Members cut deals. Within the Congresses of the 1960s and early 1970s, simple trades of urban votes for rural ones were necessary for the survival of the farm-policy game within the House. After the wheat price support bill of 1960 was soundly defeated when urban Democrats broke with their party leaders, two types of trades were made, predominantly within the Democratic party. From 1964, and in subsequent farm bills through 1970, urban support for farm-price policy was negotiated and exchanged for rural support of food stamp legislation. An exception was the Food and Agricultural Act of 1965, where urban votes were traded for rural votes on a separate labor-rights bill to repeal state authority over right-to-work laws.

These trades were classic logrolls, where two distinct minorities within Congress voted together as a majority for legislation that no true majorities favored.[22] The majority coalitions were short-term voting blocs of members who lost any sense of common purpose after votes. As individuals, members moved to other things. The interests of the rural/urban and farm/labor coalitions of that era had nothing to do with continued stability and everything to do with momentary attachment to the success of well-defined policy vehicles—their bills. From the perspective of agricultural policy, legislative success was predicated not on exclusionary specialization, but on the entry of new players into food and labor games under explicitly negotiated agreements.

New players were fully aware that their own real interests had little in common with those of others in the rural/urban coalition or on farm/labor trades. Members who saw opportunities to win for their home folks in food stamps or labor rights legislation were encouraged by the politics of a committee-dominant, prereform congressional era to hold farm programs in disfavor, even if they really cared little about them. Personal gains mandated conflicts, or at least an active if contrived contest. Logrolls and coalitions were impossible without strident opposition among member minorities. Opportunities for political advantage resulted only when active proponents of competing views met head-on, but the results of such meetings were hardly threatening to farm policy; rather, they were beneficial to that policy.

To save farm policy and to extend food stamps, the leadership of the House intervened to facilitate exactly this winning coalition.[23] Those seen in the triangle metaphor as nonroutine players mattered greatly. Leaders rallied their troops around two different types of districts and constituents, thus creating useful opportunities to serve the home folks.

After 1974, in the midst of procedural reforms in Congress, the omnibus structure of agricultural legislation took over the process of resolving policy conflict, eliminated logrolling, and lessened the need for leadership intervention. As an encompassing variety of programs—far broader than price supports and food stamps—got wrapped and packaged in single farm bills, three things happened. First, congressional committees accommodated postreform members by negotiating and reassembling a winning but growing policy package with each new bill. Second, floor action was limited to amendments, replacing detailed consideration of one or two programs that previously made up each bill. Third, a joint House and Senate conference committee convened after floor action to "restore whatever damage might be done to the bills in either" chamber.[24] Thus, a final safety valve existed in conference to shore up what was left out or too hastily added to the omnibus bills. Conferences could either fix policy or arrange a final floor majority.[25] Collectively, those features bias the agricultural policy process in favor of making a successful deal by giving each member of the eventual winning majority opportunities in the bill that they otherwise lack. Farm bills are not designed to fail. Quite clearly, there are more winners than those in just a few policy networks.

Agricultural policy works, not because it is exclusionary, but because it is very accommodative to diverse and even conflicting member interests. Lots of members can win by playing but not by sitting on the sidelines or by just voting against farm programs. So unexpected members do play. The coalitions of the 1960s, for example, are only roughly aggregated by party and region in postreform bills, which shows changing policy games.[26] Predicted positions by district on farm-price programs and food stamps fail to explain final votes. There are, as will be seen further, far more and evolving district opportunities within the domain.

Those observations indicate a far greater complexity to the ways in which Congress passes its agricultural policies than is commonly assumed. The domain is neither managed the way most observers think nor subject to the maliciousness they imagine. Whatever Washington policy networks evolve face considerable strategic obstacles to their success. Accordingly, they must be open, responsive, opportunity-laden, and permeable to wide-ranging demands from Congress and elsewhere, particularly where these demands reflect grassroots sentiments. Relationships are likely to be ad hoc as new policy games evolve around such emerging problems as world trade, environmental degradation, and food safety. The expectations of a policy domain, as opposed to a cooperative but threatened governing process, encourage that behavior.

AN ESTABLISHMENT BECOMES
A POLICY DOMAIN

The fluidity of networks and policy games does not mean agriculture is without common players and policies. Nor is it incorrect for Theodore Lowi to contend that agriculture's basic political principle, which emphasizes farm-sector development, was set in the nineteenth century.[27] Indeed, agricultural policy specialists have argued persuasively that a broad set of agricultural institutions, spread across the nation, have collectively fostered farm development and then taken on numerous new tasks of an expanded agricultural policy. These institutions were labeled by Theodore J. Schultz as the "agricultural establishment."[28] Because policy networks are so amorphous and so issue specific, and far from the only policy winners, that idea of an establishment provides a good starting point in looking for an analytical unit for studying congressional behavior in a community context.

Scope of the Establishment

An extensive but quite unplanned set of agricultural organizations form the basis of the agricultural policy domain. They date to a series of policy additions that began in 1862.[29] Four federal acts that greatly affected agriculture were passed in that year: the Act of Establishment for a Department of Agriculture, with its very specific scientific mission of discovering new plants and seeds; the Homestead Act, which opened frontier land for new farmers; the Morrill Land Grant College Act, which transferred federal lands to the states for building agricultural and industrial colleges; and the Transcontinental Railroad Act, which hastened westward expansion for farming and ranching.[30] These policies combined a set of far-flung education facilities in the states with an expanding commercial-farm population and a development-oriented federal agency.

Later legislation strengthened this institutional base. Experiment stations, tied to the land-grant colleges, were added in 1887 to conduct research. Under active farm demands, USDA gained cabinet-level status and increased political prominence in 1889. A tier of African-American land-grant colleges was added in the South in 1890. When it became clear that education and research were not yet reaching enough of the nation's farmers and ranchers to solve their problems, the Extension Service was created within USDA in 1914. Like the land grants, it was subject to state controls and management. Extension reorganized various agricultural outreach programs and delivered services from the land-grant schools at the county government level. Before the 1930s, an extended depression in farm sales and prices already touched most of American agriculture and led to more institution building. Legislation provided for a loan system for funding farm operations, allowed agricultural marketing agreements between producers and food and fiber middlemen, granted antitrust exemptions for cooperative marketing organizations of farmers, and regulated railroads and agribusinesses for farm advantages.[31] These policies each expanded the involvement of public agricultural organizations, facilitated greater ties between Washington and the grassroots, and furthered the singularly focused yet ever-expanding policy purpose of agriculture. The policy community, in short, was extensive.

It also was really about only one thing, which provided important integration. The agricultural establishment of that seventy-year period, from 1862 to 1933, was directed toward a single integrative goal, the commercial development and industrialization of farming and ranching.[32] Although influential agricultural economists of the 1920s saw development of rural community resources as critical to successful commercialization of agriculture, the implementation and evolution of policy retained its farm and ranch emphasis.[33] The combination of considerable expertise within the agricultural establishment and its dedication to developing farming away from its peasant roots led to insular and closed self-governance.[34] Because establishment experts were closely linked to one another and to farmers throughout the states, their recommendations to Congress were well received because those recommendations generally kept constituents happy with exceptionally interventionist public policies.[35] When they did not, farmers rebelled.

Congress began to be an active part of the agricultural establishment in the 1920s, when an organized farm bloc of midwestern rural state members began to work with AFBF to alleviate continuing low prices.[36] There was no longer the integrating belief that service programs were enough to satisfy agricultural needs. More direct sector support, which would provide capital for individual producers who could develop their own resources, was called for. Southern state members, after years of looking the other way, followed midwestern members into the establishment as failing cotton cooperatives also looked to relief from the national government.[37] By 1928, after a year of tenuous regional jockeying, members of the agriculture committees acknowledged their first and aptly short-lived farm coalition, the "pact between the Corn Belt and Cotton Belt."[38] By 1932, southerners in Congress again united with midwesterners because the collapse of the South's cotton economy caused them to listen to mass-membership farm groups rather than to the cooperatives.

Within the next few years, as price-support and soil conservation programs were put in place, agriculture's policy establishment was institutionally complete. Price and conservation programs added an important feature to outreach efforts. Grassroots participation was built in through local farmer committees that helped govern service delivery. The Roosevelt White House supported these efforts, but their fate, and the continued satisfaction of farmers, was left to Congress.[39]

The agricultural policy domain was showing its current characteristics by this point. Economists like Harvard's John D. Black joined those such as Montana State's M. L. Wilson and the Bureau of Agricultural Economics' Mordecai Ezekiel to bring both an outside and an inside perspective to price policy.[40] That network was permeable. It also was generally separate from the soil conservation network. Policies were varied. Direct support programs were quite different from outreach efforts. There was considerable coming and going, or change, within basic organizations, as well. The establishment initially grew in a highly partisan era of American politics that left agriculture more to technocrats and those who would support them rather than to political brokers.[41] But, as early development policies and players proved insufficient to meet the crisis of the 1920s and 1930s, opportunistic members of Congress followed earlier policies with new ones that were defended on the basis of serving better the grassroots in their districts. New influence within agriculture was given to interest groups, who both pushed for policy change and convinced Congress that they best knew farm opinions. The domain was not a cozy community. It was full of divergent forces, spread regionally throughout the nation. Its policies, though, were protected, expansive, and added to a cumulative base.

Agriculture as a Policy Domain

Although the concept of an establishment is useful in developing an integrative meaning for agriculture's policy context, while networks are not, the concept still has problems. First, the focus of attention in an establishment is on organizations, not behavior and rules, and the base of existing public policies is what seems to give the greatest order to agriculture. Second, the establishment concept suggests permanence and also implies a distinct and absolute difference between the ties of insiders and outsiders to the purposes of an economic sector. An establishment almost begs to be run by a closed network. Thus, as agriculture's organizations change, the notion of an establishment involves unanswerable questions as to whether an establishment's decline is imminent or whether it is merely adjusting in unexpected ways. These characteristics result, in large part, from contemporary agricultural policy observers defining the bounds of the establishment and their ascribing largely normative purposes to its existence. Therefore, it makes little or no sense in studying Congress to talk about the establishment role of a number of members. They do not have such a role, other than to be unwarranted agents of policy influence.

More useful in developing an integrative meaning is the concept of a national policy domain. The intrusions of government can be subdivided into a number of somewhat overlapping policy areas, or domains.[42] Each policy domain has its own substantive focus, a clearly understood set of politically interrelated issues, programs, and policies that may, because of conflict, have some social and economic inconsistencies. These foci deal with specified problems and solutions that define the boundaries for and the reasons for the domain's existence. Moreover, policy options for the domain are formulated, advocated, and selected by important and identifiable public and private sector players who have a direct interest in, but not necessarily jurisdiction over, domain problems. Because of their convergence of interests around domain problems, these players must take the actions of one another into account—but not by participating in the domain in any permanent sense.

In short, and in keeping with Arthur F. Bentley's theory that networking goes on as an expression of shared interest, the concept of a policy domain—much like a marketplace—integrates the bounded and orderly set of institutional interactions that go into policymaking and its implementation.[43] Bounds are defined by institutional rules, not simply by reference to organizations that may be changing and even in conflict as rules are altered. Most, but not all, interactions occur within, rather than across, domain boundaries. Yet, because politics is a dynamic process, the bounds of the domain and the structure of organizations and players within it are shifting and open. Not all players are identified primarily with those domain institutions in which they are active. Nor do a domain's most consistent players necessarily restrict their involvement only to that one set of problems and organizations; they come and go as opportunities are presented.

In fact, by providing overlapping opportunities, some policy domains are relatively closer to others, based on the frequency with which players follow their interests across boundaries.[44] Therefore, policy domains are also either more or less permeable, with no rigid definition required for how much self-governance is required to retain domain status. Thus, by using the concept of the policy domain in looking at congressional behavior, we have no need to dwell on the breakdown of the agricultural establishment or on the degree to which its autonomy still persists. Moreover, the domain concept allows us to go beyond oversimplifications about closed networks and institutional overlap to concentrate on what seems more accurately the thorny politics of agriculture. We can observe how the effects of postreform congressional rules and changing interest groups and agencies work together to influence congressional behavior.

That analytical advantage means that the domain concept presumes

nothing about the symbiotic and mutually supportive relationships necessary to the triangle metaphor,[45] although some of them may indeed occur
within the domain as different groups of players network around different
issues and put into play distinctly unique policy games. Internal conflict,
however, is expected in far more instances. Shared policy space, rather
than shared values, govern interactions. Some congressional players,
such as those driven by urban constituents, network in only a small range
of subdomain issues. Others, like those on the agriculture committees,
may play a more broadly integrative role in bringing diverse issues and
interests together. Nonetheless, despite differences within it, the idea of
an agricultural policy domain brings to use a precise and empirically
determined unit of analysis for studying the structure of political relationships around what its players treat as common policies. Studying
networks directly lacks that precision and empirical basis.

Four reasons explain why agriculture, in particular, should be treated as
a policy domain rather than as just a series of autonomous but vaguely
related and highly adaptive issue networks. First, the importance of the
organizing principle of agricultural development can be explored. Network explanations ignore the importance of any central values by focusing only on political expediency. The agricultural policy domain exists
because government chose to foster an industrial-based commercial rather
than a subsistence farming.

Second, the idea of a domain that exists on an institutionalized policy
base points to the commonality of domain interests, yet it also allows for
an understanding of their diversity. It explains where the opportunities lie
for resolving internally the very real conflicts that have historically
plagued agricultural policymaking.[46] In addition, the domain concept
forces a search for institutional mechanisms that bring divergent networks
of players together.

Third, the institutionally bounded parameters of the domain help explain why the extensive array of traditional agricultural organizations and
programs established between 1862 and 1933 persist despite conflict over
them within the domain. Quite literally, as we have noted in the emergence of rural/urban and farm/labor coalitions in the 1960s, farm programs define the focal point for agricultural policy interactions and allow
for the pursuit of additional policy rewards by adding to them programs of
broader social interest. Farm programs encourage contests and policy
controversy, although they are themselves inherently innocuous.

Fourth, and tied to point three, the resulting elasticity of the domain
shows how systematic expansion of new issues, new interests, and new

policy games are continuously accommodated. For instance, the concern over farmers left behind economically in the wake of commercial agriculture led to the Country Life Commission Report in 1909 and, ultimately, to a small-scale, policy emphasis on rural quality-of-life problems.[47] The transformation of broadly rewarding farm-policy benefits to include, in the 1930s, selectively distributed income transfers was another matter of program additions, as was the later inclusion of other program crops to the list of initially supported commodities.[48] Finally, after omnibus legislation came to the farm-bill process, nonfarm programs exploded. Food stamps were joined, in postreform-era legislation, by world hunger and domestic nutrition programs, consumer legislation, environmental and energy programs, regulations for animal welfare, subsidies for trade enhancement of raw commodities and processed products, and farm worker programs.[49] Almost any congressional member has some constituent interest in some part of this extensive policy base.

The result is that modern agricultural policy includes the well-modified core of farm and rural programs that were in place by the mid-1930s.[50] It also has added numerous programs for nonfarm constituencies since that time. Indeed the agricultural policy domain involves, in its entirety, far too much for any single member of Congress to care about. This breadth can best be seen in USDA's changing role. By 1993, only 20 percent of its budget and 18 percent of its employees worked on farm programs.[51] What congressional members share in common, despite their constituents' diversity, are incentives both to challenge and to accept the underlying agricultural domain principle of the economic development of the nation's farm sector. Members want personally rewarding district opportunities to be available, and this central domain tenet and the policy games it inspires, both for and against the issues, provide them. The domain becomes the well-recognized umbrella under which members of Congress and other players network and engage in individually rewarding behavior. In those terms a policy domain is, by nature, an untidy and cluttered political arena, far more subject to legitimate interference than is any version of a policy network or an establishment.

CONGRESSIONAL MEMBERS IN THE AGRICULTURAL POLICY DOMAIN

Under the circumstances described above, the politics of any historically well-established domain undoubtedly gains considerable attention from

Capitol Hill. Any time the existing policy base is reopened for negotiation, multiple district opportunities arise for numerous members if the
benefits have some parochial appeal. Because members of Congress, and
to a lesser extent their staffs, are the least specialized of policymaking
players when compared with others,[52] congressional players cross boundaries with the greatest frequency, although most participants find their
interests leading them over domain boundaries. The imperfect match
between committee jurisdictions on policy and the substantive content of
a growing number of omnibus-style bills is obviously a reason for crossing boundaries.[53] Jurisdictional uncertainty not only leads to multiple
committee referrals, it also allows members to see that their own committees' issue interests are being influenced by others. That effect is likely to
be common: when agriculture committee staff and lobbyists of the domain were asked to identify a few committees in each chamber that also
periodically handled agricultural issues, they selected nine in the House
and six in the Senate (see Appendix); these agriculture-related committees, plus those with standing and appropriations agriculture assignments,
totaled 67 percent of the members of Congress.

District reasons are also likely to be important ones for crossing
domain boundaries. But their effect on issue initiation has been subject
only to conjecture. Exploring the importance of district reasons to issue
initiation became the purpose of this book. Three random samples of
members and their staff in 113 congressional enterprises from both chambers of Congress were asked, after careful discussion with us of the many
facets of this policy base, to identify those exact agriculture issues that
they had initiated. These members were sampled so as to be representative of House and Senate committees. They also were typical in partisanship, seniority, and types of district (see Appendix).

Specifically, these sampled members were asked which issues consumed extensive amounts of office time and which ones had the priority
interest of the member over, approximately, the past one to two years. The
emphasis was on identifying *all* issues of real member interest that were
initiated from each enterprise in the agricultural policy domain or in one
where agricultural issues overlapped.[54] Initiated issues were defined as
those public policy goals emanating from member enterprises that required offensive action and which, as they were pursued, became immediate office goals. The intent of the study was to measure the *degree* to
which the agricultural domain and its polices are open, permeable, and
sources of opportunities in an individualistic Congress. (Also, see Appendix for the methods used in the study and the questionnaire. Note

especially the respondents' extensive discussion of the meaning of agricultural policy prior to the identification of enterprise issues.)

The first set of findings indicates that the parochial and fragmented agricultural domain is every bit the cluttered political arena that the domain concept and open congressional networking imply. Nothing about member behavior demonstrates the exclusivity and specialization that any forms of closed networks suggest, even those that render behavior analogous to wind-blown clouds.[55] As Figure 2.1 shows, almost all member enterprises allocated great amounts of the time of several staff employees to at least one of what *members* saw as agricultural issues. There was indeed systematic expansion of the number of players as opposed to network-induced restraints. Of 113 enterprises in the sample, 104 were the same sort of players as Representatives Gunderson and Mfume, that is, they wanted to deliver on issues for their folks at home. Moreover, 99 of the enterprises played because their members saw at least one issue as a personal priority. Even with the expectation that postreform circumstances create opportunistic networking in Congress, these are exceptionally high numbers.[56] Despite a greater history of individualism within the Senate, these high rates of participation did not vary much by congressional chamber (see Appendix, Table A.1). In the Senate, twenty-seven of twenty-nine members, or 93 percent, initiated at least one issue, and each of them set at least one of those as a personal priority. House claims are at very much the same rate, with 77 of 84 enterprises (or 92 percent) initiating at least one time-consuming issue and seventy-two members (or 86 percent) indicating at least one as a priority.

Success on time-consuming and priority issues was uniformly high in terms of final adoption in law, regulations, or oversight. When, for instance, a member seriously championed the inclusion of rural water systems in a rural development section of the farm bill, such an item would generally be included in the final act. Member enterprises, as I will explain in greater detail in Chapters 3 and 4, initiated 256 issues. Of those 256, 70 percent (48) were won by senators and 69 percent (129) were won by members of the House. Priority issues won 72 percent (41) of the time in the Senate and 73 percent (105) of the time in the House.

These results indicate at least three postreform effects that demonstrate congressional capacity to serve district interests. First, as we might expect from procedural reforms, the House and Senate are now more comparable playing fields for encouraging individual activism. Second, members of Congress are quite unwilling to defer to either congressional or network expectations that limit policy participation to those who have some degree

FIGURE 2.1. Issues Initiated by Individual Legislators, by Percentage*

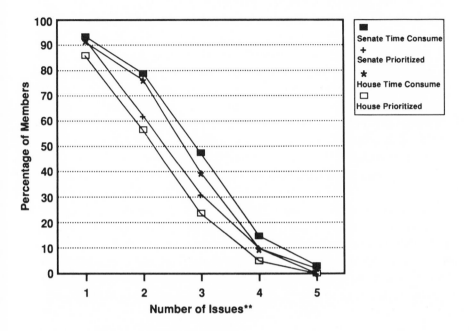

*Includes all time-consuming issues
**No one selected more than five issues

of expertise or institutional authority. Third, the results show that staffing truly matters. Of the 202 issues given high priority by members, only three did not require extensive enterprise time. Each of these three issues were in the House and were resolved by members with committee support.

As members and their staffs explained, member priorities drive office agendas, not necessarily because members value the issues, but certainly because they attach importance to those who do want issues resolved. They see that the tedious pace of the Congress and the large number of legislative hurdles to overcome for nearly any priority initiative require extensive staff resources. Doing something on an issue almost always takes time, follow-through, and a well-managed staff. Issue commitments were seen as such a drain on the office enterprise that few issues gained attention without becoming acknowledged as member priorities. Accordingly, among the 256 issues the enterprises identified as time consuming, members personally decided to support 199, or 78 percent. The remaining issues were undertaken by the staff with the acquiescence but less than enthusiastic support of members. Members, however, followed along diligently in almost all cases as loyal participants in their enterprises.

Despite the fact that staff resources exist so that they can be used for the members' purposes, the relatively small number of agricultural issues initiated in each enterprise confirms how carefully issues must be selected. As Figure 2.1 shows, the average is about two issues per office. This means that although domain intrusion is common among nearly all members, it remains relatively infrequent for each of them. No member enterprise initiated more than five issues within the eighteen months prior to the interviews. Less than 50 percent of senators and 40 percent of House members initiated three issues. Of those who initiated one issue, however, almost all initiated a second. This low frequency has the same strategic importance to enterprises as does the choice and content of whichever policy vehicles they use in following their congressional interests. Individually determined strategies, which can seemingly be directed easily to constituents, appear to be the mechanism for managing uncertainty under the conditions of a postreform Congress and an opportunity-laden policy context.

CONCLUSION

Two elements for analyzing policymaking are now in place. The first describes a policy domain that will be used as a contextual testing ground for studying how well members of Congress respond to their districts in policymaking. The second is the development of a domain theory of policy participation that meets expectations of modern congressional behavior. In a domain networking, according to the Bentleyan argument, exists as interest behavior, bringing numerous policy players together because of their immediate concern for mutual goals. No institutionally structured basis for networking needs exist, as traditional theory implied. Networking, however, as food stamp logrolling of the 1960s shows, is dependent on a public policy base that exists at the bounded domain level. Networks themselves are only situational and temporary arrangements that gather around that base. Domains, in contrast, are rule driven and exist because the general purposes of an aggregated set of public policies are commonly understood.[57] For agriculture, the structure of the domain lies in its expansive array of public policies, organized around a farm-development principle and on perceptions of the need for broader social relevance for nonfarm constituents.

Both of these points are important because, despite what was described in Chapter 1, prevailing views of agricultural policymaking still rely on the logic of the iron-triangle metaphor, especially in envisioning an exclusive and monolithic establishment. Those who follow that logic do not differentiate systems of organization and systems of rules from one another. The context for the analysis laid out in the following chapters was redefined as a domain so that the parochial confines of agricultural policymaking could be viewed as compatible with the conditions both of a postreform Congress and of more ad hoc community networking. Agriculture, in its compatibility, is no more narrow or directed to its own ends than any of numerous other U.S. policy domains. It may differ only in degrees and, therefore, remains a good candidate for explaining contemporary policymaking and its constituent basis.

As the first cut of the data base for this study indicates, conditions in agriculture are indeed compatible with the less deferential and less specialized behavior of opportunistic members of Congress and their constituent interests. Most members have highly specific issue interests in the agricultural policy domain, though not necessarily in anything they see as involved positively or negatively with farming. Although these members make limited initiatives, they effectively intrude into policymaking, changing policy and the proposals of others in both dramatic and subtle ways. If the expectations set by the triangle metaphor are used as a base, there has been a remarkable expansion of congressional players. Therefore, to continue to think of agricultural policymaking as either the sole turf of legitimate experts within closed policy networks or as the prerogatives of declining establishment organizations makes little or no sense. Rather, the agriculture policy domain should be understood as a useful set of programs that *at any one time* meets the needs of numerous public policy players.

3

Members, Issues, and Policy Vehicles

Look, the important thing is getting your language in somebody else's bill. Any place will do as long as it gets into law.
—A twenty-five-year-veteran staff assistant, explaining how he pursues his member's interests.

Agricultural policy can best be understood as a domain of political interest, one encompassing a common set of related programs that extend far beyond farming and farm interests. Although the agricultural policy domain is defined and bounded by established programs and attended to by those in Congress, USDA, and the land-grant system, the domain is also permeable. Not only have numerous programs for such concerns as nutrition and environmental quality been added to the domain, many members of Congress have also sought to pursue issues and opportunities there. In addition, the domain itself does not always contain all relevant agricultural issues. Congress has shown the same expansive tendencies as have an array of interest groups whose issues bring them a concern with far more than farm legislation.

The next task in judging domain stability is understanding the way issues change to maintain policies, or more accurately, the policy base. Thinking through the relationship between issues and policy requires better operationalizing of how political observers think about policymaking. Both academics and politicians are incredibly cavalier when using the term "issues." It has catchall meaning for many who use it, describing everything from a social cause to a bill in Congress.[1] This lack of clarity presents analytical difficulties. As Mayhew observes, members of Congress package what they *want* in salable *wraps* that others find appealing.[2] To understand the congressional process, the wants, as issues, need be distinguished from the wraps, or vehicles. According to the theory of congressional networking proposed in Chapter 1, members of a post-reform legislature shop among various alternative policy vehicles for ways to package the issues they want; issues are their discrete and precise "topics of policy concern."[3] Issues are important, if not always news-worthy, because they are the basic building blocks of public policy, with which coalitions are constructed.

Several studies point to the importance of this want-versus-wrap distinction. For example, back-door appropriations to fund wants are often made by working funding language into authorization bills, or wraps, usually by mandating entitlements. Back-door authorizations for a new program likewise are inserted as enabling language into appropriations bills or, less easily because of the larger scope of line items, into budget bills.[4] Indeed, the legislative assistant quoted in the chapter epigraph was, when he spoke, pointing to highly technical and very brief language in a Senate appropriations bill that created a new program to buy equipment for physically disadvantaged farmers.

The distinction between issues as wants and policy vehicles as wraps is also quite evident in some of the most widely known case analyses of congressional policymaking. Researchers from Raymond A. Bauer, Ithiel de Sola Pool, and Lewis Anthony Dexter, who studied the ideological splits in tariff legislation of the 1950s, to Richard E. Cohen, who looked at the far more concentrated pressures to pass a Clean Air Act in 1991, demonstrate a common finding.[5] They note that discrete and narrow substantive issues delay the policy process more than the perceived need for or the inevitability of the legislation.[6] For example, ranchers did not oppose the creation of East Mojave National Park in 1993, but only be-cause the issue of grazing rights was left alone. To pass the bill estab-lishing the park, Congress also had to deal with several other issues: protecting Pentagon flight paths, excluding existing mining operations from park boundaries, and creating opportunities for motorcycle enthusi-asts. As a result, East Mojave became a new park, but its design lacked the protections of pristine quality desired by its initial environmentalist advocates.

Passing a policy vehicle, in other words, depends on how issues, defined as the exact things wanted by political interests, are managed within it. A familiar quote among members of Congress, and one bor-rowed by 1992 presidential candidate H. Ross Perot, concludes that "the devil is in the details." Issues are more than problems identified by those who are plagued by them. Issues are also proposed solutions to specific problems, with the proponents going to some length to define what they want from policy. Cumulatively, public policy is only the sum of the issues that lead to its creation. That theme of issues constituting policy informs this chapter, first in looking at alternative vehicles and then in explaining how issue choice affects winning. The theme also underscores the importance of omnibus bills as particularly encompassing, expansive, and opportunity-laden vehicles. Yet, alternatives to farm bills are also valued in a Congress noted for, as Richard F. Fenno, Jr., says, accommodating rules to interests.

FARM BILLS AND OTHER VEHICLES

The utility to Congress of farm bills, as we saw in chapter 2, suggests that not all policy vehicles are created equal; omnibus bills seem especially useful. John Ferejohn's analysis of only two sets of issues, price supports and food stamps, shows how the omnibus structure of legislation provides numerous opportunities for pursuing issues of interest to members who contest and then pass bills in this format.[7] Institutions, which are important to congressional networking, also matter in setting and limiting conditions for member choices of issues. Kenneth A. Shepsle's theoretical work on congressional equilibrium, or the retarding of change, suggests this to be true.[8] Institutionalized structures, or established procedural and policy rules, and the complementary need for internal order obviously make some agricultural policy vehicles more prominent than others. An emphasis on the importance of institutional order, however, must be seen in light of the strategic advantages it represents to one coalition-specific format over another and of the idea that members make procedural rules to accommodate themselves as interests.[9] The implication is that favored policy vehicles serve institutional purposes, and thus gain support, but only if they are quite closely tied to the interests of a large number of individual members. The institutional Congress, that is, wins when it passes an expected bill but only because numerous members benefit personally.

The Primacy of Farm Bills

Not only do members of Congress pursue their own issues primarily through farm bills, they also select other policy vehicles with sufficient frequency to highlight the importance of the relationship between individual member interest and the desire for other institutional choices. Table A.2, which is in the Appendix, shows where members of Congress attached what they saw as agricultural issues to particular policy vehicles. Sixty-two percent of all issues that consumed considerable staff time and 66 percent of all those issues to which members gave priority attention were attached eventually to three closely linked farm bills: the Food, Agriculture, Conservation, and Trade Act of 1990 (FACT), which received most of the attention; the closely related Omnibus Budget Reconciliation Act; and the December 1991 corrections to FACT.[10]

The findings on issue placement reveal an overall pattern of vehicle use that emphasizes agriculture as a single policy domain, even with its expansive purposes. If the large number of members involved with agricultural policies raises questions about the domain's relevance as a bounded set of institutions, congressional attention to its principal public-policy playing field answers them. Members obviously are attracted to farm bills; the omnibus format is the clear focal point of domain and agricultural issue attention.

Equally striking, however, is the timing with which members direct their attentions to farm bills. Very few issues are initiated as floor amendments. Most efforts are aimed at what might be termed the front or loading end of the farm-bill process. Front-loading means that members of Congress consider numerous problems and issue solutions early in the bill-drafting process, or during the initial mark-ups. It also means the early acceptance of these issues by committee members so that they can begin to solidify support for passing the final bill. Front loading emphasizes members' selling bits and pieces of legislation to a Congress that would rather accommodate its members than force floor fights: approximately 70 percent of issues are won, or successfully attached to the final bill that passes.

The 1990 farm bill is really a misnomer because of its broad nonfarm content. It includes twenty-five titles, ranging from single-farm commodity programs to efforts on behalf of the global climate. The final, miscellaneous title includes nearly every other item of interest to the expansive agricultural establishment—for example, social outreach to support for the physically disadvantaged in rural America. Each title has several sections, constructed of problems confronted in the process of organizing the various programs under the title. The dairy title, for example, offers 16 sections—out of a total of 687. Some sections authorize one or more programs, such as dairy export incentives; others provide

regulatory changes, such as regional pricing schemes; and some emphasize research needs or other requisite administrative actions. The numbers
of provisions in each section and of sections in each title are set only by
the scope of congressional demands, as with the 102 sections of the
widely inclusive agricultural-promotions title. This practice, of course,
gives plentiful opportunities to members to participate in designing the
bill. They can either get involved with a plethora of nonfarm issues that
use 80 percent of USDA budgets, or intrude into parts of complex farm-
policy provisions without having to worry about redrafting or redefining
the whole of even a small program.

Of all 256 issues initiated by member enterprises, 151 pertained to only
a single section or to two or more intertwined sections of a farm bill. The
issues were like those of cattle or motorcycles in the East Mojave legislation that finally passed: very important to their proponents, very irritating
to their foes, but still only a narrow part of the entire legislation. But as
members of Congress all agreed, resolved issues are what structure public
policy in both big and small ways, but especially in cumulative ways. Of
all the farm-bill issues, only 16 were intended to rewrite or otherwise
broadly to redefine the principal content or purpose of already existing
agricultural programs. The vast majority of member incursions, or 135
issues, aimed only at adding to, modifying, or deleting some service or
regulation that the section governs. In a few cases, this narrowness of
purpose meant establishing by means of a single section a new single-
service program similar to other agricultural services. A good example is
funding for product- or purpose-specific research centers, for instance,
for the promotion of turkeys or for rural-development information. Such
initiatives rarely attempted to alter the purpose or operation of other
provisions in other sections. In fact, most members and their staffs
emphasized that their intent was to avoid the conflict created by any
change in section or program purpose. This emphasis on highly discrete
and narrow issues underscores the importance of the accommodative,
soft-sell approach of front-loading the bill in a Congress given to extensive networking. It also suggests why successes are likely even though, in
the end, nearly every part of the farm bill is altered by member issues or
by those of agency officials.

The comments of members who seemed to be more interested in broad-
based reform are also revealing. Several members, and their staffs, were
sought from beyond the sample because they had sponsored different
versions of farm bills in either 1985 or 1990. Over half explained that their
sponsorship of those abbreviated omnibus proposals was *not* a personal

priority concern. They acted perfunctorily and only on behalf of other interests: "Somebody had to introduce the Farm Bureau's bill"; and "We carried water for the administration." The remaining sponsors indicated that their efforts were indeed priority concerns, yet they had no immediate interest in the whole bill, for example: "My concern was with decoupling, that was it." Either sponsors were attempting to leverage their influence on a particular section of one or more of the titles in the bills that the committees would introduce, or they were trying to sell a single priority scheme for organizing those bills, such as removing the linkage between farm payments and the amount of crops produced in decoupling, or the targeting of payments to smaller farms. Thus, even those members seen as reformers were really pursuing change by small pieces at a time.

This strategy of minimizing conflict in what was, by necessity, a contentious policy vehicle is possible for two reasons that relate to the structure of these omnibus bills. First, farm bills and their programs are renewable legislation, subject to a temporary, four- to five-year cycle.[11] Each farm bill reauthorizes, adds, or deletes all programs from previous legislation. If, for some reason, the bill failed to pass, commodity titles and sections would revert to the terms of the comprehensive and "permanent" Agricultural Adjustment Act of 1938, with its parity language, or to modifications made in the 1938 legislation by the Agricultural Act of 1949.[12] Costs of farm-price programs would soar unrealistically and other programs valued by members would be gone unless Congress voted them out in a separate policy vehicle.

As a consequence, farm bills expand in scope very incrementally and predictably. Any interest that wants changes can determine how to proceed by studying the organization as well as the substance of existing legislation, or what was passed in the last bill. The member enterprise, as a result, can plan both what it wants from the next pending omnibus vehicle and, generally, where it can insert those wants within the vehicle's wraps. Then, too, an enterprise can react to problems found with recent farm bills. The months following farm-bill passage are given to cleaning up policy difficulties, as was the case with the two bills that followed FACT.

The second reason why members can avoid conflict over section purposes owes to the nonexclusive rules that govern titles and their components. If, for example, new dairy or food-stamp programs are added, existing titles will include them by adding new sections or incorporating them into old ones. Sections need not be restricted to a single program or purpose. Moreover, alterations in pricing levels, regional distribution, eligibility, compliance and so on need not redirect the principal purpose behind each section. In brief, despite their predictability, farm bills are wide-open institutional mechanisms for generating new demands and negotiating important changes. That explains why only seventeen of the eighty-six member enterprises, or 20 percent, that targeted 1990 farm-bill sections intended that their initiatives significantly alter, or reform, basic policies either by redirecting old programs or by starting new and unique ones.[13] Their changes were instead targeted far more to single problems of delivering agricultural policy.

All enterprises, however, saw their initiatives as changing the existing distribution and regulation of the agricultural-policy services that those policies provided. These issues were not inconsequential for overall policy content, both because they all at least reallocated existing policy rewards and because they were so numerous that their combined effects were felt domainwide. When, for instance, the interest of members of Congress in adding infrastructure issues to rural-development provisions increased, the jobs and human-capital emphasis of rural policy was lost in favor of the traditional congressional pork barrel. Change, in the sense of always modified policy objectives, was a constant, as was the concern for policy redistribution.[14] Incremental changes, though, were dominant. For every congressional member interested in, for example, disrupting U.S. trade practices by restricting existing foreign sales of pesticides, four were interested in much less difficult initiatives, for instance, redefining the number of days a wetlands needs to hold water to keep its classification, or allowing new conditions for harvesting plantings on conservation set-aside acreage. Although these changes might mean considerable financial gains or losses to constituents, either change could have been made and kept intact the previous intent of conservation provisions of the 1985 Food Security Act. As a member noted, "We were not out to gut anything. That's the way to be irrelevant."

As modest proposals, these types of initiatives provide easy opportunities to act on issues for members of Congress because the resulting legislative actions, on their own, seldom mandate dismantlement of existing policy.[15] Rather than on large-scale initiatives, members who pursue this option of change while maintaining existing programs capitalize on marginal shifts in domain influence that may have occurred between two farm-bill periods. "I thought I saw," the above-quoted member continued, "a reassertion of concern about farm finances, with less emphasis on costly environmental detail." Thus, the process of finding new issues to replace those successfully enacted into law each time a farm bill or other vehicle related opportunity comes up is a dynamic one. A concern with political information on the part of member enterprises allows them both to manage the expected resistance from others and to find self-serving advantages in the institutional structure of farm bills.

These members also gauge shifts in the influence of particular players over time since these are likely to affect well-understood titles, sections, and provisions and to generate timely circumstances for some kinds of change. When a western member wanted to initiate a less confining definition of wetlands, for instance, his enterprise looked for reasons why it could win in 1990 when others had lost on the issue in 1985. Changes in the environmental lobby, problems with existing policy, and national attention to water-quality were among the subjects of inquiry.

These subjects were easily targeted for analysis by the member and his staff because of the predictability of the farm-bill cycle. Those in other enterprises also noted that the farm-bill process, in effect, gave them a planning cycle for identifying their own opportunities. In the years between bills, very public discussions involve all likely players in highly ritualized meetings, conferences, and strategy sessions. This discussion goes on for much of the two years preceding each bill.[16] As a result, the ongoing flow and emphasis of policy debates is observable, and its momentum can be gauged and timed. For a rational member of Congress, supported by a staff that can overcome any natural reluctance to attend to agriculture, the decision to initiate an issue depended on an assessment of the success of a program from the 1985 farm bill in the intervening years. Members and their staffs, as they see it, are overwhelmingly rationalists who appreciate the importance of shifting participation and policies within the domain. Of the 151 time-consuming issues that member enterprises attempted to attach to farm-bill sections, only 19 were considered by their advocates to be unlikely winners.[17] And only 11 of the member-priority issues were seen as long shots. "Why pick a loser?" was one member's explanation of why some issues are initiated and others are not.

Numerous members voiced a related and not unexpected observation—that the odds of winning would have been reduced substantially if their issues had not been incorporated into omnibus farm legislation. Each saw, in other words, the standards and structures of a loosely bounded domain—and a recurring vehicle that fit it—doing more to determine policy outcomes than did the collective values of the Congress. This superiority of form over content explains why, for agriculture, there are such frequent charges of parochialism, the persistence of exclusionary policy networks, and disregard for national electoral wishes. But it also explains why there are few serious efforts to dismantle existing policy. The enhanced like-lihood of winning underscores the numerous opportunities for tactical victories that exist for members of Congress who become domain players, as long as they do so on the proper turf. As one member said, "Here was a farm bill, there was me as an environmentalist, there were all those ranchers degrading public lands, suddenly I saw my interest in agri-culture."

The Use of Alternative Policy Vehicles

Questions of turf prove important in member enterprises, decisions about where to attach their issues. Although members and their staffs value choices about policy vehicles, they clearly preferred to work within the structure of omnibus bills and the jurisdiction of the agriculture commit-tee. This preference meant that 90 percent of all issues, whether farm or nonfarm, were addressed within the bounds of the domain.

Other domain choices, as Table A.2 shows, targeted agriculture appro-priations subcommittee language (23 issues) and more narrowly focused bills (21 issues) of the agriculture standing committees. Those initiatives amounted to 9 and 8 percent, respectively, of what the enterprises identi-fied as their agricultural issues. Although the number of those choices of vehicle fall below those for farm bills, each type exceeded the combined attention to regulatory and oversight initiatives within the USDA (20 issues). Given the great amount of discretion delegated to the Secretary of Agriculture in domain legislation, that comparatively low attention to USDA initiatives was unexpected. Members and staff explained, how-ever, that they would rather legislate.

One reason for that preference stands out and reinforces the explanation of why issues stay within the domain. As a member noted, "We can better monitor our programs by addressing an issue in Congress rather than following it through the haze or maze or whatever of the bureaucracy."[18] A few members explained their reliance on General Accounting Office investigations as a way of addressing bureaucratic concerns while staying within the Congress: "A written report comes out of GAO, the press provides coverage, and USDA moves forward with change. It's very smooth." One member, for example, pushed for a report recommending limits on discernible toxins in imported Italian wines. He felt that the resulting publicity would mean faster action than normal regulatory channels would provide in correcting the problem. Thus, there are some domain issues that were handled by nontraditional means within the domain.

Why was the domain so important? One member summed it up: "Because of expanding policy intentions, we struggle to identify the meaning of agriculture." He and other members and their staffs went on to explain that a loss of the meaning of agriculture throughout the Congress would lead to an unwanted reassessment of the central purposes of agricultural policy, particularly farm programs. Wariness of that loss of definition explained why the domain was largely centrifugal in its policymaking, clearly accommodating diverse nonfarm programs for food stamps, food safety, health standards, and environmental use.

The result of a centrifugal domain was impressive. Few agricultural-issue initiatives were handled in other domains, despite the large number of congressional committees that members and staff saw to affect agriculture. Only ten agricultural issues, and of those, only five member priorities, were taken first to committees or agencies working on policy vehicles that were central, in members' eyes, to another domain: the Clean Air Act, tax reform, water standards, or pharmaceutical regulations. Members argued that the reason more issues have not been taken to other domains is agriculture's success in defining issues as farm problems and in claiming that resolutions to issues have been operational in agriculture for some time. As a result, a farm-policy focus that accommodates numerous nonfarm needs has largely stabilized the domain.

But, in an opportunistic Congress interested in and capable of choices, domain stability is far from complete. There were still numerous cases (seventeen issues) of members going beyond the domain on issues that were arguably not central to agriculture. This was evident on some single-purpose bills that eluded the agriculture committees' complete jurisdiction: the House Education and Labor Committee shared jurisdiction with the agriculture committees over the Child Nutrition and WIC (Women, Infants, and Children) Reauthorization Act; the House Environment and Public Works Committee's wetlands bill became law after being approved in an omnibus aquatics act; and the House Select Committee on Hunger worked hard to produce its own world hunger bill after its chairman, Mickey Leland (D-Texas), was killed during an investigation in Ethiopia in 1989.

The three bills, as all the involved members understood them, dealt with obvious agricultural issues. Some members treated those bills as domain properties, mobilizing agricultural interests around their own enterprise interests in each of them. One member sought to insert lan-

guage compatible with his interest in food stamps, and another attempted
to gain producer restitution for lost use of agricultural wetlands. These
members initiated their issues on others' turf to pursue benefits they could
not get in farm bills. As one staff associate explained, "This is an
influence-enhancing act." But reformers noted the reverse, namely, that
they wanted to pull poorly attended issues away from agriculture. As a
consequence, they brought issues that affected food and farm problems to
other domains. "If they won't do it, give it to someone who will. It's the
Dingell rule," said a member, referring to the then-chairman of the House
Energy and Commerce Committee and his continuing work to claim
jurisdiction over more and more bills.

There were other members of Congress attempting the same ploy on
seafood inspection, food labeling, rural development, biotechnology, and
scientific research. Although the complexity of dealing with issues
of these kinds proved to be problems for those who wanted to protect
agriculture's turf, there also were advantages in moving beyond the domain. One advantage was the farm-bill planning and review cycle, which
kept Congress directed to policies tied to agriculture's policy base and the
next omnibus bill. Members felt that their own efforts to realize agriculture policy in other domains were recognized by others in Congress as
legitimate ones taken on behalf of agricultural constituents that just did
not fit into the farm bill. For example, the Food and Drug Administration
and the Environmental Protection Agency were both cited as agencies
outside institutionalized agriculture that other members would understand
as being "good targets" because they are likely to overstep their bounds
and intrude in other domains, such as domestic economics and international trade. Members represented their issues on bills affecting these two
agencies by arguing the need for a broader consideration of agricultural
problems than either FDA or EPA were likely to give without the intervention of agricultural interests. Under these conditions, members of
Congress who went out of their domain were more willing to work with
agencies on issues than were those who stayed inside agriculture.

Another member explained in greater detail the logic of representing
agriculture's central interests in other domains: "Think of the necessity of
us seeing an ongoing agriculture component to the work of the budget
committees or GAO. They're like the sector's service centers, and we
supplement them with staff expertise to ensure their use." Thus, by
maintaining specialized institutions, budget committees and the GAO
played within-domain roles. Several members wanted FDA and EPA to be
the same type of service centers, but from clearly outside the domain. The

behavior of those members, and especially the institutional conditions supporting it, means that the bounds of domain politics are both well recognized and, paradoxically, seen to be very nonexclusive; with future change likely, they are also inherently unstable. All domains appear to be accommodating to outside interests. The same dynamics that bring so many members of Congress into agricultural policy decisions also bring agriculture, despite the dominance of farm bills, into other functions and domains within Congress. This shifting happens because opportunistic members who gain personally through their attentions stand to gain even more if the subject of those attentions is more rather than less encompassing: "If agriculture takes on minor importance, what I do there is bush league and trivial." This attitude, of course, is what brings representatives and senators who care nothing at all about farming to the agricultural domain and those who do care about it to other domains.

Members who moved beyond the domain always wanted to do so by staking out a legitimate interest elsewhere. "A third of the battles in this place are fought over turf," was one member's explanation. "You lose when [it's evident to colleagues that] you're in the wrong place." This desire for legitimacy means that members look for areas of domain overlap and see these as likely sites for opportunities. If one committee was working on legislation that other committees could claim jurisdictionally with House or Senate leaders, there was little hesitancy to move on an issue. "In fact," said one member, "that's prime hunting grounds." Enterprises simply used the leverage of likely committee conflict and leadership involvement to their personal advantage in negotiating with committees of jurisdiction. "Just the idea of concurrent jurisdiction gives us enough clout to deal with a farm issue in, for instance, a labor bill," noted one member. He went on to explain how his own efforts had gone into relaxing otherwise straightforward work rules for West Coast migrant farm hands in an immigration bill: "I just argued that the immigration bill's purpose was with national security and labor issues but that my problem was the very different one of farm economics. I needed an exception. I got it."

As did numerous others, this House member argued that the success of an agriculture issue depended on how well it was defined to others as legitimately domain property, or at least deserving of shared space. This process of definition also allowed some members to conveniently move some issues out of domain vehicles. When USDA analysis argued against tax advantages for ethanol processors on economic grounds, ethanol's congressional advocates reversed course and looked for more rewarding institutional support. Members such as Senator Thomas A. Daschle (D-S. Dak.) initiated ethanol issues on the basis of air quality rather than of agricultural production and manufacturing. Ethanol tax credits were then successfully incorporated into air-quality legislation. The proposed want superseded the wrap, or the vehicle. And the need for a new policy vehicle superseded the disadvantages of entering another domain. It appears evident from the data that when change is in order, member expectations place a premium on exploiting possibilities beyond the commonly relied-upon farm bills and their open, yet always restricted opportunities. Other policy vehicles and, less often, even other policy domains also usefully serve to achieve change, even though within them, issues may not be as easily addressed by individual member enterprises.

Winning

Despite the greater use made of farm bills than of other policy vehicles by member enterprises, members were not notably more successful in attaching issues there than the average. Members were successful about three-quarters of the time in getting either their language or new enabling provisions incorporated into omnibus farm legislation passed by Congress and signed by the president.[19] That rate of success, as can be seen in Table A.2, dropped slightly for single-purpose bills within the domain and for all nondomain bills. The quite unpopular action of offering floor amendments succeeded in only one instance for any bill. Sponsorship of an entire bill, if only to advance a single section, was used only twice and failed both times. This relative lack of success explains why respondents dwelled so much on committee jurisdictions and what was anticipated to take place in subcommittee deliberations. Committees and their subcommittees, regardless of domain, were the playing fields that brought success. They still remained the points within the process where the overwhelming number of member wants were accepted or rejected.

Of the committees most frequently targeted, appropriations subcommittees for agriculture provided the highest rate of success. Eighty-nine percent of member-priority issues were funded as passed. In contrast, the far less frequently targeted budget committees, with their agriculture staffs, were successfully breached only once. Members saw appropriations bills as ideal vehicles for incorporating narrow but often quite expensive programs that no one wanted to waste time dealing with in public: "Now who is really going to read that thing?" The size and weight of these long and bulky bills made it difficult for likely critics to discover the appropriated item and complain publicly. Appropriations bills also could be used to correct areas of neglect, for example, equipment for disadvantaged farmers, about which members could make a good case for creating better public policy. As a long-serving Senate staffer explained: "Nobody would object to the bill and the small expenditure, but I wasn't sure how I could get a markup hearing on that particular proposal in the authorizing committee. We just avoided that procedural headache." In short, relatively small items that members felt strongly about went regularly to appropriations when members had entry there. The budget committee, with its notorious interest in making zero-sum decisions, handled only multimillion-dollar expenditures on department and program generalities, and few members, as a result, gained entry to it.

Given member and staff attitudes about working with agencies, it was hardly surprising that enterprises succeeded somewhat more frequently with congressional committees than they did with agencies. Nor was it surprising that USDA agencies produced a higher rate of decisions desired by members than did the nondomain agencies that were mentioned, FDA and EPA, even if members felt they had reasons to challenge the latter. Member initiatives proposed greater changes in policy or program intent for these agencies than for USDA. Two less obvious but important findings also stand out about congressional-agency relations. The first was that members did not feel there was much to be won by prioritizing agency oversight activities. It was done only to be harsh and punitive in order to stop agency actions against a single interest, such as a consumer group that in some congressional eyes had gotten too cozy with agency officials. Oversight also was done more successfully using the General Accounting Office when and if a member saw a good reason for it and a chance to institute it.

The second relates to members' perception of greater difficulty in working with agencies than with committees. As mentioned above, the preferences for keeping initiatives within Congress are not surprising. Yet, it seems far from easy to follow that route. To insert an issue successfully in a bill entails the commitment to an arduous and long-term effort to keep the language or provision in place through endless committee markups, chamber passages, and conference committee decisions. An issue can slip out of the vehicle at any point, often at the suggestion of an anonymous player or any of several committee staff. It should be remembered though, that members and their staffs expressed their overwhelming preferences for this process rather than to following decision making in agencies. These preferences, as I suggested in a different context in Chapter 1, provide a telling commentary on bureaucratic processes and their tedium for Capitol Hill people. It also reveals an agency insulation from congressional pressures that the iron-triangle metaphor, with its focus on a cooperative establishment, neglects. If relationships between Congress and the agencies they oversee were as cozy and cordial as is often assumed, more member enterprises would pursue their issues there or seek administrative help in dealing with legislative complexities. Few members, including those on the agriculture committees, did either.

The data on winning show overall that the domain setting matters despite the distinct preferences of members for some vehicles and policy jurisdictions over others. Going beyond domain institutions on agricultural issues is harder than staying inside, but not impossible. Members still won on agricultural issues taken to other domain institutions over half the time. This rate of success reflected the degree to which domains necessarily overlap and bring some sense of linkage to the whole of congressional public policymaking. "To call something agriculture or commerce will always be a misnomer," explained one member. Yet these data also show that, by far, the greatest number of wins are made within the most comfortable institutional settings. Congressional initiatives thus become less likely on issues involving the bureaucracy or those committees that have more marginal effects on the policies at hand because these are not the preferred playing fields. Winning is mostly about keeping issues narrowly focused and defined as commonly bounded, or as particular as possible to domain bounds and committees of jurisdiction. Quite obviously, then, as Ferejohn and Fenno suggest, strategies and tactics of how best to use vehicles and committees are important.[20]

What makes these processes successful for members? Those who provided information about issue initiatives suggested that strategies and tactics are heavily but not exclusively dependent on the staff of self-reliant congressional enterprises.[21] So, too, does the data. Winning is not the result of members closeting themselves with their own informants and bringing superior insights back to the enterprise. This procedure would hardly give enterprises the time to replicate in other policy areas what they do in agriculture. However, some intelligence gathering by members themselves also goes on. In total, issues that were seen as member priorities won nearly 73 percent of the time, but they also produced only 3.5 percent more wins than time-consuming ones (see Table A.3). Issues that members did not prioritize won in but 59 percent of cases. That lower score, along with members' comments, indicates that members hone and refine their approaches to the issues that staff initially select and are often allowed to pursue. At least, that was how the time-consuming and the member-priority issues were seen: "What I really want to go after and what the staff may otherwise spend time on differ but little. It's usually a matter of my determining that we really can deliver on a priority thing."[22]

The refinement of an issue from time-consuming to priority status significantly improves the overall odds of winning: "It would be hard for me to give my priorities to what couldn't be won. . . . I wouldn't do it." In consequence, member enterprises and the extended contacts that staff provide appear as tools, which, when used with persistence and intelligence, open up domain deliberations: "My staff finds ways of gaining entry for things that I have reason to believe can be done. They also have the time available if we don't worry about too many issues." Nevertheless, discussions of members themselves contribute further to the effort to win issues, and I will later explore them at greater length: "What do I add? I have my own networks."

MEMBERS AS ORIGINATORS AND MAINTAINERS

Neither the persistence of the staff nor the contribution of members as individuals to enterprise strategies satisfactorily explain the high incidence of winning. Networking of members and follow-through by staff means only better communication; why communications enhance winning needs further exploration. Some things can be explained by old findings as well as by earlier observations from this chapter. For example, political scientists are more accustomed to thinking about winning 10 percent of all bills introduced than they are about a 70 percent success rate for issue initiatives.[23] Yet, that prereform-era committees consistently won over 80 percent of their bills, even with members poorly integrated over committee purposes is easily overlooked.[24] The reliance of committees on successful solidarity, however, still explains little of the dynamics of how either an enterprise or a committee wins. Why should better committee integration improve the odds of winning to even 100 percent, as Donald R. Matthews found?[25]

The observation that victories stem from keeping issues narrow does not explain completely why winning seems so probable when members and staff set their resources to it either. Diffuse, limited, and narrow— rather than concentrated and encompassing—member attention certainly makes it easier for the institutional rules of Congress to accommodate many demands, or wants, within a single vehicle. If most members prioritized a plethora of issues, or advocated encompassing titlewide goals, for example, it would be exceedingly hard to build effective coalitions among interested domain players. Costs of interacting would be too high, and staff would be overextended, unless, of course, members all wanted the same things, or shared issue consensus. They do not. Thus, given the problems of follow-through, winning is still formidable even in Congress.

There are, however, ways to make things easier. Other analyses of Congress and agriculture highlight how diverse member interests have become even within the solidarity of their committees. To compensate, members develop policy stories that encompass collective explanations of what they want as individuals. G. R. Boynton's study of the Senate agriculture committee is particularly instructive about this development. He finds, within the otherwise diverse views of the members, five shared "global points" of agreement on farm-price policy that integrated and bound the committee from 1960 to 1973: protection of farm income from market fluctuations, bringing commodity supply in line with demand through supply controls, voluntary program compliance by producers, emphasis on the international market, and a concern with the lowest possible program price.[26]

Committee members, throughout that prereform era, were so bound by their causal story, or shorthand and simplified explanation, of recurring high supply and offsetting prices that all solutions to individual member concerns were explained nicely from its central thesis.[27] Commodity differences, regional differences, and even cyclic conditions of the farm economy were spun off the central story of oversupply and accommodated in both its theme and the final legislation. In brief, policy was constantly readjusted for the same general and recurring reasons. The issues produced by distinctly different conditions—no matter how unique to a crop or place—were always resolvable within the paradigm, or story, that defined the interventionist purposes of price policy. As Boynton concludes, homeostasis, or stability over time, occurred because members had crafted from their shared policy experiences—and continued to refine—a sustainable policy vehicle in the ever more omnibus-style farm bills of the period.[28] He also notes evidence of the story's continued viability in policymaking through 1985. Such collectively shared stories and their capacity for ongoing adjustment seem to account for the cohesion, or high degree of integration, others have found in the House Agriculture Committee.[29] Members suggested this explanation earlier when they mentioned the significance of keeping issues defined as agricultural, which triggers the response to domain legitimacy. Agreement, as a consequence, becomes easier than diversity makes it appear.

What can be seen in Boynton's work is that the institutional structures (that is, existing policies and the committees that maintain them) of the agricultural policy domain are important to member choice and strategy. The committees organize to tell their stories, and they do so to modify and keep alive existing policies. Structures matter not just as procedural rules, but also as nonexclusive and expansive policies linked to the essential farm-development principle of the domain as it becomes encapsuled in more sweeping congressional lore that spreads through House and Senate. This broader structural importance means that within certain centrally defined value positions such as that of the agricultural-development paradigm, central rules about policy purpose mythically accommodate many diverse wants as these reflect various social problems. In consequence, individualistic members of Congress win on their issues not just because they create narrow issue demands; they also win because those narrow issue demands fit the existing institutions of Congress and the policy base, as well as organized interests. Thus, winnable issues emerge mostly as a mix of several parts maintenance of longstanding policy purposes and a more modest dose of original prescriptions for newly responsive policy reform.

That several-parts-maintenance/a-few-parts-reform formula is evident in two earlier observations. Only 16 of 256 initial issues were intended to rewrite or otherwise influence, on their own, the principal content of existing programs. Successful policy changes in these issues essentially maintained existing programs and made them look timely. Also, of the 86 member enterprises that targeted any 1990 farm-bill section, only 17 initiated any sort of broadly reformist policy: issues affecting either the entire status of an existing program or adding new policy directions to the 1990 bill that were not related to the 1985 legislation. There were few original issues among the initiators.

Members win, in other words, because they tend to build new policy for the future on an extensive and storied base of existing agricultural programs. The action taken on policy, in other words, is logically incremental—but it can take unexpected swings in the direction of reform. Individualism thrives amidst institutional restraints as members find open and accommodative omnibus farm bills supplemented with numerous other policy-vehicle options that meet their particular needs. The availability of alternate vehicles serves three useful ends that make winning less difficult: (1) gaining a strategic opportunity within the domain if farm-bill dynamics are incompatible with specific issues, (2) extending domain-relevant issues to vehicles that are more appropriate than farm bills for reaching out to nonagricultural institutions, and (3) giving new life through nondomain vehicles to existing policies and programs that may no longer fit acceptable conditions or tenets of domain politics. The latter, for example, was used when tobacco price programs were thought to be vulnerable in the 1985 farm bill and moved to a small, deficit-reduction bill.[30]

Despite the difficulties of redefining issues and moving to new turf, the nondomain option is also useful to some members because of zero-sum budget rules. For example, some members have been concerned about the ways agricultural programs or those of another domain have been run, and they want to force program changes or dismantlement. Program costs, if moved from the agriculture to the environmental domain, for instance, can be transplanted by the budget or finance committees along with the issue. Agriculture, in this example, loses its control. USDA gets no net savings to make new expenditures elsewhere, and the environmental domain adopts these issue interests at no costs in revenues. EPA, however, gains new authority in what constitutes a serious reform. In sum, the numerous choices for members, despite their farm-bill accent, litter agricultural policy with considerable institutional subterfuge. That subter-fuge makes it particularly important that each issue and its proposed intent be examined carefully to actually compare maintaining versus originating, or reformist, behavior in Congress. Only some reaggregation of the issue data is necessary to make that comparison.

As we would expect, the mix of maintaining and originating issue initiatives is strongly biased toward the protection of existing programs. However, the mix is not so directed toward maintenance that the whole of the agricultural domain and its relationships to a broader policy environ-ment appears in a state of equilibrium. This cross-sectional data suggests that the domain is in another of its periods of evolving policy games.

To assess the data, all member-initiated issues were divided between those that were intended either: (1) to preserve existing pre-1985 programs with only incremental modification; or, (2) to dismantle old programs or to add or advance new ones that could give some distinctly new policy direction to agriculture. All issues clearly fit one type or the other. This distinction provides a relatively relaxed standard for determining reform-ist behavior because originating issues can be piecemeal additions to newly proposed program changes emanating from other congressional sources. Members, in other words, were making partial contributions to what were new policy directions. A reformist's interest did not have to be in rewriting an entire title or section of a bill for her or his issue to be defined as "originating behavior." Indeed, only sixteen of the ninety-four time-consuming issues that aimed at new policy directions proposed such title- or sectionwide changes.

Using this relaxed standard, 37 percent of all time-consuming issues and 39 percent of all member priorities were linked to congressional reforms affecting agriculture (see Table A.4). Change, in other words, was advanced narrowly, as congressional network theory would predict; but it was still actively being sought. Many observers mistakenly infer equilibrium because of the remaining initiatives, or the maintaining issues. These clutter and crowd the congressional arena, emphasizing policy preservation. Maintaining initiatives filled nearly two-thirds of the total agricultural agenda of those office enterprises loading issues into committee and administrative policy vehicles. The preponderance of maintaining issues, however, cannot refute the importance of reform initiatives within the larger picture of domain and interdomain politics.

What confirms the consequences of reform initiatives are their widespread appeal to members of Congress and their high incidence of winning. Fifty-two percent of office enterprises pursued at least one originating initiative that was a member priority. In contrast, only a quarter of the enterprises engaged issues on the basis of member priority only for maintenance purposes. The mainstream appeal of policy change shows also in the small number of members (12 percent on time-consuming issues and 16 percent on priority issues) who were interested only in agricultural reform. These "originators" carried only 33 percent of member-priority reform issues forward, with fifty-two of seventy-eight originating issues initiated by members who also performed maintenance duties within the Congress.

The slightly higher prioritization by members of originating issues is expected, given issue outcomes. Originating issues also were won more frequently than maintaining ones. Whereas 69 percent of all time-consuming issues were won, 72 percent of originating issues of this type were won. Comparable rates for member-priority issues are 73 and 75 percent. These statistically insignificant differences show quite clearly that no impossible obstacles exist for members who elect to change at least some types of domain policy. Reforming behavior can be at least as successful as that which tinkers with policy readjustments in order to keep old programs intact or which incrementally shifts service and regulatory effects from one beneficiary to another. As Table A.5 shows, these findings are consistent for both the House and the Senate, as well as for the types of policy vehicle used.

Another important point is that most originating behavior goes on within the domain. Eighty-two time-consuming issues were initiated within the domain and only twelve in other domains. Those numbers fell to seventy-two and six, respectively, for member priorities, which reinforces the idea that members—even as reformers—are reluctant to leave agriculture's turf. In contrast, fifteen maintaining issues that were time-consuming and eight that were priorities were initiated for nondomain vehicles.

What these data reveal is an agricultural policy domain where the members of Congress make extensive use of existing institutions and structures to pursue the dominant number of issues of interest to them. Members seize most of their opportunities, as individual issue entrepreneurs, from present policies. Preservation of these policies has obvious utility in keeping old agricultural constituents happy. Yet, in maintaining present policy, members suffer few of the disadvantages of being labeled either obstructionists or opponents of change. Most members refute those charges by merely referring to their own prior efforts at reform. They can easily argue that the maintenance of high price supports over time are accompanied by real reforms that have made other parts of agricultural policy more socially relevant. Attention to originating, or reformist, issues by so many members with so great a rate of success defuses all but the most strident reformers in Congress. Most members find, as the data indicate, that policy can go wherever individual office enterprises take it, usually by expanding farm bills and following other legislative vehicles. As one member of Congress noted: "I have ardent environmental interests but arguing that agriculture refuses to change is never easy. There's always too much evidence of change to the contrary, even as things stay largely the same." In short, the domain is dynamic and changing because a static set of policy vehicles would serve no useful purposes to opportunistic members of Congress. This, explains former Secretary of Agriculture and ranking member of the House Agriculture Committee Edward R. Madigan, is why the 1973 farm bill was 29 pages long and that of 1990, 713 pages. More postreform members felt free to look for opportunities.

CONCLUSION

Most members of Congress intrude effectively into agricultural policy-making for what seem individually determined strategic reasons. Two factors facilitate their issue initiatives. First, the plethora of policy vehicles by which agriculture issues can be advanced makes strategic options plentiful. Although farm bills are at the center of congressional action for this domain, other legislative wraps, including some from beyond the domain, are no less useful. It would be foolish to think that issue accommodation of agricultural interests stops with farm bills or USDA. Numerous vehicles for an expanding array of policy games exist.

The second factor that facilitates intrusion is the odds for success. Successful issue initiation appears highly probable once an issue is targeted by a member enterprise, especially if it has the member's priority interest. Winning is likely not only because staff resources are formidable and members network to somehow insure success, but also because member enterprises, as congressional networking suggests, keep their demands quite narrow in order to keep conflict low.[31] They seldom try to change whole programs or entire legislative provisions on their own. Such networking members rarely face either the high costs of policy dismantlement or a great likelihood that they will confront numerous adversaries without potential coalition allies of their own.

That tactically conservative behavior, however, does not mean that the agricultural policy domain lacks dynamism or an ongoing sense of reform. If either were the case, given nonfarm demands for broader relevance to society than farm policy offers, the domain would collapse. Most issues are best advanced by building on existing policy intent, yet a third of the issues are served by nonincrementally shifting or adding to this policy base.

Reform, though, is seldom encompassing or overtly threatening to the agricultural domain and its policies, at least as initiated by most individual members in these policy games. This scale of reform suggests that reforms seldom aim at farm-price programs as the central policies of the domain. These programs are adjusted incrementally through maintaining initiatives, as the reliance on an integrating principle and its accompanying story suggest. In contrast, originating issues focus on adding a new agenda to agriculture: less environmental degradation in production, safer food, and improved nutrition are all examples. The reasons why reform is so alive and nonthreatening lie within the foundations of that institutional rule-base. Over the decades of agricultural-policy debates an extraordinarily flexible set of substantive rules was created; through postreform congressional processes and the accommodation of more and more interests, they can be amended, expanded, and added to without any real loss in core intent. "Getting something from agriculture is like punching your pillow," said another member. "It gives up when you keep hitting it but it doesn't get hurt a damned bit, at least if you and your protagonists play properly." All of those factors—numerous issues, multiple vehicles, winnable odds, flexible policies and committees, and constant punching—suggest that participation in agricultural policy entails strategy and order rather than random involvement from the many member enterprises that become players.

PART TWO
The Politics of Places

You're making this too complicated. If it's good for [our state], we're for it. If it's not good for [our state], we're against it. It's that simple.
> —A senior member of Congress, giving directions to his newly arrived, doctorate-clad staff analyst preparing for the 1990 farm bill.

4

Peak Interests: Farm Issues and Reform Issues

Agricultural politics goes on at two levels, the illusionary and the real. The illusion is that all old and new parts of the establishment matter. The reality is that farm problems flood [congressional] offices and we have to develop means of attending to them. That means is complex.
— A ranking agriculture committee staffer, discussing the strategy of insuring that each new omnibus farm bill is not the last one.

Issues are not selected by member enterprises because they appear to be good ideas in some neutral policy sense. Although issues can be seen as good ideas, "good" seems to be determined by a combination of enterprise appeal and certain strategic advantages associated with each issue. Both the appeal and the advantages are also associated with beneficiaries and their interests within the expansive array of agricultural programs, both those of the domain and those handled by nondomain policy players. Issue intent, or purpose, shows the ease with which issues can be brought to a Congress that has worked hard to become even more permeable than it always has been. Fenno's home-style explanation of congressional behavior, with its emphasis on doing Washington work for district interests, serves as the rationale for linking types of beneficiaries and types of members.[1] The explicit concern is with typing members according to the characteristics of their districts.

As I have suggested in Chapter 1, three factors condition congressional responses: numerous individual freedoms, plentiful opportunities to provide legislative services, and increased uncertainty as to which congressional players affect any given member's fate. These factors are likely to push home-style behavior into the policymaking and issue-selection process. There exists little reason to think that issue demands are created solely from within the Washington policy community.[2] As Jeffrey M. Berry states so well, members are in position to "have it all."[3]

The most compelling reason to focus on beneficiaries and their relationship to district and—for senators—state constituencies, beyond Fenno's argument, is suggested by scholarly work on congressional committees.[4] Steven S. Smith and Christopher J. Deering portray agriculture committees as primarily constituency directed, in contrast to committees where members seek assignments to shape policy solutions to national problems.[5] Members serve on the agriculture committees because that work brings returns to the district. Smaller-than-average but comparatively centralized committee staffs facilitate House efforts in much the same way that staffs do in the generally more freewheeling Senate.[6] Noncommittee members who network with the reportedly open agriculture committees have similar district purposes in mind.[7]

Smith and Deering's portrayal of House and Senate agriculture committees squares with observations from this study. Members and their staffs, without exception, described the agricultural committees and their programs as parochial and directed toward district politics: "What goes on here, even on the most important national issues, reflects what members see as local problems." They also described more than just a localized domain politics where members and staff determine district interests. Those in each member enterprise emphasized that their policymaking was exclusively reactive, responding to what others identified as policy wants.

Those in seventy-nine enterprises volunteered that opinion at the onset of their interviews: "Keep in mind one thing. We only work on issues brought to this office. We don't think them up or search them out, other than to monitor the home front for dissatisfaction." In other words, dramatic or subtle, these issues are important to one or another political interest. Whereas members and their staffs attributed specific nonenterprise origins to each of their time-consuming and priority issues, they also indicated that nothing was unusual about this domain's reactive policymaking. As one legislative director noted, "I don't pay my staff to conjure up issues. We have too much to do in all policy areas to worry about our own ideas. Agriculture is different only in that you can more predictably pinpoint those places that bring you problems and issues."

The consequences of reactive policymaking for Congress are evident. Localism and responsiveness, as components of home-style representation, play out in generalized patterns of legislative behavior rather than at random. Predominantly narrow issues are framed as beneficiary-specific initiatives, at least so far as these represent organized interests and distinct causes associated with the agricultural domain.[8] For an encompassing and expansive policy domain, with its 130-year policy history, this framing creates the potential for a widely varied pattern of issue interests and initiatives. As the following sections will show, that potential is unrealized. Although the pattern of selected issues is broad and despite varied vehicle choices, it is far more concentrated than representative of all domain policy problems. All types of domain issues most emphatically do not have high levels of congressional salience. Rather, the most salient types of issues exhibit two alternate tendencies—either long-term constituent use or recent high-profile introduction into the domain. Along with that mixed interest are formed adaptive issue choices that encourage members to follow both traditional and reformist policy paths.

FARM-INCOME FEVER

Given the large number of members who intrude into agriculture, the low salience of most issue types within the domain is surprising. One might well have predicted that the extensive range of agricultural issues would cause widespread member involvement. Wouldn't the broad range of topics create a great number of opportunities? After all, the Washington policy community has had a growing number of interest groups and proliferating branches within agencies. As the earlier discussion of the agricultural establishment implies, traditional types of agriculture issues include direct farm assistance, education and technical outreach, product innovation and research, regulation of agribusiness middlemen and farm-provider services, rural infrastructure and development, as well as those of price-support and conservation policies from the 1930s. Types of issues institutionalized within agriculture since the 1950s include low-income food assistance, nutrition, consumer health and safety, international food aid, promotion of world food and fiber trade, value-added exports, energy use, environmental degradation, low resource-depleting or sustainable farming techniques, family farm and land preservation, animal rights and welfare, rural community problems, and assorted others. Yet, only a limited range of these issue types were the subject of much attention from member enterprises; many were of little or no interest. Apparently, they failed to generate more than limited opportunities for reacting to valued interests.

Congress, at least insofar as its agenda is set by its members' issue initiatives, neither seriously debates nor considers all those topics of concern that exist among other organizations and institutions of the domain. "Just because it's important at the university," noted one administrative assistant, "doesn't mean we give a damn." Attention is directed toward specific types of problems and, for the enterprise, well-defined beneficiaries. Most attention is given to a base of extensively used or timely policies that reward specific stakeholders and clearly identifiable social activists who tend to be distributed in numerous locales. Yet many prominent and emotional issues of national scope are largely ignored, even when extensive efforts are going on in agencies and in the states to implement existing policies that address them.

In essence, because of timeliness, individual members focus on issues that are hardly representative of agriculture's encompassing agenda or of the workload of its other policy organizations. As we have seen issue initiation is more than widespread, limited in the intrusiveness of each member, narrowly directed, maintenance intended, and somewhat reformist; initiatives are also generally the central policy concerns of the domain or, alternatively, they are limited to a few obvious appeals that best link members and constituents within some current context that helps define relevant policy games. The orientation of members to centrally important causal stories suggests that collective attention to a current, or at least a recurring, context is important in shaping congressional attention.

When issues were categorized by their proposed intent, five types dominated enterprise interests. Eighty-three percent of time-consuming and 85 percent of member-priority issues, by rank, went for farm-income enhancement, environmental problems associated with farm and ranch production, trade programs for food and fiber products, rural-community needs, and nutrition efforts (see Table A.6). Almost all the issues for each of these types were handled within agricultural domain vehicles, most frequently in farm bills. That ranking actually understates farm-policy attention. Although 31 of the time-consuming and 22 of the member-priority issues overlapped somewhat in purpose between two issue types, all of these issues shared a farm-benefit emphasis as well as another more dominant intent. Accordingly, all of these were labeled nonfarm-issue types.[9] Good examples are an environmental program that led to land set-aside payments to owners, or a research project for a land-grant university that established care providers for a specific cattle breed.

The result of this farm-benefit emphasis is a policy domain that reflects heavy biases in the attention and interests of congressional members, something not entirely unexpected in a domain that has long followed a central farm-development principle with only a few transitions in its high-profile policy games. Excluding the small number of rural and nutrition issues, the politics of the domain in the late 1980s and early 1990s concentrated primarily on supplementing farm incomes, exporting low-priced commodities and value-added products, and imposing environmentally responsive standards on farm practices. The prevailing politics of the 1970s and early 1980s, with its farm-for-food-assistance trades, was replaced by a changing set of member interests that reflected the domain's dynamic tendencies and its attention to timeliness. The old food-versus-farm policy game was being shoved to the back burner of member interest, demonstrating, it seems, that those disputes were resolved in the eyes of most of the members of Congress.

The Centrality of the Farm-Income Problem

Considerable irony can be seen in the data on issue selection by members, at least if the concept of majority rule is taken to mean servicing specific majority interests. Food and fiber producers constitute less than 2 percent of the U.S. population, including part-time farmers. Yet, in a policy domain with jurisdiction over a large number of industries that account for more than 15 percent of U.S. gross domestic product, farmers and ranchers get the lion's share of personal support from enterprises in both House and Senate. Of the 256 time-consuming issues, 44 percent were concerned with somehow influencing the financial distribution of federal support to producers. An even higher 47 percent of member-priority issues served that purpose. Moreover, because of the overlapping effect of the issue types, another 12 percent of time-consuming issues and 11 percent of member-priority issues also affected farm beneficiaries. Producers of one kind or another were direct beneficiaries of over 55 percent of member initiatives within the domain, not counting indirect benefits from agricultural research and extension that were issues for other beneficiaries.

The range of this intervention on behalf of farmers was extraordinarily broad, going far beyond direct price-support and commodity-loan policies. Too often, farm payments have been thought of only in price-policy terms, but not among contemporary members of Congress, who no longer believe in single solutions to farm-income problems or, apparently, in the triangle networks credited for that policy's existence. Anything that could be done to provide additional resources to producers seemed fair. Some initiators were involved with direct payments, others aimed at lowering farm-business costs. Numerous proposals emphasized free or low-cost commercial subsidies. Tax incentives, tax breaks, federal commodity purchases, lower operating- and investment-loan rates, subsidies for reducing production capacity, disaster assistance, proposals for increased idling of land and facilities, cost-containing inspections, assumptions of cost obligations for federal and state regulations, payments for lost use of property, low-cost leasing arrangements for federal land and water, marketing assistance, new check-offs for commodity-advertising promotions, and such cost-containing federal services as breeding programs and disease control were among these initiatives. Twelve of these issues were pursued in other domains.

As one veteran senator observed: "My feedlot ranchers get no price-support payments and, by God, they pay a high price for corn growers who do. I use government policy to even that out. Veterinary services, grain-standards pricing differentials, and tax and loan programs do it." This type of behavior brings intriguing results at times. For example, Texas feedlot owners have found themselves buying downgraded corn supplies and feeding their cattle far more cheaply with these "damaged goods" than could Midwest competitors. Explained a second member, "When Congress got into supporting basic crops through price policy, it just opened up the door to provide some damned federal mechanism for every other crop or critter." Members and their staffs emphasized that their agricultural issues, for as long as they can remember and even in a changing policy era, were dominated by farm-income problems and creative responses to them. A northeastern congressman who entered the House at mid-term observed: "I've been here only weeks and I've already two pressing problems, saving my shipyard and helping local apple growers with some disaster assistance. My work here is about jobs, and both kinds count."

As these comments imply, farm-income politics is not generally a mixed bag of maintenance and reforms, as is the domain as a whole. Of the 112 time-consuming farm-benefit issues, only 7 were reformist, or originating, issues. Only 5 of these were member priorities (see Table A.7). Three sought payment or program-reductions, 2 limited payments to large-scale producers. None of the overlapping farm-beneficiary issues that were typed with rural, environmental, trade, or miscellaneous issues sought program reductions. At most, they marginally redistributed farm benefits among different producers or aimed to reallocate administrative costs to growers' payments. For example, one enterprise sought to move some conservation payments from those who grew erosion-prone crops to those who introduced "new crops" with less erosion potential. This initiative, in effect, was subsidizing a core of existing producers of those environmentally friendly crops: "We were getting money in those guys' pockets to aid that conversion. It was a good policy."

Such efforts and their wide use explain why farm-price-support reforms have so far failed in an otherwise dynamic policy domain. While the many profarm initiatives were being advanced, a well-publicized reform effort to end income programs for peanuts, sugar, and honey was being fought. Representatives Dick Armey (R-Texas) and Charles E. Schumer (D-N.Y.) organized the Coalition for a Common Sense Food Policy to bring market-oriented Republicans and liberal, largely urban Democrats together against, in Armey's words, the "folly of central agricultural planning." After generating the greatest amount of publicity for any single conflict in the entire 1990 farm-bill debates, these initiatives were stalled in both coalition and committee negotiations. The coalition's subsequent floor amendment to limit each farmer to $100,000 per year in commodity subsidies was defeated 159 to 263. As Armey explained: "Powerful interests just killed us. I had no realization of their influence here, badly underestimated."[10] Both commodity and environmental interests attacked the coalition, arguing that there was a need to protect the agricultural-policy base.

Armey's surprise is the surprise, at least in view of these data. Some reforms are popular, but not those whose effects are antithetical to the domain's emphasis on agricultural development and its encompassing policy stories. Not only were the greatest number of issues framed on behalf of farm producers, but most member enterprises also acted as farm-income proponents. These initiatives were proposed across the Congress. When issues are considered for each member, as in Table A.8, 74 percent of all enterprises, or 84 of them, worked on at least one time-consuming farm-benefit issue. This was more than the 63 percent of those (or 71) that initiated any and all other types of agricultural issues. Member-priority issues were almost equally skewed in favor of producers, with 69 percent of members (78 of them) initiating farm issues and 57 percent (65 enterprises) pursuing those of any other type.

Quite clearly, and expectedly, the critical issues of this domain remain those of farm-income policy. The collective influence of farm interests, supported by an existing policy base, is extensive. Members, through their intervention on a wide array of income issues, well serve the central development tenet of the agriculture domain by keeping alive numerous components of public-sector support for private-sector producers.[11] At least they serve that organizing principle and central tenet as they see its current applicability: "Agricultural development, to me anyway, means keeping those well-educated young farmers in business. All the work of the land grants and [USDA] research units around the country means little if the resource folds. Beyond that I'm not convinced, even as a liberal Democrat, that agricultural development today doesn't come more from the private sector than it does from public institutions."[12]

Members, through their individual initiatives, follow with little reservation the decades-long agricultural-policy struggle of keeping farmers in business through government intervention. What committee deliberations reduce to a causal story to justify intervention gets played out by individual members as the central and critical part of past and current policy games within the domain. Myths matter, in this case because they are followed by numerous members from throughout the Congress. That these ventures on behalf of farmers are so widespread and more frequent than all other domain initiatives is startling. Agricultural committees are not the only parochial forces in Congress. Parochialism extends beyond members' having jurisdiction over domain institutions to far more members playing than were expected even within expansive congressional networks. They all find opportunities in the relatively easy manipulation of an open base of numerous public policies.

The Politics of Domain Balance

Neither Congress nor its individual members are blatantly profarmer in their agricultural issues and policy choices. The data on use of policy vehicles and member and staff explanations of that use affirmed that point earlier. Congressional issue initiatives are exercises in balance: they select some issues that reward farmers, as the oldest constituencies in agriculture, and other issues that identify the initiating member with reform.

A brief look at the data shows this balancing of issues by individual members. Less than a quarter of all enterprises (26 of them) initiated only farm-benefit issues (Table A.9). Somewhat fewer (20 enterprises) initiated only issues for other agricultural policy purposes. Most members emphasized their interest in both farm and other issues, although they expressed it slightly less often through priority issues. This latter set of members also intruded the most frequently in domain politics: the 58 enterprises that proposed time-consuming initiatives for both farm and other purposes were responsible for 194 issues, or 76 percent of the total; the 53 enterprises that initiated 154 member-priority issues for both farm and other purposes were responsible for 77 percent. The most active players, quite certainly, were those members who engaged in issue balancing. As one of them noted: "I like being seen as someone who takes care of my farmers and other bigger problems."

This congressman's emphasis on "bigger problems" meant linking some of his farm issues with reform initiatives, "the well-covered ones, you know, agriculture's new directions." Such concerns directed the most heavily involved members to a mix of initiatives that was more likely than not to include, as we saw in Chapter 3, both originating *and* maintaining issues. Originating issues, quite surprisingly, were rarely those of members who could be considered the most distinct domain outsiders, or likely outliers; committee members had reform interests. Over two-thirds of the issue initiators of farm and other programs, despite numerous options, pursued both reformist and maintenance goals. This meant that few members were involved in the domain only to advance originating issues.[13] While fourteen members initiated only originating issues of a time-consuming type and nine advanced only originating member-priority issues, many more members (forty-two of them) were willing to work only on policy maintenance.

A strategy of issue-identification and -selection becomes evident. While the preferred position for most members is one of balancing what are seemingly the domain's least compatible issues, taking care of only existing policies is acceptable for many other members. However, only a few members appear willing to intrude into agricultural policy as ardent reformers without also evidencing an interest in traditional programs that provide domain stability. The lesson seems simple: don't be only a reformer.

"I think," explained one staffer, "that you have to advise your boss not to be like a Pete Kostmayer [D-Pa.], who goes from being an entrenched incumbent to rumors of being on the borderline (of electoral defeat) next year. He thought all of his environmental reform ideas for western public-lands management would play in his upscale suburban district." After Kostmayer's 1992 defeat, the same subcommittee staffer continued: "I told you so. I could see by the letters that it was hard to convince people back home that a cattle-free environment in Wyoming was in the best interest of Bucks County. . . . Attacking private property rights is dangerous."

In contrast, other members were held out as being far more representative of their home places in their behavior—and, accordingly, electorally more secure. "I'd like to be Ben Campbell [D-Colo.]," a colleague observed, "he doesn't have to wear a tie and identifies with all those Native-American problems, yet his cattlemen and oil guys from the rest of the state know him as approachable and no less inclined to work for them. He takes care of all state interests and is seen as fair back home, not some single-issue or turn-the-world-upside-down type." While Kostmayer was being defeated in 1992, Campbell was moving to the Senate.

More than some generic desire to mix farm benefits with just any other reform type issue moves enterprises, however. The timeliness of a specific cross-section of issues becomes apparent. Strategies appear quite issue specific. Trade and environmental initiatives are both the next most popular issues after farm benefits and the dominant originating types. Although all but one of the members who were interested in nutrition issues also proposed farm-benefit issues, that consumer and welfare topic generated little member interest. "No currency," summarized one member. Currency, or timeliness, in issue mixing was found principally in the popular issues of trade and the environment. Thirty-one of the fifty-eight enterprises that mixed farm and other time-consuming issues chose to mix with trade or the environment. Roughly the same ratio, twenty-six of fifty-three, selected those issues as member priorities.

Accordingly, within this policy domain, the typical reformist member of Congress was most likely to be mixing farm-program involvement with trade programs, or alternately, with environmental initiatives. Reformists wanted significantly new features in agriculture along with farm-income protection: "[T]he reformists want either better ways to protect environmental health, or they want significant trade expansion. They're serious about new stuff." As all who mixed these issues with ones for farmers explained, these topics were opportunities in both the changing post-reform Congress and the expansive Washington community: "hot issues you can ride"; "the ones that get attention"; "where coverage is focused."

Issue selection, it appears fair to conclude, is more than just balancing the central concerns of a domain with emerging ones. In addition, selection entails identifying a small range of especially timely issues from among all those possible. Members discover the dominant policy games of the moment for the domain as they became linked to more traditionally recurring farm-policy concerns. The environmental problems of farm-production practices led to collectively shared accounts, or stories, of farmers overusing resources. Likewise, problems of oversupply in production permitted trade initiators to tell how their issue initiatives added to the collective story of how to deal with the problems. This emphasis explains how, if not exactly why, animal-rights and welfare issues were mostly ignored even while animal activists from People for the Ethical Treatment of Animals (PETA) were sending large delegations of constituent supporters to blanket congressional offices—these groups were unable either to break old links in domain collective stories or to establish new ones. "It takes some courage to do something different on the Hill," charged a member who combined farm and environmental attention, "I'm not [courageous]."

OTHER ISSUES AND THEIR POLICY SUBSTANCE

Two sets of behavior reveal much about the opportunism of members in their issue selection: (1) issue mixing and (2) the concentration of attention on but a few timely nonfarm programs. Yet decisions about issue selection must also be seen as somewhat more complex than these. Members and their staffs felt that the extensive base of domain policies makes it especially feasible to include a farm-benefit component in any issue mix. Working for farmers is relatively easy, for reasons of policy history that were explained earlier. These people also emphasized that that policy base generates great numbers of demands from the likely beneficiaries of issues for incremental adjustment and for corrections of perceived inequalities. Therefore, there are numerous but rather homogeneous claimants to satisfy. So farm-policy opportunities are both low cost and high payoff.

Inherently reactive enterprises, facing periodic rewriting of basic policy in adjustment-oriented and contentious farm-bill cycles, feel pressures to take some—often any—kind of actions for particular beneficiaries. As one would expect, then, behavior within the postreform Congress is indeed due to larger contextual factors in politics. As Jess Gilbert and Carolyn Howe note, there exists a kind of synergism about agriculture, in which public institutions and grassroots forces converge to prompt policy momentum.[14] As a junior member with no previous experience in the domain explained, "With that farm bill just snowballing through the process, you feel foolish if you don't put something in it for one of your many plaintiffs. You don't have that many chances to show gains up here." As a consequence, that urban member was working on a low-income food program for, as he saw it, inner-city children and an income-protecting scheme for his state's apple growers. Often these pressures to act eventually led to the choice of alternate policy vehicles: "The tempo of demands gets so high and so intense that things that fail to fit in farm bills have to be pursued elsewhere. You've publicly committed yourself. Pressures won't go away."

Because of unrelenting pressures from claimants and from busy office schedules, the element of timeliness in issue selection is, again, evident. Farmers, of course, are always in vogue because their issues recur. For issues of trade and the environment, the impression of contemporary timeliness facilitates the same low cost/high payoff decision making identified with farm issues. When members and their staffs select a nonfarm issue that becomes the responsibility of their enterprise, the ease of action and the prevalence of beneficiary demands both come into play, just as they do for farm issues. Accordingly, the selection of nonfarm issues, like that of farm issues, involves more than simply juggling issue attention or identifying with any handy reformist challenge. These individually opportune issues, too, are timely in that concentrated member attention can be linked to specific events and trends within the Congress, creating political windows for what will probably be a time-bound but intense policy game.[15]

Relatively neglected issues, though, lack that sense of congressional timeliness. They create much less of an impression of immediate relevance. Member initiatives seem to matter only when the creation of public institutions can be identified with widespread social wants: "What the hell good does it do to pass something when nobody pays attention."

Other Maintenance Issues

The association of public institutions and public wants is especially necessary for most other issues that maintain policy. Only three types of nonfarm maintenance issues were initiated by several members—rural, trade, and research. These, however, included thirty-two of fifty-seven such time-consuming issues, or 56 percent, and twenty-one of forty-two member priorities. Thirteen members were interested in rural issues, and eight were concerned with expanding already existing federal trade subsidies in agricultural-products promotion. The rural issues were aimed either at community infrastructure supports, water projects, or at economic development grants.[16] Trade issues targeted either specific commodities or products for assistance, encouraging in each instance increased shipping and handling of overseas exports. The other frequently initiated nonfarm maintenance issues were less single-purpose and included in the miscellaneous category. Nonetheless, eleven members initiated issues for individual public-research centers and other related projects. Some of these issues organized institutes, some awarded project funds, others mandated new research directives.

One thing that rural, trade, and research initiatives shared was the initiating enterprise's commitment to framing each issue as beneficiary and place specific: "Remember these are for certain people." Members and staff were working on behalf of communities with rural bridge problems, those with water supplies from depleted local aquifers, universities with poultry programs, grants to particular colleges, and very specific types of manufacturing and shipping firms; they targeted the user of the allocated funds, never some generic purpose. As a committee staffer candidly remarked, "These projects are all designated for exact interests. A university or firm or a set of regional municipalities will benefit and, for all practical purposes, get earmarked appropriations."

What helped to account for the clustering of attention on these three types of issues is the dimension of low cost/high payoff timeliness in Congress, in addition to the emphasis on beneficiaries who generated demands. Community context sets the stage for individual members who see common opportunities. Rural issues gained attention because the Senate agriculture committee chair, Patrick J. Leahy (D-Vt.), had gone to great lengths from 1987 to 1990 to try to get a marginally popular rural-development bill through Congress. In attempting to win, Leahy opened his policy vehicle to whatever kinds of issues potential supporters wanted.[17] Similar deals were struck in the House. He also activated noncongressional interests. Although the bill failed, all but one members' initiatives were then retargeted to the farm bill. No one, however, sought the policy reforms that the Leahy vehicle's purpose implied. Members and their staffs merely used the low-cost situation Leahy had created to slightly alter and expand existing rural programs.

Research interests were accommodated in a similar fashion, dependent on the momentum of congressional action. As members and their staffs were quick to point out, Congress has for some time been systematically removing research funds from competitive grant appropriations to earmarked institutions. As one agriculture committee staffer explained: "We could not say 'no' to a ploy used throughout the entire House in every area of federal research support. The argument for taking research grants away from peer reviewers and agency administrators is a compelling one on the Hill. Once it started, members knew they, too, could deliver very useful research projects to the folks back home." Again, as was the case for rural issues, members simply redistributed benefits from the margins of on-going programs in low-cost fashion. These initiators were not starting new policy games based on a reformist agenda; rather, they were resurrecting policies from games that had been eclipsed within domain policy vehicles.

Nor were trade issues part of a new and high-cost game when linked to old policies. Trade maintainers were initiating issues appended to the longest and most narrowly written farm-bill title, agricultural promotions, with its 102 sections. "Those programs," as one southern congressman explained, "started out as particularized bailouts and handouts." Yet maintenance-style trade programs were seldom targeted within that total set of initiatives. Larger congressional trends made international-trade programs a much better and more timely target for reformists and opportunistic originators.

The Dominant Reform Agenda

Originating activity was more concentrated around certain issues than nonfarm program maintenance was (see Tables A.6, A.7, and A.8), and for good reasons. Trade and environmental issues were so numerous that (1) they covered nearly one-third of all initiatives, (2) they encompassed over three-fourths of the originating issues of the entire domain, and (3) each of the two types gained the attention of over one-quarter of all office enterprises. However, trade and environmental issues were never mixed by the same enterprises. They were distinct games, operating through conflict to bring the domain together, just as the rural/urban coalition did in the 1960s. Maintenance issues of all types, in contrast, were frequently mixed. Accordingly, trade and environmental issues were two popular but uniquely unrelated reform types—the interests of distinctly different members. Trade issue advocates were far more likely than environmental initiators to mix their issues with farm-benefit initiatives (see Table A.9).

Both sets of issues included numerous topics. Originating trade issues were intended to specify items within the North American Free Trade Agreement (NAFTA) or General Agreement on Tariffs and Trade (GATT); to establish new markets for new products; to subsidize rural enterprise zones; or to extend export-enhancement programs from the 1985 farm bill. Nearly all these initiatives depended on exporting or otherwise using more farm commodities to reduce oversupply. Environmental reforms emphasized wetlands conservation; public lands protection; regulations for environmental degradation; limits on farm use of land and water;

pesticide-use-and-supply restrictions; incentives for lowering pesticide use; water quality standards; and air quality standards. For the most part, these initiatives decreased farm production or raised the financial cost of meeting current production levels. They were thus in direct contrast to trade programs, which of course explained the appeal of the two programs to two different sets of members. Nonetheless, the further incorporation of both programs into the agricultural policy domain elevated their collective importance to a growing number of opportunistic congressional members.

Despite major differences, both in their impact and in which members were interested, these two issue types were quite alike in two important ways. First, each was seen as producing beneficiary-specific proposals. Second, both were reactions to reform initiatives begun in the 1985 farm bill, the Food Security Act. That is, within their timely policy windows, trade and the environment were extended and ongoing games—ones that at the time of the 1990 farm bill entailed low costs of entry despite their reformist bent.

Trade initiatives are the issues most obviously of interest to selected beneficiaries. The purpose of all trade initiatives was to advance U.S. foreign-trade sales, but each proposal worked by setting specific protections or subsidies for distinct crops, products, or firms. While the environmental programs provided collectively received benefits for the public, they were also written to please very identifiable constituent beneficiaries.

Members and their staffs saw actions being taken on behalf of one constituency group as coming at the expense of another group, even on environmental questions. Farmers and landowners paid when actions were taken at the request of municipal and industrial water users, outdoor recreation advocates, state government officials, and those citizens and activists who simply gave high salience to one or more environmental-quality issues. "Environmental advocates are directed toward favors for themselves in the same way that farmers or firms want favors," explained an interior committee staff associate.

As a consequence, member enterprises tailored environmental initiatives both to specific user groups in local places and to the particularistic demands of other complainants: "The trick is identifying what people want on those issues. . . . For example, clean groundwater is important where homes depend on wells but not much of an issue where the emphasis is on river and lake water standards. What you do as a member of Congress is attuned to very specific problems that come to you

and get discussed in local communities." As another member emphasized, "Environmental programs are for the common good but are well
received only by a few. Those are the ones you work to please." As these
comments suggest, enterprises that initiated environmental issues are able
to claim credit for them for pleasing those who consider themselves
direct beneficiaries rather than for reasons of general social well-being.
Although these issues produce collective benefits for the general public,
members find them good opportunities because at least some beneficiaries
receive them with selective appreciation.

Finding opportunities in these two types of reform issues again depends
on timely congressional events and the ease of working with existing
policy games and on an established policy base—or low costs. Trade and
environment issues were both follow-through reforms. The Food Security
Act of 1985, in its impact, was much like the omnibus farm bill of 1973,
the Agriculture and Consumer Protection Act. Both farm bills institutionalized "new agenda" issues into the domain and then led to continuing
controversy and conflict. The 1973 act permanently institutionalized food-
stamp programs as part of farm bills, even though this program had been
established previously and would still demand negotiated settlements to
ensure support.[18] The 1985 act began the process of building both
foreign-trade enhancement programs and environmental policy into the
agriculture domain, expanding considerably on a base of product promotion and soil- and water-conservation legislation.[19] The 1985 act, too, was
only a second step on the way to potential policy equilibrium.

Issue-initiating reformists in Congress simply were capitalizing on the
conflicts and accommodations of 1985 as the 1990 farm bill and other
policy vehicles advanced. Since trade and environmental issues were
perceived as gaining in popularity with both the Congress and the public
over that period, concentrated issue initiation flourished in several individualistic member enterprises. Under postreform congressional conditions, each of them had the flexibility to become real policy players, and
they used their clout to insist that any policy they supported must include
provisions for the solutions they offered.

Other closely tied congressional events helped solidify perceptions
about the importance of these ongoing games. NAFTA and GATT trade
agreements and scheduled Clean Air and Clean Water acts furthered the
congressional awareness of impending reform opportunities. The growing
awareness and sense of comfort with those two sets of opportunities can
be seen in the degree to which enterprises turned to them over time. As
it became evident that these types of issues were especially popular,

members were asked about similar interests of their enterprises in the mid-1980s.[20] Although twenty-six members initiated environmental issues as the 1990 farm bill approached, only two of them had done so for the 1985 legislation. Only seven of those twenty-eight who had initiated trade in the 1990 act had done so in earlier acts, even for the maintenance issues of product promotion. Thus, members who pursued newly available opportunities in the domain were affected far more by the timeliness of demands made on them than by any recurring interest in those issues. As open congressional networking suggests, new opportunities create new intrusions. But the opportunities are not distributed equally among all issues.

Neglected Issues

To an extent, the very few members who exhibited an interest in less well-attended issues, like nutrition programs, reflect neglect of important policies, at least when compared to the large number of trade and environmental initiators. With a children's nutrition act on the congressional agenda; with Representative Leland's death provoking a legislative reaction; and with widespread stories of U.S. nutritional needs and a health-conscious public in the media, member opportunities would seem more likely. Those events, however, generated no concentrated member interest, nor did they lead to well-publicized congressional reforms in any domain vehicles in the late 1980s. Only five members initiated nutrition issues, and none felt much recognition for that work. As one of them summarized, the subject "generated a weak but intense response, and we created some useful and significant changes. Not many members saw opportunities, though."

The comments of that member suggest the opposite of what the clustered and concentrated issue attention of members might imply. He continued, "It doesn't take a lot of members working on similar things to make something happen." That belief in opportunities without concentrated attention undoubtedly led several other legislators to initiate numerous types of agricultural-policy issues that, at most, two other members also pursued. Roughly 15 percent of issues were typed as miscellaneous. Although most of these were of the maintenance variety, they were of interest to nearly a quarter of all enterprises. As was the case for research issues, with which they were typed, other miscellaneous issues commanded somewhat less member-priority attention than did other types of initiatives. Nonetheless, one of every five members with a priority issue in agriculture selected one or more issues of the miscellaneous type. Quite interestingly, these members—like those who initiated rural and nutrition issues—almost always mixed their initiatives with other issues providing farm benefits.

Miscellaneous issues were remarkably varied. Topics of concern included animal and plant health-and-safety regulation, human disease control, animal rights and welfare, organic agriculture, farm workers and their problems, child labor, energy supplies, new product development, genetic standards and biotechnology, food labeling, food-industry support, restaurant regulations, consumer protection, support of private-sector research, extension and education programs, shipping restrictions, commodity standards, commodity trading, and regulation of boards of trade. All that distinguished these initiatives from other, more concentrated issues was the lack of related congressional and media events; there were no functional equivalents of the highly publicized GATT and Clean Air negotiations for these issues. Nor were there emerging farm-bill games that elevated their importance, at least of such a well-publicized and timely scope as trade and the environment.

To be successful and win, members had to depend on more than the momentum of timely issues. Accordingly, thirty of the miscellaneous time-consuming issues and twenty-four of the member priorities were targeted to catchall farm bills or their administration: "These are like a trash bin," linked with on ongoing game of unbound proportions.[21] The other issues, with the exception of one attached to a labor bill, were divided between omnibus and single-purpose bills that were the subject of debates over domain turf, such as food labeling. More than for all other issues, miscellaneous initiatives were directed toward legislative vehicles in general and those of agriculture's domain in particular. Members let the agriculture committees handle these issues if at all possible. Initiators recognized the central institutional rules and organizations of the domain as being encompassing and expansive enough to cover most of their assorted opportunistic wants in typical low-cost fashion.

Beneficiaries of these issues were both varied and specific, with agri-business firms and regionally based commodity growers affected by twenty-one of the time-consuming issues and fifteen of the member-priorities. So, rather than trying to capitalize on larger events, miscellaneous issue initiators, like those of farm-benefit issues, worked the easy gambit of tying their issues to existing and naturally expansive legislation—that is, the old policy base—on behalf of those they could please. What their efforts showed, though, was that postreform congressional conditions gave even iconoclastic members opportunities, if they could work with existing policies and traditional players.

Winning

The success of iconoclastic members proved the malleability of Congress. Remarkably little variation occurred in the winning percentages of the six issue types (Table A.10). Only 54 percent of the small number of rural issues were won, primarily because a much briefer version of the Rural Development Act was incorporated into the 1990 farm bill. All other beneficiary-type bills passed with winning percentages of 69 to 71 percent.[22]

Member-priority differences did show interesting and statistically significant differences. The events surrounding trade and environmental issues—with their reformist context and their identification with timely domain changes—meant that these issues were the ones most frequently won. Maintenance issues for farm and miscellaneous beneficiaries were only slightly less successful, reflecting the relative ease of using an existing policy base to support identifiable beneficiaries. In comparison, nutrition-reform issues and rural-maintenance issues were more difficult to win. The lack of widespread congressional momentum on those two issues, even with more than occasional interest in them, seemed to work somewhat to their disadvantage at the member-priority level. The same was true of research issues.

Even so, the high rates of success for all issues are more notable than the relatively minor differences and advantages among them. Congress shows a remarkable ability to give balanced attention to divergent types of policy in keeping its many members satisfied. If member enterprises wish to win, and if they follow the appropriate strategies of formulating narrow content and moderating their goals, the odds of succeeding on any domain issue type that members select appear to be quite good. Mixing nonfarm issues with farm issues, however, seems an integral part of that success for all members except those with an environmental agenda. Other than that practice, the biggest factor in winning lies in what seems to be the greater prevalence of opportunities associated with some issues, such as farm and environmental programs, over others, such as rural affairs and animal welfare. This uneven distribution brings far more wins for some beneficiaries than for others. Of course, the absolute number of wins, if high, is a far more important factor for beneficiaries than is a high winning percentage on a small number of issues. Farmers, accordingly, really are the major winners, followed by trade and environmental interests.

As a result of the cumulative effect of wins, a Congress reacting to numerous farm interests on many issues is hardly ready, under these policy games, to dismantle widely important farm price supports. At the same time, Congress demonstrates its flexibility by being willing to move its attention from farm interests to trade interests and even to environmental interests that impose costs on farmers. Winning in Congress shows just how dynamic a policy domain can be under the appropriate relations between timeliness and traditional responses.

CONCLUSION

Agricultural institutions have long been seen as constituency directed, both in the intent of traditional farm programs and in the operation of congressional agriculture committees. With a constituency purpose embedded in what is mostly handled as domain policy, it hardly seems surprising that those in member enterprises view their work as both reactive and specific to beneficiary and place. Members view policies of the domain in select and small pieces. At least, their enterprises treat agricultural policy that way in their issue selection and prioritization, even while acknowledging that important central features govern domain intrusion. There appears simultaneously a distinct openness to the domain and to Congress, yet a set of dynamics that remind members that not all types of issues offer the same opportunities.

The choice of issues, on the surface, seems unconnected to widespread popular appeal. Distinguished agricultural economists have long warned of declining farm-sector influence.[23] Their basis for such assessments is the assumption of majority rule in establishing the importance of issues and, with a farm population in perpetual decline since the mid-1930s, their belief that urban voters simply will overpower farm district representatives. Their concerns have merit, but only if politics is viewed as a zero-sum game dividing constituents in clearly obvious and competing ways; after all, not a single congressional district has a 20 percent farm population in the 1990s.

As congressional members approach issue selection in agriculture, however, they see few such zero-sum constraints. That is why even issue successes that surprise policymakers seldom create a ripple in the media.

There are no obvious losers since there has been little open conflict. But members and staff understand the importance of issues to narrow constituencies and for their own futures. As one northeastern member noted, "I'll be responding to the sector as long as one producer exists to make noise in my district, at least as long as people eat." From that perspective, anticipating the effect of majority rule seems to be an academic version of the tedium of *Waiting for Godot*, far removed from real-world politics.

What the data demonstrate quite conclusively is a preoccupation of members—across the Congress, it seems—with farm-income problems. Members suggest that congressional opportunities in reacting to farmers are linked to their tendency to be active politically and to the wide respect accorded them by a food-dependent public.[24] That conclusion will receive further attention in later chapters. Nonetheless, when a member intrudes into agriculture's domain and one of its policy networks, at least part of that effort is usually taken on behalf of farmer beneficiaries. This kind of effort frequently adds new farm-program benefits for specific producers, and it strengthens congresswide support for farm income assistance.

Although farm-directed behavior is relatively easy because of the large and existing policy base, that low-personal-cost is insufficient to explain why so many members engage in it. The base of rural programs and that of policies for the organization of the agricultural establishment are also extensive, but are relatively neglected by issue initiators. If the number of wins in Congress are indicators, farm power still dominates the politics of agriculture even though the agricultural establishment is far less relevant than it once was. This persistent power prompts members of Congress to see the central purpose of the domain as direct income assistance to farmers; as John Kingdon would suggest, members like this regularity as a means of reducing uncertainty about their role in agricultural policy.[25] In contrast members, as individuals and enterprises, are far less interested in providing indirect policy support to the farm sector by funding professionals who deliver agricultural-policy services. The traditional establishment of land grant and USDA employees seems to matter little as a result. Members in the main choose to intervene, for whatever high-payoff reasons, in behalf of producers and growers, at least in the front-loading of available policy vehicles.

Interestingly enough, farm influence permeated much of the issue-mixing strategies of members, which certainly seems another factor in why farm policies avoid reform. Only two sets of member enterprises were not conspicuous in balancing one substantive type of issue with another. Twelve members intruded into the domain only for environmental beneficiaries. Yet twenty-six members initiated issues only for farmers. However, issue-mixing—or looking attentive to various policy problems—still is the most typical form of issue-initiating behavior.

The reasons for issue-mixing remain somewhat unclear, other than the obvious advantage of serving more than one minority interest such as farmers. Members gain the strategic advantage of making commitments to others in a broadly responsive domain. These commitments can refute, symbolically at least, those frequent charges of parochialism in agriculture. In addition, by facilitating issue mixing, the domain itself becomes a more opportune one for an expansive range of members. Enterprises, however, do not improve their winning percentages by mixing issues. Issue-mixers won roughly 70 percent of all their issues. It appears, then, that issue-mixers simply select more issues in order to pursue a greater number of opportunities, as they are encouraged to do by the expansive procedural rules of Congress. Every conceivable issue looks to be fair game, even if it is underutilized.

Certainly the data on initiators of trade and environmental issues suggest the strategic advantages—or increased personal opportunities—of these two sets of initiatives. Both, next to farm-benefit issues, dominated the issue-selection choices of member enterprises, and they primarily involved members who had not previously been attracted to them. The emphasis on these issues also shows the dynamic tendencies of domain institutions, shifting as they do the prevailing policy games and controversies from food-versus-farm programs in the 1970s to efforts to enhance foreign sales and to resolve environmental degradation problems in the 1980s and 1990s. But member enterprises did more than just help shift policy games; many of them also added important components to trade and environmental policies in agriculture.

That shift in concentrated attention and the relative neglect of so many other issues strongly suggests that members react more to an initiative's timely appeal than farm-income choices imply at first glance. External forces truly do affect changes and adjustments going on in Congress. Members flaunt strict assumptions of majority rule. Yet they gravitate to hot issues. And committees accommodate members to retain support. Trade and environment problems certainly occupied prominent attention in media accounts and in numerous congressional districts during this period.[26] Numerous interest groups galvanized around these concerns as well.

Thus, members undoubtedly were reacting to a changing community context and newly mobilized segments of the electorate. Like the question of why farm politics dominates the domain, the reasons behind those shifting reactions need further exploration. The next two chapters will turn to why members have more interest in these dominant issues and games than they have in others.

5

District Effects

How do we select issues? Quite simply, on what's good for our district."
Issues are selected in our office because of one thing—does it get the congressman on national network news? That's what gets district and state attention, more than all the local news combined."
Good policy gets issue attention, and nothing is better policy for us than something that enriches the district.

> —Three legislative assistants explaining how they selected issues and the rationales they needed to sell them to their legislative directors and the enterprises' administrative assistants.

Chapter 4 emphasized the emergence of five principal types of issues. Each type, members explained, was initiated on behalf of designated beneficiaries who saw these as important, or at least useful, policy changes. Three of those types of issues reflect the two most recent policy games of the agricultural domain, balancing farm issues with those of trade and challenging farm interests on behalf of environmental quality. The other two, nutrition and rural issues, remain from previously important policy games within agriculture. The considerably smaller number of issues of each of those two types result from fewer member opportunities available in these less recurrent or timely policy-domain problems. The existing policy base for each, though, makes it still likely that some members will react to interests that express wants about nutrition and rural issues, as well as others, occasionally. These factors facilitate the strategies of opportunistic members who react to diverse policy claimants, choose among numerous issues on their behalf, and emphasize winning as a means of creating client satisfaction.

How do clients in the district influence issue selection? There are relationships between types of issues, as defined by their beneficiaries, and types of districts represented by those members of Congress who initiate them. Congressional members from similar districts meet similar demands for a comparable type of issue, that rewards policy claimants commonly found in these individual locales. As congressional enterprises react, many members from similar places frame beneficiary-specific initiatives that are quite alike in intent and purpose, at least for the five types of substantive issues that gain the greatest attention of issue initiators. In essence, then, even the most national of agricultural policy takes on an inescapable local cast.

DISTRICT INFLUENCES AND THEIR EFFECTS
OVER TIME

The localization of agricultural policy should not be surprising, even across its broad spectrum of programs. Even in the prereform Congress, members never escaped the influence of place-specific politics. District influences were the subject of lengthy commentary in the 1950s.[1] Since that earlier Congress had stronger parties restraining its members and less frequent reporting of individual legislators' activity than does the current one, district influences should only have grown.[2] Constituents have the capacity to know more about what their members do on the issues that affect them: enterprises send newsletters and personnel to the district, local news media pick up congressional press releases, and interest groups send messages to the grassroots. Thus, mobilization of the selectively interested, or affected, can be intense. Indeed, Congress, in the midst of the reforms of the 1970s, emphasized stronger concerns with constituents than was found earlier.[3]

Member adjustment to the conditions of a postreform Congress, with its greater uncertainty over who controls the policy agenda, only escalates district importance. R. Douglas Arnold develops a convincing theory of why constituents have influence.[4] Citizens, he argues, are aware of their most important policy preferences; they evaluate candidates through their known connections to policy effects on the basis of those preferences; members in turn choose policy positions by estimating citizen responses;

and committee and party leaders develop strategies for vehicle passage by anticipating how individual legislators will respond to district factors.

Attending to policy preferences by being timely certainly explains why the already safely moving reform issues of trade and the environment gained the attention of so many issue initiators while other reform topics got much less interest. With uncertainty always a concern, why would a member want to be associated back home with risk-taking positions that constituents probably have yet to consider? Better to go with what in all probability plays well.

Arnold's logic also helps explain congressional interests in recurring farm-income issues. Why would any member want to be associated in her or his district with issues that further impede local farmers' business? With farms and farm populations declining annually, why not be identified with what will be perceived back home as help for beleaguered growers? Steven S. Smith's analysis of postreform behavior supports that logic. His modern Congress has more issues, more members involved, and more floor action than earlier ones.[5] The strategy members learn to adopt from this logic is to be identified with as many locally significant safe issues as possible.

Districts and Farm Policy

The importance of district influences are likely to be especially observable in the agricultural policy domain. Agriculture is seen as parochial and constituency directed precisely because those in different congressional districts and states vary quite dramatically in the benefits that they gain from any single program. Observers often note that, unlike many industries, agriculture is extremely location specific. The unique ecosystems, weather, soils, and terrains of specific places determine the conditions of production, productivity, and problems of individual crop and livestock growers. Although producers and growers are distributed nationally, their numbers vary markedly by region. So, too, do the types of commodities they grow and the conditions they face.

This regionalization of farming characterized the income-support policy game, which provided the cornerstone for twentieth-century agricultural politics. The oldest and most persistent regional commodity split in farm policy eventually aligned the southerners around cotton, peanuts, and tobacco programs while midwesterners depend on corn, soybeans, and wheat.[6] In the 1920s, some commodity programs were set for the South and others for the Midwest. Once compromise resolved regional conflicts, otherwise disinterested farmers supported one anothers' policies.

Even that division oversimplifies regional interests in farm politics. In the Midwest, wheat dominates the western Great Plains while corn and soybeans dominate its eastern regions. Other crops are interspersed locally and become important parts of those economies. For example, dry beans in eastern North Dakota and tart cherries in northwestern Michigan are large crops, and they both have forceful congressional advocates. The South and the West have similar circumstances. Industrialization of agriculture has only intensified these patterns by encouraging intense specialization where there was once a diversity of commodities produced on most farms.[7] Accordingly, members who intervene for farm beneficiaries have every reason to be issue specific. They expanded farm policy games on behalf of producers of specific crops grown in specific locations as well as through the creative design of various income-enhancing mechanisms that are not necessarily part of basic price and income policy.[8]

In brief, there would seem to be no shortage of uniquely local opportunities for issue initiators in at least the farm-policy portions of this policy domain. There are numerous and diverse constituents and an extensive base of public policies to tinker with in serving them. But the question is, where were the strategic advantages in other issues and in mixes of issues?

For one, advantage has been in further place-specific differences that affect agricultural policy. Crops, farm size, costs of production, and other characteristics are not the only district variations among program beneficiaries. Since human welfare programs such as food stamps were purposely framed for an urban constituency, where far greater numbers of low-income recipients were concentrated, than in rural areas, central-city, often minority, members of Congress supported agricultural policy, including its farm programs, in all-or-nothing farm-bill votes. By broadening the appeal of farm bills by linking urban wants to farm-constituent wants, Congress only intensified the politics of places in the domain by institutionalizing an urban policy base alongside a rural one. Strategies that are now commonplace were developed by members for correcting neglected local inequities, which added to enterprises the tasks of initiating more numerous issues than they had in prereform eras of Congress.

As a consequence of these new tasks and resulting conflicts, representing specific places has taken on greater importance than it had when agricultural policy was only farm based or when the Congress was more rigidly controlled by committees. At least a bare-bones pattern of district influence has been evident. Since the 1970s, numerous scholars have provided a collective framework for identifying types of congressional districts made up of the many different kinds of agricultural beneficiaries. Farmers come first because of farm policy, but they are not the only ones to have an interest in healthy farm economies.

Those who fear majority rule and adverse reactions by those who do not receive direct payments argue that the percentage of farmers and farm-dependent workers in a district leads members of Congress to support farm programs.[9] They allude to a necessary long-term willingness of farm producers to support one another regardless of crop or region. They assume the need for an alliance to defend against urban critics. The creation of the congressional Farm Bloc in 1921, the bloc's informal maintenance as a recurring coalition through the 1940s, and the rise of vote trading between regional commodity representatives in subsequent years led scholars to this view that farm numbers and mutual support are agriculture's only strengths.[10] Despite regional variations by commodity, these scholars gave the impression that farmers from everywhere were seen in Washington as basically alike, even as programs were tailored by crop and, accordingly, place.

Nonetheless, other differences between districts logically affected interests in farm policy and, indirectly, helped expand farm influence. John G. Peters's analyses show that the degree to which a district was urban or rural also explained support for farm legislation.[11] In less densely populated districts and states, local economies are less likely to include diversity of economic and social interests.[12] Farmers and ranchers, when present in such places, found it easier to develop an effective political voice than they did in more urban places.

That influential producer voice also was enhanced by a third factor, place-specific proximity to blue-collar workers. Some of this influence was simply owing to politics over time, or once again, the residual influence of former policy games whose impact is still felt in existing programs. Labor's congressional representatives built farm-and-urban coalitions that were effective within the Democratic party from the 1950s through the 1970s because farm and nonfarm workers shared an interest in building their own respective policy bases, in getting substantial protections from government on prices for farmers and wages for labor, and in opening up respective domain politics to new programs.[13] Food stamps, as permanent policy, emerged from that cooperative coalition.

But more than past national politics mattered; district and state economic conditions provided even greater local linkage between farmers and labor interests. Where farm and blue-collar populations were both high in a district, especially in more rural and less pluralistic places, blue-collar laborers generally were involved in agricultural businesses; whether in supplying products for farm use or in processing and manufacturing from farm commodities. In effect, they were dependent on locally sound and inseparably linked farm and agribusiness economies for their own jobs.

Thus, place-specific district politics, as feared by those who adhere to a strict view of what interests the majority, have been more complex and less intimidating than expected. Measured by relative level of opportunity for members, those most interested in farm programs probably came from districts high in the percentage of farm and farm-dependent workers, low in population density, where few other jobs matter to the economy; and high in the frequency of blue-collar workers who were likely to be dependent on agriculture.[14] The combined effects of the three variables were, in all likelihood, much more important than just the number of district farmers.

In doing something for farmers, a credit-taking member of Congress seized several opportunities: (1) providing a direct producer benefit, (2) bringing federal policy gains to the district in a setting where chances to do so are relatively limited, and (3) appearing responsive to an economic sector broader and more integrated than one just for farmers. Strategic actions were intended to do more than win farm votes. Initiating a farm-benefit issue showed the congressional member's identification with some encompassing sense of the district interest—one in which various localized components *felt* they won when farmers were served. Where could a member of Congress find better opportunities?

That sense of the district, as will be seen, explains the continued popularity of farm benefits for issue initiators. Conversely, it also shows why farm-income policy remains popular, or at least beyond substantial reform under existing policy games. Not only are these issues relatively easy to advance as especially germane to specific regions; not only does the large, fragmented, farm-policy base and similar issue-initiating behavior on the part of so many colleagues add to this ease; these issues also serve the member's purpose of building an appropriate home-style image.

Moreover, because most members also use the policies and vehicles of the domain for advocating other types of issues, there exists no necessary downside to selecting farm-benefit issues. Members can identify in a very tangible manner with the policy wishes of some of their local electorate, even while remaining noncommittal about what the collective agricultural policy base should include. Striking this balance is pragmatic, not philosophical or partisan. A member need not cultivate the image of being solely a farm advocate, he or she must just be seen as someone willing and able to help farmers while also advancing other social and economic interests in a dynamic agriculture.

Districts and Other Issues

This multidimensional rationale for issue choices appears to have been equally applicable to other frequently selected agricultural issue types. At least, given the preponderance of farm-benefit issues, that logic applied as long as alternate issues were complementing farm policy rather than competing with it. Once they acknowledge agriculture for its farm emphasis, members of Congress can move on to address other district or state problems. The contentiousness of the domain also comes into play. As a member noted: "By claiming that the committee always responds to producers, I almost guarantee that I get a hearing for my environmental interests." The modern history of agricultural policymaking suggests that new policy choices were made and agreed to in order to solve problems of inequity between districts. Policymakers collectively agreed to meet some specific need that deserves to be served by an ever more socially responsive agricultural policy. In short, members mounted place-specific challenges that brought agricultural policymaking its contentious, coalition-dependent reputation.

Thus, the same district dimensions—farm employment, population density, white- or blue-collar labor force—that influenced farm-benefit issue choices seem important to nonfarm issues. What benefits some interests, nearly by definition, brings complaints from others. District effects on policies have been felt under two conditions: first, when the electorate in several districts found interests in domain policies that were alternatives to some features of current farm programs, and second, when members from those districts were sufficient in numbers initially to threaten and then to provide winning margins or otherwise important security for domain vehicles. As with urban food programs in the 1970s, agricultural reform initiatives have come from congressional members who did not threaten to take benefits from their own farmers. Issues identified with reform for those policy games were, it seems, initiated by members from districts with relatively small percentages of the combined farm and blue-collar workers in the workforce, along with relatively high population density.

But policy games have changed, and issue initiators had little interest in low-income food problems.[15] Others interested in nutrition chose food-safety and health issues, which shows more about the transition in policy games from food politics in the 1970s to health-conscious politics in the 1990s.[16] Along with policy games, the origination of reform issues has also changed.

Environmental, consumer, and other public-interest food issues have middle-class, white-collar appeal; additionally, their advocates hold policy preferences that jeopardize current farm practices in ways that food-stamp programs did not. With greater disposable income, white-collar workers are less concerned with the monetary costs of farm-sector losses and more focused on lowering the social costs of environmental degradation in farming and on consumer safety in food. Advocates of middle-class, white-collar issues also tend to have fewer direct constituent ties to the farm sector.

Accordingly, places would seem to matter in structuring current games, just as they did to those of the past. Both nutrition- and environmental-issue initiators in Congress seem likely to come from districts that are low in both farm population and associated blue-collar workers, which means that the size of their districts' white-collar work force is likely to be relatively large. But, because it seems unlikely that central-city residents would develop salient policy preferences about the somewhat remote environmental problems of farm production, members' places probably differ from one another in the degree of their urbanism and their respective responses to issues. Densely populated urban districts seem likely to give rise to nutrition issues, whereas less densely populated and more suburban districts lead to environmental initiatives.

Previous research, unfortunately, suggests little about the congressional districts in which trade and rural issues emerge. Nonetheless, these issues should be linked to the three population variables that affect other agricultural issues. After all, members were seen to strategically select and balance those issues with ones for farmers. That process indicates that some types of districts make it useful but insufficient for members of Congress to satisfy only farmers. As we will see, these districts, like others, do form a pattern.

DISTRICTS, ISSUES, AND RECENT POLICY GAMES

The data on recent issue initiatives find that patterns of districts where satisfying only farmers is an insufficient strategy to be important in understanding current agricultural politics. The most recent policy games of the domain are a product of concurrent attention to all five types of issues, with the expected shift in political emphasis from policy games of the past evident.

To analyze each member's issue involvement by district characteristics, a logit model was used that explained, without multicollinearity problems between the three statistically unrelated variables, their combined effects.[17] That model estimated the logit odds that each member would initiate, in turn, a time-consuming farm-income benefit, an environmental, a nutrition, a rural, and a trade issue.[18] The logit analysis then measured the degree to which legislators from demographically similar districts initiated similar types of issues.[19] The intent was to predict from which places different issues would come, not to prove, as Richard F. Fenno, Jr., warned against doing, that members from similar districts would initiate the same types of issues. Results are found in Table A.11.

Several findings stand out. First, only one-third of the determinant, or independent, variables used to explain selection of an issue type proved statistically significant on their own. But, each issue type was linked significantly to a specific type of district, even with the small number of nutrition and rural issues. As expected from previous explanations, it was the combined results of several population factors that matter, not congressional responses to single types of constituents. The predictability of the model is all the more impressive because so many members mixed different types of issues in their initiatives. Thus, the types of districts overlap by issue. As in Figures 5.1 and 5.2 show, each issue type produces a cluster that represents where members and their districts are ranked on the three-dimensional scale.[20] These clustered pods of issue-initiators are quite different from one another despite the overlap that comes when most members pick two or more issue types.

Other important findings that are linked to strategic considerations made in Congress on specific issues can also be seen. Given the large number of members of Congress initiating farm-benefit issues, there were only a few obviously distinct congressional outliers who did no policy favors for farmers. The pod of farm advocates in Congress, while reflecting the same constituent interests, has grown considerably from what existed under old policy games. Outliers, the data on individual members

FIGURE 5.1. Spatial Plotting of Legislators by Farm, Trade, and Rural Issue Types, by District Characteristics*

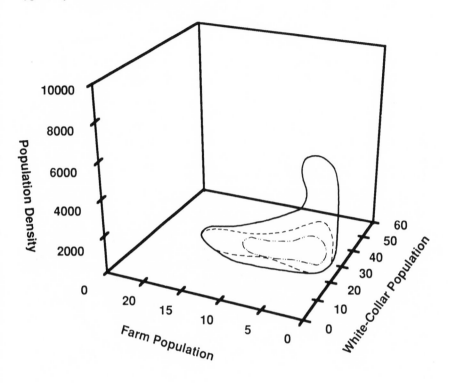

Farm	———————	(n=84)
Trade	— — — —	(n=31)
Rural	— ·· — ·· — ·	(n=11)

* **Best fit as determined from locus of pod.**

FIGURE 5.2. Spatial Plotting of Legislators by Farm, Environment, and
Nutrition Issue Types, by District Characteristics*

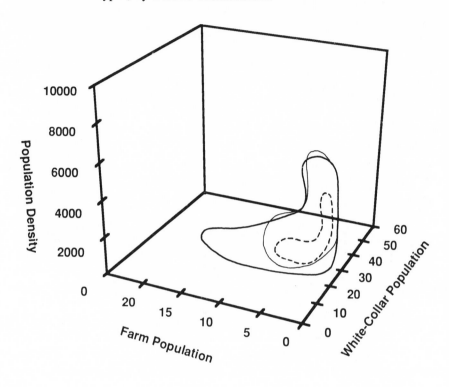

Farm   ——————   (n=84)

Environment   ——————   (n=28)

Nutrition   – – – –   (n=6)

* Best fit as determined from locus of pod.

show, were from urban districts with especially high concentrations of white-collar population where local farmers were extremely rare. So, farm-benefit initiators were not from everywhere throughout the entire Congress. Nonetheless, it seems very clear that, given the low cost of representing farmers, most members who find interest in the domain will be supportive of farm constituents even if they form no large district voting bloc. Numerous members attended to farm-income problems and acknowledged that they had few farmers in their districts: "Its not numbers, its their noise level." In other words, the number of farmers matters less than the level of mobilization and resources they use to make themselves heard. Some degree of district farm presence, though, is necessary before a member of Congress works on farm problems.

The issues most complementary to and most often mixed with farm policy—trade and rural initiatives—are of greatest interest to the core of districts represented by farm-benefit initiators and of little concern to urban, white-collar places. Trade benefits are for districts high in farm employment and even higher in blue-collar employment, with accordingly greater population density. Members who initiate these issues do so to dispose of farm products and also to generate commerce for processed and manufactured, value-added commodities. These members clearly have local business interests in mind. Rural issues, in contrast, address the infrastructure needs of smaller communities and come from districts with a high number of small towns.[21] These communities also use low-income FmHA and development programs that are less needed in white-collar places. The districts associated with trade and rural issues, as a result, are moderately populous places with high percentages of farm and blue-collar populations.

These similar patterns of trade- and rural-issue initiators put the locus of their pods some distance on the three-dimensional scale from those of either environmental- or nutrition-issue initiators. This indicates, once again, and despite overlapping attention by members to different types of issues, that district forces are significant in their influence.

What does that significance mean? For most of the domain's issue initiators, the characteristics of their districts make it apparent to their enterprises whether a rural or a trade issue is more appropriate than an environmental or a nutrition initiative. Given both the limited number and range of choices that a member can pursue, members find their opportunities on those less timely rural and nutrition issues restricted by the diminished choices that the characteristics of their districts impose. Opportunities expand for the dominant originating issues of trade and the environment. Accordingly, for those uncertain members who want to be identified with a safe and mainstream reform theme for agriculture, district factors determine quite logical choices. The most influential factor that separates these two reformist types, moreover, is the relative lack of farmers in environmental districts and their notable presence in trade districts.

This pattern presents an intriguing dichotomy for congressional domain politics. There are numerous members from both of these two kinds of issue places willing to act on behalf of farmers. But these two types of reform-source districts also exhibit an important difference. There are as well a number of members representing some of these districts who have only an environmental interest. Thus, members from modestly urbanized areas receive, it seems, mixed cues about possible soil and water reforms that are most likely to change farm-production practices and impact national and local producers.

This ambiguity leads to some moderation in existing policy games. By pointing to the dynamic nature of politics, it also indicates that these somewhat urbanized districts are the places most likely to become swing districts in the future if members feel it no longer appropriate to do *both* farm and environmental favors. If local political conditions ever alter resident perspectives on agroenvironmental questions, these farm/environment places are likely to become important centers of politics in choosing nationally between farm and environmental interests. No other places seem likely to play this role. Neither of the extreme types of district, very rural or highly urban, have encouraged congressional issue initiators who were willing to load environmental issues into domain policy vehicles. Since these extreme districts are unlikely to change much in their demographics, members who represent such places seem unlikely to change their interests. They will still be able to identify safely with reform from a trade or a nutrition perspective and to avoid environmental debates about farm practices. Farm/environmental districts, though, are likely to change, especially by losing farmers and gaining other residents.

While farm, trade, and environmental issues appear to be especially dynamic in their relationships to one another and to congressional district politics, nutrition and rural issues appear remarkably stable in their effects on domain politics. Nutrition issues generate congressional interest from urban legislators who also do farm favors for the few dairy or fruit and vegetable producers in their districts. As was previously true of food-stamp policy games, none of the nutrition-issue initiatives restricted farm practices or increased farm costs; existing balanced treatment of local places explains why, at least from a member's perspective. Low-income food programs, well-supported in committee and entrenched in the domain's policy base, apparently needed little support from issue initiators: "These are not at issue on the committee level. They remain a given."

This equation for equilibrium would soon change, though, if food-stamp and other assistance programs were opened for renewed contest over entitlements and, therefore, became a policy window for change. A reinvigorated game would result, restoring the coalition-building patterns of the 1970s.[22] The same could happen if consumer-health-and-safety advocates effectively pointed to a crisis situation, activating a new policy game where farm interests had to open doors to white-collar food interests who wanted to challenge food-safety standards rather than accommodate the farm sector.

Rural issues are in sharp contrast to nutrition ones. Members from only a very small range of districts share an interest in them. All are from somewhat low-population places that rank high in farm and blue-collar worker populations and where the greatest member attention goes to farm-benefit issues. In short, rural issues depend on the most traditional of farm-program supporters for moving them along. Even with the importance of issue-balancing, this dependency bodes poorly for rural policy. These programs appear to be of little interest to anyone who matters. No reform initiatives, such as investments in human capital, were advanced in rural policy. Moreover, budget pressures of the late 1980s and the 1990s made it difficult for proponents to initiate issues whose costs would be borne at the expense of farm programs. Accordingly, members responding to opportunities created in considering a rural-development bill gave relatively modest attention to rural issues that were likely to be of short-term interest. As one member explained: "I saw a chance to serve the district there, satisfy some complaints. But without the mood that Leahy created, these wouldn't have been my issues." In effect, rural initiatives are really just another miscellaneous issue unless someone opens an unexpected and short-term policy window. As a former member of Congress said, "I'd say rural development was a mid-1980s issue. Time passed it by."

So district effects not only matter in selecting issues, they also matter within the context of the institutional dynamics of the Washington policy community. Members shop in the Capitol for what to provide through their initiatives, but the opportunities are also presented from home in very logical and orderly fashion. For strategic reasons involved in doing district work in Washington, members pursue some service opportunities and fail to follow others.

However important these dynamics are, they do not reflect institutional characteristics of the members as initiators of certain issue types. When the logit model was more fully specified by adding committee assignment and leadership, there was no clustering, and none of the new variables proved statistically significant for any issue type.[23] Their inclusion, both individually and collectively, actually weakened the significance of the district model.[24] In short, the model for predicting which issues would be initiated by which members worked because of complex population characteristics at home, not because of institutional factors in Congress.

OTHER DISTRICT EFFECTS ON RECENT FARM POLICY GAMES

More evidence attesting to the importance of districts and their problems with policy neglect exists. Selective attention by members to district politics can be seen by looking in greater detail at issue selection for the biggest category, farm beneficiaries. Two patterns of members' issue-selection are particularly revealing: (1) emphasis on regional commodity interests and (2) responsiveness to the impact of higher-than-average district farm costs. Each pattern offers additional insights into congressional representation of district interests beyond that seen in the broad clustering of initiatives within the five issue pods.

Regional Commodity Differences

The regionalization of farm production is a significant factor in predicting who initiates which issues. Of the eighty-four time-consuming farm-benefit issues, seventy-five of them had a specific commodity focus. In other words, only 11 percent of these issues were not intended to benefit producers of select commodities and livestock (Table A.12). Very few members of Congress were concerned with general farm problems such as credit or taxes.

Nor were members worried about whether these were major commodity programs that caught their attention; only forty-one of the seventy-five commodity issue initiatives were directed at the eight major program crops: corn, cotton, dairy, peanuts, rice, soybeans, sugar, and tobacco. Moreover, only twenty-six of these aimed at the major programs themselves. Initiatives were also intended for wine, potato, honey, vegetable, poultry, and assorted other specialized producers; and, with major crops, disaster assistance and other income-enhancing initiatives were prominent. The highly location-specific nature of agricultural production causes a regional fragmentation that cuts deeply into congressional politics to convey to members their sense of the district interest.

Attentiveness to local economic conditions shows how deeply fragmentation of farm interests affects representation of the farm sector. Paradoxically, however, that same attentiveness shows how encompassing the sector's influence remains in national politics. Sixty-five of the seventy-five commodity-specific initiatives came from members of Congress whose states ranked among the top ten in cash receipts for that particular commodity or livestock. Fifty-two actually came from the top five states. In other words, members were taking actions that had the effect of concentrating issue attention on already dominant national producers. Only a small number of issues, ten, aimed at capturing a larger share of production for less intensely cultivated grower regions. For example, where cotton is king, local issue initiators controlled the congressional cotton agenda.

What makes this concentration possible, and contributes greatly to collective farm powers, is the large number of beneficiary states. For the numerous commodity producers whose interests were advanced in issues, forty-one states were represented in the top ten rankings. Moreover, these states accounted for 93 percent, or 495, of all senators and representatives. Thirty-seven of these states, with 467 members, ranked in the top ten for major program crops or for cattle, hogs, and chickens. As the next chapter will emphasize, congressional delegations are moved by the logic that their state is a major producer of a specific "crop or critter." Delegations, in turn, according to members, work to create internal agreements in support of important state interests, especially in agriculture, with its attention to such diverse farm and nonfarm issues. The reverse claim—that, overall, their state might be a relatively small beneficiary of cash receipts from farming—seems irrelevant to risk-averse issue initiators and to the delegations that support them.

This extensive distribution of relatively important crops among the states makes the choice of representing farmers' issues from the district greatly appealing and helps show why the farm-benefit cluster of issue initiators is so extensive. This wide distribution does even more to explain national farm influence because more than just the traditional price-supported commodities gain policy benefits. Contrary to beliefs about the dominance of majority interests, and just as contrary to those who see extraordinary influence in only a few farm industries, such as dairy and sugar, with their unusually large and well-organized campaign contributions, opportunities in representing the diverse grassroots farm sector are plentiful.[25]

The Production Cost Factor

A second fragmenting effect was evident in the issue-initiatives data that showed how farm policy serves multiple interests. However, it demonstrates a very different splintering of policy. While the focus of members on farm programs in general and commodity programs in particular deals with a sense of serving locally prominent interests that matter economically, the secondary factor of their representing neglected district interests can be seen in another set of geographically distributed farm initiatives. In this case, economically disadvantaged districts get special attention. The two related variables that affect initiatives serving the interests of those districts are costs of farm production and their determinant effects on farm-policy solutions, specifically whether programs should limit or control the supply of farm production or let the market exercise those restraints.

Member initiatives aimed at creating mandatory controls came from districts that have higher-than-average costs of production for major commodities. Because farmers in such districts are not competitive nationally and often grow at prices below costs of production, their congressional representatives attempted to raise local incomes by limiting U.S. product supply and, theoretically, raising prices. Government price programs, however, based as they are on subsidizing the amount grown, do nothing to correct inequity based on differences in costs of production. For example, if limits are placed on the amount of corn grown in highly productive and low-cost Indiana, prices will be relatively higher for everyone—at least in accepted theory. But Indiana growers will lose income while those in high-production-cost regions such as the Dakotas gain in profitability as prices rise further above their expenses. Whether such plans to limit production work in an internationally competitive agriculture is highly questionable.

What is beyond question, however, is that government programs often limit farm production, either by retiring and setting aside land or, for example, by buying out some farmers. Oftentimes, as programs are put together through the combined influence of disparate interests, subsidies and control principles are put into simultaneous effect. So too, occasionally, are market principles. Moreover, responsibility for maintaining a mandatory supply-control approach to policy rests with a very small number of congressional members (Table A.13). The possible advantage to constituents who face high production costs led nine members to initiate all of the issues intended to limit or control commodity production. When the average cost of production for feed grains was added to the logit model as a fourth variable, the model accurately predicted that those from a cluster of high-production-cost districts would initiate supply-control issues.[26] But the low-production-cost districts were not the ones that led to twenty-four market-enhancing issues, which aimed at increased sales and profits without increasing unit prices for all producers; those initiatives were distributed with near randomness, even among some supply-control initiators.

This pattern indicates that while members were prompted to correct economic inequities for major crops within their districts, they did not respond predictably to the likely advantages of market enhancement.[27] Market issues were only one among many approaches to farm benefits that numerous members were willing to propose. These members were commodity specific in their proposals, but apparently, differences among commodity producers presented obstacles to linking the most favorable district economies to market-oriented principles. Pragmatism about their districts, not a market ideology that might have driven farm-benefit choices, once again moved members of Congress. Given earlier findings, their pragmatism is hardly surprising. But it raises questions of whether other intervening political variables are responsible for it.

To test this hypothesis further, partisanship was added as a fifth variable in the model. Production-control issues have been part of recurring partisan policy games since the late 1940s; Democrats frequently favor production-control and oppose a Republican emphasis on market-oriented policy.[28] Was the distribution of Democrats really what was measured in predicting production-control issue initiatives? It was not.[29] Partisan influence was clearly transcended by that of the cost index, with no statistical significance for the former and a high correlation for the latter. The postreform rise of the caucuses apparently has not affected agriculture much because of the local nature of its issues.

These two patterns of initiatives bring considerable insights into the behavior of members of the postreform Congress as they venture into whatever traditional policy networks remain in the agricultural domain.[30] When their issue-behavior entails challenges to the Washington policy community, those challenges are made on the basis of more than some vague sense of the district; the five pods of common issue initiators, plus the production-control pod, are far too clustered for district effects to be anything other than fairly precise.

Even the apparent anomaly of the simultaneous massive representation of farmers and the problems of their income can be explained in logical district-first fashion. First, members generally represent commodity components of the farm sector that matter in their own or nearby districts more than they do in other places. Second, however, these members will argue on behalf of distinctly different policy approaches than their colleagues if their own district producers face especially inequitable circumstances for a major crop. The result is widespread shopping by member enterprises among old and new agricultural policies, tempered by an issue-selection process that employs appropriateness to the district as its guide. Douglas Arnold is quite right in claiming that members of Congress can follow constituent preferences in logical fashion, especially if constituents may feel disadvantaged.

CONCLUSION

The issue-initiating behavior of congressional members has a clear, district-based explanation. Across Congress, in front-loading policy vehicles, constituent effects seem greater than those suggested by studies of committees.[31] Members of Congress who address issues in common represent places with something in common. Of course, not all members from similar districts represent the same types of issues because other conditions and circumstances are variable, as are member perceptions of them. The capacity of member enterprises to act on their own strategic district needs can nonetheless be seen in members' addressing certain issues. Quite clearly, members are not responding to them, on the basis of committee assignments, or only at the encouragement of the Washington policy community; at most, they are responding to policy games set in motion in Washington. Constituents and districts matter in policy work in a postreform congressional era.

Constituency effects aggregate the responses of small clusters of legislators around a few either traditionally recurring or timely issues of the domain. Both types—the traditional and the timely—are emphasized. Moreover, these issues gain emphasis for different reasons.

Traditional farm-benefit issues, as we have seen earlier, gain from an extensive policy base that can be maintained with ease. An added part of that ease relates to the involvement and the interest of so many issue initiators who recognize farmers within their districts. The regional circumstances of commodity production encourage numerous players, not just a few, to represent what they see as important district concerns linked to a problem-plagued farm sector: "Dry beans count in my district, we're one of the nation's largest producers." Members, however, do not see themselves as just doing favors for farmers in general and collectively, as the coalition tactics of the regionally split farm bloc once suggested. Instead, contemporary members of Congress view their work rather accurately as responding to unique districts, as opposed to some national farm interest. Given the extraordinarily broad range of farm-benefit issue initiators and nationally distributed commodity types, farm power achieves successful expression by playing multiple ongoing games on its extensive policy base.

As congressional districts become more heterogeneous, however, members provide other agricultural-policy benefits for nonfarm constituents. For example, considerable interest has developed in doing things for agribusinesses, whose leaders often ask why farmers deserve special income consideration. Accordingly, trade benefits grow. Farmers, though, gain the most even as heterogeneity increases. Their structural and institutional advantages in the policy base insure their gain and, surprisingly, lead to the comparative neglect of all but the most timely nonfarm agricultural issues.

Timely issues also can be explained by a district rationale, however. When common member interests are articulated through the initiation of separate but similarly intended issues, district circumstances explain those actions. A general sense of neglect, usually related to a timely set of circumstances, seems responsible for those initiatives. Rural, trade, and environmental issues were all inspired by new—or reinvigorated—policy games of varying dimensions, but their issues emerged from quite specific types of districts. Nutrition and mandatory-production-control issues were not "hot" issues, but rather were resurrected from previous games still embedded in existing policy. However, initiators of these issues are all linked to certain types of districts that could permit them legitimately to assert the unfairness of traditional farm programs for many of their local constituents. Members from these places apparently wanted more consideration from the domain.

Such circumstances, of course, create real opportunities for uncertain members of Congress. Given ambiguous district characteristics, members might just as well represent important local interests and those with particular problems that can be addressed through expansive agricultural domain institutions. Representing both is all the better, because of electoral needs and the chance just to take good care of the district. Through open congressional networking, this strategy carries members and their staffs into whatever networks of shared interest now exist within the agricultural domain and even, on occasion, across to related ones.

6

Networking: Who Listens to Whom

After all the analysis in the world, decisions would come down to a member who suddenly said something like "On the contrary, I know a man in Illinois. . . ." Then we drafted language to avoid that man's problems as if they reflected all of agriculture. What a life!

> —A former staff economist who found that analytically determined solutions were often superseded by observations made from a nonrandom sample of one.

What do the data show so far? Members of Congress are far more active on issues in agriculture than was expected.[1] In a postreform Congress, with its emphasis on individualism, members pursue personal opportunities in policymaking when they confront a substantial policy base and the legislative chance to manipulate it with relative ease. But this Washington-style issues work also merges with district politics. Members from demographically similar districts pursue similar types of issues and have quite logical reasons for their interests in them.

But to whom in the district are these members and their enterprises reacting? One possible answer is that players from the Washington policy community provide the incentives, or point to district opportunities.[2] Previous research on agricultural domain interests underscores the importance organized interests place on currying congressional favor by giving district and electoral intelligence to member enterprises.[3] "I seldom see members in person anymore," observed one lobbyist from that study, "unless I have some inside information from home to drop on them."

Lobbyists also routinely bring constituents with them on calls to members and staff.

The alternative answer is that members go home for their own information and use local sources as respondents. As the lobbyist quoted above added: "My biggest problem is that members react to my proposals by seeking out other information back in the district. These are people I have no control over, even if it turns out that they actually belong [to my group]. They have their own opinions." Or, as a former House member summarized: "Going home is a powerful experience. You learn pretty fast what your problems are." Of course, aspects of going home occur daily: traveling to the district, managing independent campaign committees, developing functional district offices, and meeting with constituents.

Members and their staffs, often in the strongest words, acknowledged that home-style concerns provide them with a clash of ideas since those in Washington's policy community disagree frequently with district informants. As one agriculture committee member explained, "The dairy program and nearly every other commodity problem gets worked out by organizations that lobby for a nationally applicable policy. What comes out of a national [interest group] conference, even with their lobbyist's advice about representing all regional producers, screws somebody. We find ourselves working to correct those situations because, believe it or not, most of the farmers that come out of [a group's] policymaking sessions are [very angry]."

The result is that members of Congress, individually and collectively, respond to divergent pressures. In reality, they keep grounded in two worlds, Washington and the district. Yet their attention gets divided in surprising ways as they try "to have it all"; the most surprising emerges in the dominance of the district in influencing issue initiation as well as in evaluating the proposals of other members. But what is the home-style process of identifying with constituent policy preferences to the member's advantage?

PRIMARY INFORMATION SOURCES

How much do members mix Washington and district work? When asked why they intrude in policymaking, members and their staffs point to district constituents as both the primary informants and the principal beneficiaries for whom they initiate issues. A series of questions were asked about seven likely information sources: constituents who are identified with living or working in the home district; interest representatives who are identified with Washington organizations; USDA officials; other agency officials; other recognized agricultural or policy professionals; the news media; and the professional or technical media. Questions were asked about responsibility for issue selection; the importance of different sources in determining issue content or solutions for each problem; the extent of member and staff involvement with each source; and the relative value of—including the perceived trustworthiness of—each informant. Finally, each office ranked the overall importance of all relevant sources and explained that ranking for each of their issues (see Table A.14).

Why Constituents Matter

Constituents from the district were ranked highest in importance in all five use-indicators: issue selection, determining issue position, trust, overall ranking of informants, and seeking out information. Eighty-five of 110 enterprises, or 77 percent, selected their issues because of constituent contacts. Another 11 percent selected issues on the basis of contacts divided between lobbyists and constituents. It was exceptionally rare for these reactive members to select issues for any reason other than constituent ones: "Why would I otherwise tie up my limited capital?" If an issue was not linked to constituent policy preferences and, therefore, to a larger sense of the district interest, few members were willing to consider it.

Over three-quarters of those who selected issues based on constituent problems also determined their exact position and defined solutions to those problems through district contacts. Because issues were commonly narrow in content and pursued as small pieces of policy vehicles, the gap between assessing the problem and doing something about it was generally small. The problem quite easily defined the solution once the enterprise understood the complaints. Little technical information was used by issue initiators in formulating language or developing a proposal; even in technical matters such as environmental standards. As a ranking House Interior Committee member suggested, "Don't be fooled into thinking that we use a lot of facts around here."

A few enterprises faced more cumbersome circumstances in moving to solutions. Their tasks entailed initiating bills, major provisions, or controversial agency requests, which required staff to go beyond figuring out what language to draft and where to suggest that their request be inserted in a pending policy vehicle. Enterprises then faced the more complex tasks of actually designing their initiative and connecting its various pieces while also collecting data on how the proposal would affect other aspects of policy. The tedious nature of doing so drove twenty enterprises to select issues through constituent requests but then search elsewhere for help in determining content. Explained one staffer, "Drafting complex language means I need a lobbyist." Yet that did not end district contacts. Over half of these offices then cleared the detailed content of these more complex issues with informants back home.

Constituents gain access for good reason. When discussing the value of informants, those in two-thirds of the offices spoke of trust as a criterion for listening to any information source. Members believed that constituents openly and honestly shared their problems. So they listened. Numerous studies of interest groups show that members have the same receptivity to an honest presentation from them. If a lobbyist fails to provide reliable information, however, he or she rarely gets a second chance.[4] Member enterprises listened to constituents as informants whom they could count on because they felt the quality of their information to be more reliable than that of other available sources.

Some constituents mattered because of a one-time contact with the enterprise, but not many. The unusual constituent pathway to influence is familiarity, not just geography.[5] The district is more than a place. It is a collection of recognizable people and their recurring problems. Members and their staffs who initiated issues on the basis of one or two contacts with an unfamiliar district informant were always moved by an unusual request, one that meshed with an idea on which they were already working or one that would meet the media's interest. An example was a Northwest logger who identified an environmental problem that, when addressed, got national network news coverage for a member in a hearing. Even in these cases, though, enterprises followed through because they trusted their constituent informants and the experiences those people detailed to them.

Five factors that enhance the usefulness of constituent information were cited by enterprises. First, and most important, from among numerous constituents, over time, staff can most frequently determine the reliability of a few key informants. They test them, and in the process Richard F. Fenno, Jr.'s geographic constituents, or those who live within the district's bounds, become primary ones.[6] Second, district informants can always be counted on to address both immediate and local conditions. Third, they address those conditions with far greater accuracy and expertise than nationally active informants. Fourth, local informants also carry information back to the district and, because they have positioned themselves to talk to those in Congress, are thought to serve as local opinion leaders. Once again, enterprises test to see if these impressions are accurate: "We ask around, very simple." Fifth, enterprises can easily reach constituents.

For most types of issues, enterprises can readily identify informants through district work. They can also contact informants quickly via available communications technology and, if desired, can monitor their views on a routine basis. When enterprises consider these five factors together, they perceive that some identifiable constituents are nearly perfect for judging the effect of Washington work on back-home politics. That type of information and feedback should be more than good enough, members believe, for a particularly parochial domain with an extensive base of very localized programs: "Why get more data?" In short, the economist quoted above accurately charged that agriculture operates at length on one important premise: "I-know-a-man theory."

As those combined factors indicate, member enterprises tend to be as concerned with securing constituent information as they are with processing it. Of the 103 member enterprises that purposely sought out *any* information sources (only 9 did not), 71 of them, or 69 percent, had developed strategies for improving their use of constituent contacts. Of these, 37 had organized farm-advisory committees composed of a small group of invited district producers with whom the member regularly met. Although a few of these groups met but once a year, some others convened monthly.

As in the offices without such committees, staff interspersed personal face-to-face meetings with outgoing calls soliciting information from district contacts. They kept files on contacts, their issues, and background characteristics. Farm-advisory committees, however, were not the only forums for organizing constituents cited. Seventy-five percent of enterprises had some type of issue-specific constituent committees; many were important to agricultural policy. Two were rural advisory groups, twelve were environmental committees, and twenty-six were business groups that involved agribusiness leaders. All were attended avidly, even as members and staff continued to rely on more routine contacts to generate issue solutions. One legislative assistant explained, "We provide a setting, they provide the problems." That distinction is important. Office procedures and organization are proactive. The enterprise's interest in any issue is reactive.

District contacts can be thought of too dismissively, as mere correspondents—just another district face—whose problems are anonymous. Members and staff disagreed with this simple view, referring as several did to trusted informants as "district confidants."[7] Three traits elevated the stature of these constituents from correspondent to confidant. First, many contacts are recurring; second, they originate both from congressional offices and from the constituents themselves. For example, Senate Agriculture Committee Chairman Leahy's staff spoke of his use of a Vermont dairy farmer as a routine sounding board. "What's interesting about that one," a committee employee explained, "is that the guy doesn't even vote for Leahy. But his opinions are trusted." Third, they have previously provided information that has been tested and proved valuable. In other words, was it useful in structuring a positive issue response that played well? Testing also commonly includes determining the stature of the individual confidant back home among peers: "I'm always asking people what they think of one another, in very subtle ways, mind you, but very pointedly." Sometimes the process for testing reliability takes on added dimensions, even going to the Washington policy community for help. One lobbyist spoke of being contacted by a newly organized Senate office about a state farmer: "They wanted to know if he was active in our group. When I said he wasn't and suggested an alternate choice, they said their thanks. Later I found out that the person they inquired about was chairing their farm-advisory committee." A staffer corroborated that story: "We wanted someone who wasn't in bed with a Washington Beltway view."

An agency assistant administrator provided a very different type of assistance in testing a constituent. He was asked by a USDA legislative liaison office to examine a district producer's farm financial records. "What they wanted to know," this official explained, "was how typical this farm was of larger regional units as well as [of] national producers of the same crop. Later I found out that this farmer was a close advisor of a congressman who requested the analysis." That member's staff confirmed the anecdote: "We wanted to know whether [that producer's] problems were typical, were his complaints valid?"

These and similar statements underlined one important point. Members of Congress understand quite well that interest groups mobilize many of their local constituents, creating an artificial surface of astroturf opinion rather than real grassroots sentiments. Members want very badly to avoid astroturf opinions, which they consider to be generally short-term and not very salient to those who hold them.[8] Avoiding inauthentic opinion was as important as avoiding local group leaders who were likely too closely linked to the interest group line.

District Confidants

The process of securing district information is important in explaining district effects on issue initiation and, perhaps, on other aspects of policymaking. It helps to explain why so many, but not all, members from similar districts get interested in similar issues.[9] The use of district confidants does not imply that there is a congressional concern for representativeness, mass democracy, or even counting voter preferences. To the above staffer, "typical" did not mean average: Certainly, no one samples local opinion about what to do with farm, trade, environmental, or other agricultural problems through this process. The emphasis—with but one notable exception—is on the attentive grassroots activist, the person of high political interest with more issue interest than organizational concern.

Members were asked, regardless of where they ranked the importance of constituents, about which constituents were informants on each issue. Surprisingly, on all five of the clustered issue types, members could point to some constituent influences. The types of constituents they commented on are revealing (see Table A.15). Not only are there high levels of district networking, but quite different patterns of contact exist for each type issue. For four issue types, moreover, there is almost a stereotype of the proper district confidant that emphasizes rewarding selected beneficiaries back home.

Nonactivist farmers, without regard for their interest-group status and membership, were chosen by 81 percent of enterprises on farm-income issues. These constituents were the key to understanding accommodation within Congress since they provide a common reference group that many members shared. Enterprises always described the same producer as their informant: owner or operator of a large farm, involved in capital-intensive production, independent in his or her political views, involved in numerous statewide farm events, and inclined to address little more than production-agricultural problems or those of vertically integrated industries such as mills and processors: "I don't want to listen to someone who carries on about everything." Most enterprises also emphasized the use of farmers who understood and employed a complex array of finance and marketing tools. In short, primary contacts were politically and economically consequential, usually coming from that 15 percent of large-scale farms that produce nearly 80 percent of U.S. farm cash receipts and receive almost 75 percent of all government payments.[10]

Members did not see confidants as yeoman farmers but rather, even if they were financially troubled, as businesspeople who had succeeded at industrialized agriculture. This made discussions with 70 percent of the nation's farmers largely irrelevant. Their one and one-half million small farms were hard to see as vital to the farm sector. Small farmers account for only about 8 percent of farm cash receipts with their average of less than $40,000 per year in sales; they also—as a group—derive 96 percent of family income from off-the-farm revenue sources.[11] "Those are hardly typical producers," noted one staffer, "they are really not farmers and business folks."

Most of the other district confidants on these issues were also farmers who, in these instances, were group leaders (11 percent) or USDA officials in county offices who are appointed by local farmers (6 percent). Two percent were employees of county extension offices. Once again, members emphasized informants from large farms or those who worked closely with them. The difference was that these members of Congress, for all three subtypes, wanted someone closer to the process of developing and implementing public policy. Each of these nine members who relied on group-affiliated farmers also chose their farm issues either because Washington interest groups were most important (three cases) or equally important (five cases) in issue selection. As one member noted, "I look for the owner operator who will someday be president of the wheat growers, or the county agent who really makes programs work for my guys [district farmers]. I personally don't want to encourage these very independent producers who [change their position and oppose] established government programs in order to milk out a few extra bucks for people in their county. I want local views but people who have experience with a bigger picture on commodity programs."

Most members and their staffs, for the same reason, disagreed: "Nationally, these policies are bankrupt. I want someone to tell me what to do who's not inclined to protect old programs just because they remain in place." The efforts of these members, of course, square with such comments, and members work whatever policy vehicles they can to exercise changes for their local producers. Despite their status as policy maintainers, members emphasized far more than just keeping traditional price-support policy intact; they played the gamut of farm programs, as explained earlier, from marketing orders to tax policy.

Farmers, however, were not frequent contacts on other agricultural issues. The usual response was, in one member's words, that "farmers have a limited interest in changing policy, which overstates their level of cooperation with one another." Only 10 percent of trade-issue confidants were farmers, all local leaders from commodity groups who were working closely with agribusinesses on developing policy. In contrast, 7 percent of environmental-issue informants were farmers. But they were chosen, even more than on farm issues, for their independent status: "There are only some local farmers committed to listening and learning on these issues who then push for change. All are outside the farm-group mainstream."[12]

The contrast between farmers interested in issues of trade and those interested in the environment was sharp. Trade informants were part of a more traditionally organized effort to continue old production priorities: "These guys want to sell more and still put the 'pedal to the metal' on production." That is, they want to grow more, and exports foster such increases. The environmental proponents were in a new network of local activists who sought changes and limits in basic production practices.[13] These farmers came from the different types of districts characteristic of the two issues and, as a result, reflected a sector split more by place-specific politics than previously seen.

Apart from farm informants, members generally relied on a few obvious stakeholders in issue politics. This reliance underscores how members act on behalf of what appear to be obvious beneficiaries. For information on rural issues, members depended on local government officials who wanted community funding for public works and local service needs; two members responded to business leaders who had downtown development interests. With those exceptions, many members and their staffs spoke of how very few constituents addressed these issues: "Rural development just doesn't mean anything to the typical rural resident. They just look at you blankly when you raise that topic. It's not specific." Similarly, agribusiness leaders who wanted export assistance dominated the confidant ranks for trade issues. Unlike rural issues, however, trade issues had no shortage of constituent informants: "Everybody with a product comes at you."

Community-health activists and one local government official involved with food inspection and consumer safety reached receptive congressional enterprises on nutrition issues. These constituents were described as being surprisingly similar to the most frequent farm informants: they were owners or operators of health programs or businesses, involved in efforts to change existing nutrition habits of consumers, independent in their political views, involved statewide in food and nutrition events, and single-purpose in their devotion to these issues: "They don't bend your ear on every liberal issue.". . . [They're] up on new technology and health care." Of course, unlike farmers, these were policy reformists who advocated reformist issues. Their interests as beneficiaries were just as clear, however. As with rural and trade initiatives, members selected their issues because each of these constituents were the most important of all information sources.

About one-third of the environmental informants were also grassroots activists. Most of these confidants were seen as stakeholders, not some set of public-regarding civic leaders. All but one were responding to very specific crises or widely debated degradation trends, such as groundwater and well-water contamination, in their districts or in places they otherwise frequented. These constituents were not involved in the operation of businesses, government programs, or statewide environmental events. "What we hear from the home district, at least it seems, is people who have encountered a very specific hazard," summarized a committee staffer who works routinely with local environmental complaints. "That [hazard] becomes their cause, and you have to react to it." In enterprises where such relief-directed informants were visible, constituents were always considered the most important reasons for selecting the issue. But constituents did not always express opinions, even when members felt local environmental problems seemed worth addressing.

Half of the members who initiated environmental issues had no environmental confidants. Constituent information emerged from multi-public discussions where individuals met on community or regional problems. Unlike their actions on other types of issues, and on all but two of the miscellaneous ones, environmentally interested enterprises initiated 50 percent of their issues with but nominal district feedback—no shopping among recurring complainants and no testing. In each instance, there was plentiful discussion of environmental issues in the district, however. These discussions were always unfocused dialogues, and they provided little specific guidance in formulating an issue initiative. Either public meetings or a series of complaints to staff in the district normally triggered selection of these environmental issues. "What we picked up was a strong mood within the district, a tempo or a beat." The member continued, "so we ran with it." Those sentiments were true especially of eastern members of Congress interested in western public lands issues: "We heard a great many complaints [back home] and it became something we checked out further. It looked like a good opportunity." Nonetheless, constituents were the clear reason for issue selection in only three of these fourteen cases. Enterprises relied on lobbyists (five cases), a mix of lobbyist and constituent information (three cases), and agencies, policy professionals, and the media (four cases) with greater frequency.

Other than half of environmental initiatives and a few farm-benefit ones, the sense of a district interest appears to be communicated primarily through a selective set of relatively well-known confidants. In all cases, constituent informants matter. Moreover, constituent informants within each issue type are remarkably alike, especially given the number of different districts from which they come. Because many confidants are encouraged and because most are tested by reactive enterprises, such similarities seem far from accidental. Members feel especially comfortable with certain kinds of informants, ones understood to be local stakeholders in policy decisions. The fostering of peculiarly local networks, sometimes linked to the Washington policy community but far more commonly valued by member enterprises for their capacity to generate locally independent positions on national policy games, is evident.

Constituent Networks

In pursuing issues, members overwhelmingly responded to district informants when they mobilized. Mobilization, though, appears a two-directional phenomenon. Obviously, citizens bring their complaints to government. Yet extensively organized member enterprises, through their Washington and district offices, do some of the mobilizing. To a great extent, they make interests come together. In fact, as those in nearly all enterprises emphasized, members and their staffs reach out to the district when they have an issue to initiate and when they simply want to judge local reactions to issues brought forward by others. These relationships to district informants were highly valued. Members and staff, in particular, expressed frustrations with the lack of confidants on environmental issues. As one member put it: "It gives you an uncomfortable sense. Issues are brought to you as important, but it's hard to see a district interest emerging." She went on, "You gotta go home to find an answer. But really established points of views on [environmental] specifics are rare. You ask yourself, are these claims real or reflections of hysteria?" Or, as the member noted of his mood theory: "Its hard to trust in the abstract. Opinions shift dramatically when a hypothetical situation becomes real and costs on the district are clear-cut." As a consequence, this member routinely brought opposing interests from the district "around the table to talk over very specific problems and likely solutions."

So, what seems important about district confidants? Kenneth A. Shepsle's "changing textbook Congress" appears at least as dependent on constituent networks as it is on securing a place within the Washington policy community.[14] Like those in Washington, district networks are policy specific, but they are far more able than Washingtonians to comment on a policymaking problem from a local stakeholder's position. Thus, constituents have credibility. An issue-experienced interest defines a constituent's participation and his or her utility to the member enterprise. In a classic Bentleyan statement of political interest, people with similar concerns are seen to be coming together. Of great importance, this merging of constituent and congressional interests leads to some recurring relationships with enterprises.

Yet that routinizing of district relationships explains only so much about the relationships between confidants, other district informants, and the enterprise. Members and staff described far greater flexibility than the exclusionary iron-triangle metaphor for Washington politics implied would be there. Members usually met with and sounded out several constituents on any single issue, anticipating that a diversity of views would sharpen their sense of the district and lead to the appropriate position on that issue. Although the farm constituent network is longterm, reform issues of trade and the environment quickly galvanized into local networks. Permanence, recurrence, and continuity seem dependent on what time-bound policy games are going on in Washington. As Christopher Bosso suggests of policy networking in general, a focus on the present—that is, on currently credible ideas and who mobilizes effectively around them—leads to the linkage of member and constituent interests.[15] As a member noted, "I work diligently with local forces when I can do something for them. Otherwise I try to avoid such discussions and even downplay the importance of issues that are brought to my attention."

CONGRESSIONAL NETWORKING AND DISTRICT REPRESENTATION

How does a diverse set of members of Congress come to understand those Washington policy games that are going on at any given time? Members and staff were in unanimous agreement: Congress is its own best information source in assisting enterprises with issue choices and in analyzing appropriate issue positions, "But its a backstop. You ask your colleagues how they feel about what you think you might propose." Members and their staffs agreed. No one went to other members to look for an issue, although nearly everyone went to others for assistance to successfully pursue ones already targeted as likely prospects.

Members emphasized two conditions about congressional networking, one that somewhat restrained congressional contacts and a second that definitely facilitated them. The restraining influence was the members' time. Because considerable business on a wide range of issues from many domains was on nearly every enterprise's agenda, member-to-member contacts were generally brief. Shared comments were usually restricted to whether an anticipated action was politically expeditious. However, members saw floor and corridor opportunities for conversation as plentiful, as they did quick office visits and telephone calls. As a midwestern senator said: "I make it a point to ask these types of questions while we're standing around waiting to vote. You always find those to be empty moments where you can get a thoughtful reaction." No one cited any contacts other than a plethora of hurried opportunities to see and gain help from other members.

All agreed, however, that the results of such brief and restrained encounters needed additional scrutiny before an issue was prioritized. Staff are the facilitating mechanism.[16] Once a member had an issue in mind, the enterprise took over in testing the water for acceptability—both in Congress and, of course, back home. Staff emphasized repeatedly that they were hired to network: "You might think we spend our time reading and analyzing data, but you're wrong if you do. I have not had time to read documents in fourteen years. I talk, and I telephone." To some, that networking with other staff made the job feasible. Others redefined their jobs to include greater amounts of networking because it made their positions more enjoyable. As one legislative assistant explained: "The reading and study part of an issue is tedious, so you minimize that part of it. You take advantage of the large number of interesting people around here, spread out in five big buildings like college dorms. We hire staff who are people-people rather than bookworms so they'll go out and get all the real opinions, pro and con on each issue. When you think about it, we finally select issues after we know there's no good reason for avoiding them." No member or office staffer offered a competing explanation of staff purpose.

Enterprises see congressional networking, in consequence, as integral to issue success. Members find brief but satisfactory collegial encounters; staff follow through on them, expanding the networks of contacts further than do members' own meetings. It is important that member and staff networking emphasizes the personal rather than the analytical, the opinion-centered rather than the data-based approach to pending issues. Enterprises developed information-gathering processes that led them to assess district-inspired issues less from a specialized or a committee perspective than from that of more compatible state and regional interests. These processes then made it evident to cooperative members which industries and products were important to their places and to proximate ones.

This description of the issue process shows even more clearly both the diversity of issue initiators and the freedom members feel from prereform institutional restraints. In the prereform Congress, members learned about issues, as Fenno suggests, through more or less well-integrated committee deliberations.[17] It was not committee assignment and its potential for generating selective concern for particular issues, however, that explained member initiatives for modern enterprises. When we consider traditional committee jurisdiction as a factor in the issue process, a member's committee assignment does little to predict the choice of one or another issue type for an intrusion into the agricultural domain (see Table A.16). This lack of correlation is most surprising for the two dominant reform types of issues. Trends toward these issues did not attract those with expertise in other domains. Trade issues did not come to agriculture through initiatives of members of the House Foreign Affairs and Senate Foreign Relations committees. Of the twenty-eight environmental issue initiators, only ten sat on a committee with environmental jurisdiction, and two of these also had agriculture committee seats.

Other issue types showed no committee-specific ties. The eight sampled members of the House Select Committee on Hunger initiated only one nutrition issue, even after that committee emphasized the passage of a bill to recognize its late chairman, Mickey Leland. Only one other nutrition issue came from a committee having shared jurisdiction over food programs, in this case the House Education and Labor Committee. Rural issues generated minimal response from committee members who had a jurisdictional interest. Although eleven members proposed issues for the agriculture committees' rural-policy bills, only one was a member of those committees. Seven were from House and Senate committees dealing with environmental and interior matters that had no responsibility for the rural issues they initiated. The only common link among the eleven members was their districts, all clustered in the pod of rural initiators.

Farm-benefit issues show a different pattern, but the same disregard for committee assignments. Sixteen of twenty agriculture committee members selected farm-benefit initiatives. However, most members of the five agriculture-related types of committee offered similar proposals. Even members from what were often noted by colleagues to be the aloof foreign-policy committees were aiding farmers. The highest percentage of members initiating farm benefits were from committees that had the least substantive policy overlap with agriculture. Eighty-three percent of such members initiated a farm-benefit issue as opposed to 80 percent of agriculture committee members and 67 percent of those from the other five types. Institutionalization of issues by committee meant little or nothing in restraining the effects of districts and the impact of district confidants on congressional-issue initiators. This lack of committee influence applied even though there were chances for members to use concurrent committee referrals to advance their issues. Surprisingly, only one member followed that option.

On the basis of the larger number of members initiating agricultural issues, the lack of relationship between committee assignment and issue interest makes sense. Indeed, it fits what would be expected in an open process of congressional networking. This disregard for traditional views of congressional dependence on committee specialization does not necessarily mean, though, that committees are ineffective gatekeepers for domain issues. The intense sharing of both their ideas and the basic political intelligence that members emphasized might indeed have been committee-centered. Contacts with one another and staff networking within Congress could aim at securing committee permission to initiate an issue. If the committees—that is, their members and their staff—approved of an idea before an initiating member committed to an issue, then the committees, not the rank-and-file members, retained agenda control.

That effort to secure committee permission was far from the customary practice, however. Few members, only 11 of 104, went to members of the agriculture committees for advice before selecting and determining a position on an issue. Yet 71 of them, or 68 percent, always went to some colleague for such advice before determining a position (see Table A.17). Even though not many members sought committee counsel, there were not any who initiated issues in this domain and *never* sought collegial advice. Thus, the pattern was to ask and trust one's colleagues when doubts about the value of an issue existed; but, there was no expectation that the committee should be the clearinghouse that determined an issue's worth. As Bentley suggests, networking depends first and foremost on the accommodation of mutual interests.[18] Meeting institutional expectations seems a distant second.

But a place-specific pattern does appear where an institutional pattern does not. The overwhelming number of members use colleagues from their home state as their primary source of congressional advice on agricultural issues. Sixty-nine of 104 members relied on another member from the state delegation; only 16 chose member contacts on the basis of regional or ethnic ties; 9 selected partisans. The committee of jurisdiction fared little better than party, with only 11 members going to a member of an agriculture or interior committee or related appropriations subcommittees for advice. Even though an issue would eventually go to a policy vehicle under the jurisdiction of one or more of these committees, most members did not see committee sources as instrumental in selecting or positioning their issues.

Enterprises attributed that lack of networking with the committee in front-loading policy vehicles partially to the conditions under which congressional networking takes place. Most of those who relied on the state delegation for advice—66 of 69—contacted no other members while initiating an issue. Nor did their staffs call the staffs of committee members for information on what to initiate and how to go about it: "I never would, that would signal our intent too early, and committee people would derail [our initiative] before we had a chance to firm up support." As a legislative director explained, "Committees are turf-conscious. They won't help you on a developing issue, they'll steal it and pervert it. Either that or kill it." Not surprisingly, in view of such comments, members ignored the committee of jurisdiction even when no member of the state delegation served there.

Some comments about committees, nonetheless, merit attention. Members and their staffs expressed interest in the committees on two points that stand out. First, it was somewhat inconsistent that staff "looked everywhere to find a sound reason for avoiding an issue" but claimed to ignore committees and the expertise of their personnel. That inconsistency was explained without hesitation: "That's no problem. You approach committee staff carefully. You flood them with a dozen questions a month on other issues anyway. So you can always ask questions. But you don't ask questions about whether our constituents need this or whether the committee is willing to provide that." Those in every enterprise that initiated agricultural issues felt opinions from the committee to be, at best, of secondary importance in accepting or rejecting a likely issue. At worst, enterprises ignored committee opinions. Members and their staffs acknowledged, however, that the processing of their initiatives eventually led to increasing committee contacts and dependency, "Way down the line."

Second, those members on the five types of committee that most closely shared jurisdictions in agriculture frequently commented on their desire to avoid starting battles between their committee chairs and those chairing agriculture or interior committees. Ten members voluntarily expressed that desire, as did four staffers. This concern for the chair's reaction led to more active solicitation of advice, but not from domain committees. Within the related committees, 74 percent of enterprises always sought member-to-member issue advice. However, only 55 percent of agriculture committee members and 57 percent of those from committees furthest removed from agriculture always solicited such collegial advice. Members from the five related committees saw soliciting advice as risk-reducing behavior, but not to the extent that they threatened their issues.

Members and their staffs offered a simple and uniform explanation of the committee's nominal importance in choosing and initiating their issues. In networking, the advice-seeker's goal was always more information about and better confirmation of constituent need, especially in determining whether the issue under question could hold the state delegation together and produce a win. That unity which produced success, of course, was why products and commodities in which the state ranked high were so important. This emphasis on the win raises a point that first was mentioned in Chapter 3. Issues that were potential losers were dropped in favor of other expressed constituent wants: "You can always find one issue for the same group that has a better chance of winning than another." Very rarely did anyone worry about committee or partisan solidarity since members seldom saw them as necessary for an issue's eventual success. Agreeing that rules were accommodative, a member noted that "both the committee and caucus exist to win supporters, not antagonize them."[19]

The creation of as many as fifty agricultural-domain discussion networks rounded out constituency networking within Congress. Each seemed constructed on the basis of how much internal political power the state delegation had accumulated and how much perceived interest its membership, as parts of the whole, had in any aspect of agriculture. At least, that was the members' claim. No one, though, pretended that the delegation worked together as a single entity on these matters. Yet the diversity of policies in agriculture did keep most delegations collectively interested, especially at farm-bill times. As a result, informal state networks were primary congressional conduits for bringing entrepreneurial-member initiatives to the committees. The principal attraction of state networks was their compatibility with district-driven issues. Accordingly, although some state delegations met regularly, their involvement in assessing state policy goals was largely ad hoc and specific to member requests: delegations did not put issue areas, such as agriculture, on their agendas for regular review.

Nonetheless, enterprises put great stock in state delegation relationships. While members and staff acknowledged committee jurisdictions on agricultural issues and rarely sought concurrent or sequential referrals to multiple committees, they also denied that committees handling these issues had much actual choice in accepting a strongly supported proposal. If there was strong state delegation support, or when other regional interests joined, enterprises saw the committee as being responsive out of necessity. Strong opposition from another state was one of the few things issue initiators feared. The only other note of caution they sounded was that issue successes depended on occasional rather than routine initiation by each enterprise. This pattern of initiation explained why issue selection, as seen earlier, was limited to so few issues per member but involved such a high percentage of all members: "There exist but a limited number of chances any committee will give you, but they'll give them to any member whose support the committee needs."

DETERMINING THE PLAYERS

The existence of constituent-based networking begs the question of why members play policy games. Members may initiate issues simply because policy games present themselves, and congressional enterprises merely claim an opportunity. That is, districts matter, and so, members serve them by choice. Alternatively, however, the degree to which members initiate increasingly more issues for more beneficiaries might well be a function of direct electoral pressures. Members might have initiated nothing in the domain if they felt safe. Yet they might have selected multiple beneficiary issues if they perceived electoral risks. Thus, as opposed to there being choices, this view argues that districts matter most when electoral pressures are severe and members serve them by necessity.

An argument defending choices has been developed throughout the last three chapters. From among numerous vehicles members identify and select ongoing or potential policy games that provide benefits appropriate to the district and desirable to constituent informants. There is one other finding about district effects that supports that view. Six of the nine members who initiated no agricultural domain issues (who as a group were unrelated to one another) came from outside the very extensive farm-benefit cluster in the three-dimensional model. Their districts were highly urban, highly white-collar, and low in farm-dependent population. The other three were very senior members of Congress with demanding committee assignments that left them no time for agriculture. A senior staffer said: "We trust (Agriculture Committee) Chairman de la Garza to take care of us. We take care of him on something else. Our boss is old school." These nine members, as a result, all knew that their intrusion into the domain would be of limited district interest, either because of a lack of constituents or because of attention to their constituent problems by other members.

Another finding suggested, however, that increased intervention is an electoral necessity for everyone. There was no statistical difference in district characteristics between those members initiating only farm bene-fits and those members selecting issues for farmers and for one or more other beneficiaries.[20] This finding meant that members might well be engaged in balancing issues only because of observable electoral threats, a point that potentially divided the two groups when types of district did not.

To test this hypothesis, districts were divided into three categories based on the members' average winning electoral margins in the last two elections. There was not the slightest difference between the small num-ber of members who won by margins of between 50 and 54.9 percent, those who won by between 55 and 59.9 percent, and the great majority of members who won by 60 percent or more (see Table A.18).[21] Doing nothing, serving one type of beneficiary, and initiating multiple types of issues for different beneficiaries were distributed equally: "I told you so, we just take care of our districts because we feel compelled to do so. Besides we're all avoiding electoral threats, not meeting them." Other enterprises also talked of similar preemptive district strategies as a way to help build big electoral margins.

What exists then is a very uniform set of district-specific responses. Members feel, as individuals, that they should choose to be district-directed regardless of their electoral margin of victory. Of course, predominantly large winning margins help reinforce that view: "It gives me the latitude to experiment in my responses to specific demands." Members, in turn, listen to voices that help them keep that focus and that winning edge. Congressional domain players, in other words, respond to the openness and fluidity of the process and the generalized desirability of listening to district forces. Although they may feel unsafe back home despite any previous electoral margin, members do nothing to structure issue-initiating behavior on the basis of increased evidence of risk from the last campaign.

CONCLUSION

There is a largely ignored dimension of policy networking that is determined by the home-style needs of the membership, as opposed to the interactions of a specialized Washington policy community. This constituent-based congressional networking points to one phenomenon that argues against the survival of more than a few very isolated iron-triangle relationships within the agricultural policy domain. The argument follows: lobbyists have long provided electoral security back home by way of their Washington knowledge. John Mark Hansen demonstrates why by pointing to lobbyists of the 1920s as better and more reliable sources of information than parties on recurring issues.[22] Interest groups reduced legislative uncertainty as a result. Information and electoral security kept interest-group representatives players in the networking loop.[23] Modern congressional enterprises, however, seem to find lobbyist information less of a basic need; enterprises have the means to secure their own district information. They can secure it to prepare preemptively for upcoming electoral strategies; with the result that members of Congress, although forever electorally unsafe, can indeed choose to manage the home district with some important degree of effectiveness. As can be seen in their issue initiatives, most members and their staffs make that choice.

Members and staff in twenty-nine offices volunteered the opinion that districts were easier to manage than in-house congressional relations because they could satisfactorily shop for one issue among many to placate constituents. However, they had to find just the right issues and policy games to load a particular issue into any policy vehicle. As one southern senator concluded, "You can learn to read your own district well when you can't read the Congress. First, everyone has their own districts and, second, power is spread so widely that you can get blindsided without warning as new issues are brought up on the Hill." Members such as this one continually referred to the competing powers of committee, subcommittees, caucus, and chamber leaders as obstacles to effective issue management. So, too, did senior staff. Both members and staff also referred in countervailing fashion to the sharing of power by each enterprise: "We can muck the process up from our office as much as anyone else in Congress. That means [others] have to work with us on district problems. We're as unmanageable as the rest of Congress. No, that's not right, we count as much at the rank-and-file level as does the leadership."

Accordingly, the conclusion is *not* that domain interests and traditional standing committees have suddenly lost their importance in a postreform Congress. The ambivalence of members about the influence of committees shows that it lingers. Both organized interests and committees have come to share influence with others in ways that are too frequently ignored; both have been squeezed by more pronounced enterprise networking. Constituent and state-delegation networking produce more domain activism among more members of Congress because legislators and staff have great capacity to be in contact with the district. This pronounced activism sets in motion a continuing cycle that brings increasingly more district contact, more constituent demands, and still more issue initiatives.[24]

The combined effect of this cycle is regular and recurring constituent contacts that take—or, perhaps, push—members into more networks of Washington influence. Whereas networks were once prized for bringing about specialized and expert deliberations, proliferating member attention and the rise of more Washington interest groups continuously changes networks' perspective. As Barbara Sinclair observes, power and influence now also goes to those who institutionally and substantively far exceed the previous parameters of policy domains and have little to do with their old networks.[25]

Although, as John Kingdon finds, the rank-and-file have long been important opinion molders and de facto policy leaders for their colleagues, the effects of rank-and-file influence today are more pronounced than they used to be.[26] Members seem to matter more as individuals, traditional groups are sharing power, and new competitive advantages for new confidants seem to be emerging.[27] The cycle of the 1920s, where groups replaced parties, may be yielding to another cycle of shifting constituent advantages. With modern constituents now more trusted and prized than interest groups in issue selection, and with selected and non-traditional networks of district forces articulating both timely and recurring issues, another institutional change seems to be at hand in Congress and for agriculture. Domain dynamics explains more about these institutional shifts.

PART THREE
The Politics of Institutions

The new legislative dance is a complex step . . . Old rules and rulers are intriguing to confront and twirl around the floor. It's nice, though, that they know and you know that they're not the ones who brought you to the dancehall.
— A twelfth-year House member explaining the comparative impact of Washington and district forces.

7

Groups and Agencies: The Downside of the Triangle

I find that I just don't need lobbyists anymore, not like I once did. They're just not as useful to my problems.

　　　　　—A twelfth-year member of the agriculture committee explaining his changing dependency on interest groups.

Our attention now shifts from the politics of constituents and districts to institutional changes and the ways they facilitate and limit policymaking by places. The district takes on increased importance as old institutions become increasingly suspect. In a more individualistic Congress, responding to the district first helps members reduce the uncertainty of confronting multiple demands. As one member acknowledged, "You can at least stay elected by taking a district approach to policymaking," thereby adding a new wrinkle to the old saw about reelection being the first priority of the enterprise. But, as he continued and as members with large electoral margins suggested, "It's more than just reelection that matters here. You vote with your district because you know what's there and you usually don't have much faith in the views of others who want your support."

Earlier studies help explain how the cross-sectional data presented here point to a changing politics: the postreform Congress has more congressional players, more involvement, and more issues than the prereform one; specialization, expertise, and committee controls matter less; staff and enterprises matter more. The current data in this study add two points: first, when confronted by district opportunities, most members become players, even in what most consider an insular and parochial policy domain and even when they lack appropriate committee assignments. Second, members pursue opportunities not just through floor votes but by developing a more intense interest in initiating their own issues.

The current data also adds understanding of the changing Washington policy community and its impact on Congress. Interest groups and administrative agencies both have been seen as growing in numbers and as narrowing their issues. Constituents, represented by informants and confidants, fit right into the changing situation as important and narrow parts of the policy process. Combined with increasing participation from rank-and-file members of Congress, the response to constituent demands in an already crowded universe of policy activists explodes the iron-triangle metaphor. Neither that metaphor nor any of its extensions are any longer appropriate analytical tools for summarizing complex political relationships.

Two other findings discussed earlier emphasize a changing politics. Both show that the dynamics of politics are as important as the unique policy problems that identify one domain and differentiate it from others. Both also result from what scholars tend to overlook, namely, that agricultural policy has had to become far more than farm policy.

The first finding is that policy games are evolving, not static; the one constant is that they have district importance. There have been three major game-related stages in creating an extensive and multipurpose agricultural-policy base in Congress. At each stage, the dominant issues shifted within the domain. The first stage, in the 1920s, created an agricultural-development policy game that culminated in the cooperation of farm interests representing the dominant crops of their respective regions.[1] The second stage of policy games generated rural/urban and farm/labor coalitions in the 1950s and 1960s and led to support of food-stamp programs inside the domain and labor policies beyond the domain. Once reform interests were integrated into policy bases, coalition-building ceased to be necessary, and low-income food programs became part of a standing domain agreement. The third stage followed in the 1980s, as other social and economic interests, most notably those concerned with trade and the environment, confronted the permeability of the agricultural-policy domain. Opportunistic members of Congress opened their enterprises to these, and sometimes to other policy challengers *because doing so provided more chances to represent their districts.*

What was different from earlier policy games, though, was the nature of this new confrontation. In a postreform Congress, members care little if farm development and new programs are compatible. Rewarding some beneficiaries without depriving others was, however, a central concern in conflict over food stamps and between midwestern and southern crop producers. Disagreements about policy arose over liberal and conservative beliefs about the scope of government, not about the ability to coexist. Finding compatible policy objectives no longer seems the rule among members. For example, public-interest advocates argue that food safety and nutrition have more to do with the mission of the Food and Drug Administration than the farm-to-market interests of the U.S. Department of Agriculture. Many will not negotiate that belief. Thus, with rigid positions proliferating, coalition building by Washington interests may no longer be a workable means for structuring agreements within the modern domain. Finding common ground on public-interest and farm-benefit programs is hard. Animal-welfare advocates, for example, want to limit farm production and, thus, producer income. The data set in this study, in consequence, reveals stresses that undermine the domain's bounded purposes: the agriculture domain's capacity to work things out is declining because its players no longer resolve contentious policy games.

This brings up the second finding about the importance of domain dynamics. The agriculture domain has seen significant changes in relationships between information sources and members of Congress over time.[2] The data set in this study show yet another shift in primary informants. Constituent informants appear to be replacing interest group representatives, just as group leaders replaced partisan leaders in the 1920s. Constituents are surprisingly prominent sources of information for members.[3] And they have that prominence because members, as enterprises, have the capacity to reach and to listen to anyone and everyone in whom they are interested.

The surprise derives from the long-held and very institutional view of how agricultural policy is made, what "everyone knows."[4] Closed networks supposedly emphasize distributive politics and avoid regulation. The data set in this study, however, provides a more complex explanation of congressional processes. Members and their staffs are opportunistic but also restrained: they limit enterprise demands, both in number and in the scope of requests; they also seek congressional assurance that their demands are credible and legitimate, or winnable; they supplement distributive policies with regulatory ones and also pay considerable attention to redistribution within the farm sector.

This process suggests an interplay between individual enterprises and institutional centers of influence that has been ignored since Chapter 2.

What is the result of a greater-than-expected dynamism? To what extent do old institutions order Congress? They must do something. Keith Krehbiel identifies institutional influences that limit member self-interest—in agriculture, "the system works against high-demanders and preference outliers" and in favor of those members who reflect more moderate committee values.[5] Members want the results they anticipate, or Kingdon's sense of congressional regularity. This was seen in the data in the way members direct the great majority of their issues to maintenance— mostly for farm constituents—as well as in the neglect of many potential nonfarm issues.

Although most members of Congress clearly network on behalf of issues for constituent interests, it remains to be seen how their initiatives are processed and what goes on to ensure that they win. As mentioned in Chapter 1, this process, searching as it does for regularity, appears to be an iterative one where issues recur at different stages before resolution. It is necessary to examine how, in this changing policy domain, members respond less to organized interest groups and other policy professionals, particularly those from government agencies.

INTEREST GROUPS: NEW CHALLENGES

The problems faced by interest groups can best be seen by returning to Arthur Bentley's theory of groups and what was said earlier about the problems of policy networks.[6] Members of Congress now see agricultural issues as very precise ones that meet the needs of specific beneficiaries. Groups find it difficult to identify themselves with issues in a manner congenial to Congress's view: many groups are not well organized and established, so they lack a policy history. Others emphasize superior organization but, for various reasons, fail to develop policy consensus among leaders and followers. Also, the existence of so many groups with similar interests is confusing. As a result, members of Congress often ignore both new and old groups for their lack of relevancy on issues that group leaders identify as critical.

At the same time, however, with networking now quite ad hoc, both new and old groups find certain advantages. Less established groups can contribute to some of the most timely congressional initiatives. Traditional groups, with a long policy history, remain important in any reexamination of recurring issues and policies. In both cases, however, the crowded group universe, along with competition from district interests, limits organizations that want to design policy. "Remember," said one member of Congress, "we organize and pass agriculture policy. It's not the administration and certainly not a collection of lobbyists who get it done."

Critiques of organized interest groups made by those in most congressional enterprises emphasized that members and their staffs were more concerned to identify real interests and agreed-upon needs rather than just well-recognized organizations.[7] Most organized groups failed to communicate a representative interest. As often observed, interest groups are "problematic phenomena whose existence and activities" are not necessarily owed to concerted and coordinated public-policy attention by leaders and followers.[8]

The reasons for their problematic status are numerous. Groups are heavily dependent on entrepreneurs for their success.[9] There seems little natural evolution of organizations from their beginnings in the shared public-policy concerns of like-minded voters. A congressional member said it best, "These are contrived organizations." Nonpolicy interests such as insurance programs and other selectively received benefits of membership attract and hold many duespayers.[10] Maintenance of many groups depends on financial patrons rather than an interested membership.[11] Accordingly, those in Congress know that some groups have few ties to voters, others have memberships divided over group goals, and still more mobilize effectively on public policies only because they keep their ranks very small.[12] Skepticism about interest groups, then, was, not surprisingly, prevalent. As one congressman puzzled, "Is this group a group? . . . Those you talk to in Washington . . . seem to be way out of line with the public on water quality demands." A legislative director responded, "Every year, with every new group that sets up shop in Washington, I get more cynical about interest groups and why I should listen to them."

There were three kinds of criticisms about interest groups.[13] First, those in seventy-three enterprises saw inordinate conflict between interest group leaders and grassroots informants from their own districts, especially among confidants. Second, distrust was a factor in forty-one enterprises. Members and their staffs expressed doubts about the nationally determined policy solutions of most groups. They also felt that lobbyists were unable to explain how their proposals affected others. Third, those in twenty-three enterprises felt many Washington lobbyists to be more interested in proving their own influence than in reaching an agreement. These points interrelate.

Conflict was reported by office enterprises on 116 of the 256 time-consuming issues and on 1 of the 7 priority issues that were not included in the time-consuming list.[14] Two sets of conflicts were identified on 26 of these issues. Eighty-two issue conflicts were between constituents and Washington organizations that shared, in congressional members' views, a similar interest. Those in only nine enterprises thought such conflict to be useful or, as one senator stated, "a healthy checkpoint for securing more information." The others saw it as confusing and detrimental to the use and reliability of both group and constituent informants.

Members and their staffs repeatedly told of being presented confusing and contradictory information. For example, the effects of cattle and sheep grazing on public lands was always perplexing. Environmental groups laid out a litany of degradation problems; constituents told other stories. Western residents, except for a very few highly active iconoclasts, saw little of the degradation; rather, they told of the charm of cowboy ways. Those from other districts who visited the West also saw little degradation but complained that their favored visiting sites were in danger of being overregulated and taken away. When the Bureau of Land Management was asked for clarifications, BLM never gave a straight answer. They proposed mitigation, which left the enterprises out of the picture; they presented data that had little concrete information to use in sorting out conflicts; or, most offensively, they dragged out a computer-based model that made the issues "so damned abstract that no one gives a rip." Similar stories were told about the conflicting effects of trade, groundwater contamination, and nearly every other new issue for the domain.

Examples of conflict included disagreements between local environmentalists and the National Wildlife Federation or the Sierra Club, between animal-welfare activists and People for the Ethical Treatment of Animals, and between dairy farmers and the National Milk Producers Association. These were *not* conflicts between supporters of already competing groups, such as the American Agriculture Movement and the American Farm Bureau Federation, or the radical Greenpeace organization and the centrist Center for Resource Economics. Said another senator, "I mean disagreements between my middle-of-the-road farmers and the Farm Bureau and Corn Growers."

Fifty-three of these conflicts were within what members and their staffs saw as similar farm interests, twenty were within similar environmental interests, seven were within business interests on trade issues, and one was within a rural interest.[15] All conflicts were over district versus national policy implications. Quite clearly, however, district views challenged national views and, because members were worried about their own initiatives, those challenges fragmented the concept of interest. In a Bentleyan sense, these were really conflicts between, not within, interests. They existed because political groups were not effectively integrated. A House member says: "Most of those who lobby me have a membership problem when you look into it."

District-versus-national conflicts produced, in one agriculture committee staff analyst's words, "the failure of interests." Such failures were far more evident to issue initiators than were conflicts between constituent wants and Washington organizations that represented opposing interests; for example, farm groups against local environmentalists or business associations against farmers. A senior member explained, "A constituent can come and talk rationally and with great information about a dairy or wheat program that operates to that farm family's disadvantage. That same person will gripe about environmental regulations, however, and not give me a clue as to what options are feasible. The bottom-line interest [for that constituent] is the commodity program." Accordingly, congressional members and staff saw little real conflict between constituents and directly antagonistic interests because neither party was able to address solutions to the problems of the other.

Even so, the number of disagreements involving distinct interests was high. Thirty-five of these were constituent conflicts with competing national interests. Only nine issue conflicts were between Washington interest groups.[16] Constituent conflicts with agency officials, agricultural policy professionals, or the media (12) were also more common than conflicting positions between interest groups and these other sources (5). An appropriations committee staffer summarized: "For most members, the only disagreements that matter are when someone threatens their district. They're oblivious to a lot of the conflicts in Washington, mostly because they don't care, but also because this a conflict-avoidance place where groups resolve a lot of differences themselves. Constituents, unlike even hardened lobbyists, are bold and brazen and go after those they don't like." Lobbyists were suspect for the spin they always placed on issues, particularly in downplaying disagreements.

Criticisms did not reveal a new or changing impression of the veracity of interest groups and lobbyists, however. No one suggested that group representatives were dishonest, spread falsehoods, or lacked integrity.[17] The lobbyists' problems were with what they represented and knew.

Thirty-one member enterprises criticized interest groups because they represented policy objectives that failed to take into account localized problems. Most enterprises saw interest groups as setting their objectives after either holding national policy conferences or meeting with recurring coalition partners from Washington; failure to reflect local needs was rooted in existing policy and the processes for making it. Members and their staffs criticized nationally determined commodity programs, water standards, rural-delivery systems, and so on for not being well adapted to substate or state differences. One member explained that he and his staff cooled on a rural lobbyist when it became clear that there was no more for their state in the group's proposal than for any other rural place. Even highly regional commodity programs such as peanuts, sugar, and tobacco brought district-based complaints to members of Congress over local inequities. The same was true for environmental proposals that sought to improve national standards on land use, water quality, and chemical-input restrictions. Although regional considerations were often incorporated into interest-group proposals, members saw them as overly broad generalizations that seldom took into account variations in local conditions.

This attitude exists, in large part, because of a major shift in farm economics since the 1920s and 1930s. Production agriculture has long been location specific, as the differences between farming in the South and in the Midwest shows. Thus, there were always competing local views. That effect worsened, however, with the intense specialization and capital-investment emphasis of modern agriculture. Once-minor differences in climate and soil now have major impacts on productivity and the use of such inputs as fertilizers and herbicides. The importance of local places further intensifies with the introduction of biotechnology products geared to specific environments. So, in significant ways, economics and politics are both rationally local far more for modern producers than for their predecessors.

Enterprises heavily criticized lobbyists and groups for a lack of concern about things local. Policies were designed for large areas of the country or for the entire nation, and little information was available from established lobbies about how local farmers, businesses, and economies would be affected. Twenty enterprises voiced criticisms of this sort: thirteen about farm groups, nine about environmental groups, six about rural organizations, five about business associations, and two about consumer groups. As a southern member exclaimed: "The soybean group didn't tell me the same thing about planting reductions that I learned back home." Another member went on, "No one knew the economic consequences of the plan or what it would do to my local cattle industry." Although the examples were different, the common complaint was that information was inadequate, given what was expected of informant groups. Accordingly, members saw lobbyists as less important to issue initiatives *and* in deciding committee and floor votes than were constituents.

Not all the blame for the decline of the importance of lobbyists was placed on the governing process and the need to develop a national policy framework, however. Members and staff from twenty-three enterprises were intensely critical of the goals of organizational maintenance and the personal priorities of group leaders, believing that they worked against their policy effectiveness. These critics also argued that all, not a few, lobbyists were suspect because so many of them no longer followed political conventions. Congressional members saw too many agricultural group leaders developing new policy goals that they, as targets, just could not accept.[18] Leaders would make issue choices in the face of divergent pressures, become inflexible about the choices they made, disregard important information that was extraneous to those choices, and continue to promote issues even after extensive criticism.

"Its the biggest change I've seen in Washington," observed a veteran of thirteen Congresses, "lobbyists and groups who won't bargain or listen to reason in the face of compelling evidence and advice from even their own cronies." A lobbyist responded to the complaint, "I no longer must bargain. I can take my complaints to the media through what you would probably call public scare tactics." In essence, numerous interest groups chose not to trade politically on their policy expertise and usefulness as information sources. Rather, they amassed political influence because of popular and media appeal. In particular, as several oft-criticized lobbyists explained, they issued ultimatums and then went to the media with charges of neglect by certain policymakers. "The first thing I do," explained one executive of a patronage group, "is threaten to publicize district news releases of voting records . . . it's my way of winning."

What do these changes mean for old policy networks? As critics of such tactics and groups argued, lobbyists often fail to show any compelling reason for policymakers and groups to join forces on an issue. Nor do lobbyists provide evidence that either group members or the public supports the issue under discussion. "How the hell do we support something," argued a senior staff analyst, "when there's no good data about policy need or, from a Senator's perspective, state popularity." Lobbyists had lost respect in at least some important quarters because several of them pursued influence in ways that only increased rather then resolved congressional uncertainty.

These criticisms help explain why members of Congress are drawn to their districts and to constituent confidants for cues and advice. Contentiousness and conflicting implications in contemporary agricultural policy games lead to escalating political tensions and less sense of common purpose in the domain. Not only are constituents critical of the positions of nationally organized interests, but leaders of groups that represent those interests open themselves to critiques of their strategies within Congress. Members see lobbyist information as lacking in precision, especially about matters back home. Perhaps in response, many groups have adopted other mechanisms for exercising influence. As another long-time lobbyist concluded: "I could never assemble the data to satisfy Congress on these issues anyway. They want to know the impossible because they're so insecure." The result is that congressional enterprise and group interests are often badly divided. When members sense that division, organized Washington interest groups become less relevant to the needs of a modern Congress.[19] Member enterprises still use groups, but not with the same degree of trust and with much greater scrutiny than they used to.

INTEREST GROUPS: SOME DECLINING STRENGTHS

Interest group leaders who discussed congressional influence acknowledged a decline in their capacity to represent constituent opinions.[20] This decline occurred despite the actions of many of them to mobilize the grassroots; there were several problems in developing agreement between Washington and district folks. For example, public interest groups often had no direct memberships. Moreover, few of them had participatory mechanisms for involving their supporters in policy deliberations. Environmental, consumer, and rural groups had attentive publics and committed Washington activists, but they lacked, as one interest-group director stated, "informed members who locally back our specific demands." Farm groups, in contrast, faced divided memberships, often more fragmented than ever after policies were prioritized in local, state, and then national conferences. As one lobbyist concluded, "We have to practice too much democracy." Business interests had a third membership problem. Firms involved in similar products and industries were often divided over public-policy wants. Most firms therefore lobbied actively on their own, leaving their trade associations more to monitor legislation than resolve divisive issues.

Those factors help explain why most organized groups fell far short of overcoming congressional uncertainty about the direction of future policy, as a House member says: "There always is a risk in listening to a lobbyist's pitch." Groups, as a consequence, seem only moderately successful in final negotiations with members, whether over which issues should be included in a policy or over how the policy should be directed.

Assessing Group Strengths

Contrasting sentiments among members about group influence show much about how interest groups are received in Congress and what they do in policymaking. When asked whether these organizations drove the agricultural policy process, congressional members and their staffs in only 27 percent of the enterprises either strongly agreed or strongly disagreed with that assessment; slightly more disagreed than agreed. Ambivalence was the dominant view.

Committee assignment was the biggest predictor of opinions, primarily because members and their staffs saw group influence varying at each stage of the policy process. Agriculture committee members all agreed— but none fully acknowledged—that organized groups drove the process. All saw distinct limits on group influence, particularly in proposing issues. Those on committees that periodically dealt with agricultural issues tended to disagree, oftentimes strongly that groups drove the process. Members who strongly agreed that interest groups drove agricultural policy were mostly those with assignments only on nonrelated committees; they, of course, were the ones least likely to be involved in committee deliberations where policies were finally negotiated. They also had the least experience with agricultural interest groups. As one of them said: "My opinion about their great strength is based on what I see as very slow change in farm policy and the great scrutiny I felt when this office wanted something. We got it but had to really justify our constituents' needs." These members strongly suspected groups of too great an influence. Members who faced groups in their own committees saw, according to a House member, "both their vulnerability and strengths."

Member and staff comments were more important than their rankings in explaining why lobbyists still matter, especially as parts of constituent-linked networking. Within the agriculture committees and the agriculturally important House Interior and Insular Affairs Committee, members felt an obligation to listen to and work with interest groups, owing to protocol, or longstanding congressional etiquette: "I still have to listen to them before I act. I really have to give them a chance to work things out first." These committee members saw their own constituent issues resulting from the failures of groups to provide politically adequate solutions. They still acknowledged, however, that they worked with groups in structuring final legislation.

But protocol extended to only some groups, particularly commodity interests, and for four reasons, all more important to committees than to individual members. First was historical influence; decades of congressional and group partnerships went into making commodity programs the dominant parts of agricultural policy. Second, commodity groups still had the greatest expertise in the operation of what several members called "their own programs." They knew more than other information sources, including constituents, who were seldom versed in more than their own policy problems and solutions. Third, the complexity and the often arcane language of each program encouraged reliance on group representatives, who provided institutional memory. The enterprises of agriculture committee members understood one or another program, but only in a less technical fashion than commodity lobbyists and their economists did. Fourth, Washington farm groups were thought to be especially effective in mobilizing grassroots discontent when commodity programs were actually threatened, as opposed to being redrafted. Commodity groups seldom stifled dissent and opposition within their own grassroots factions, but they did maintain loyal followings when it came to the need for income assistance. Thus, members of the agriculture committees found it advantageous to let Washington lobbyists propose the first solutions to changes in commodity policy, even when constituents at home were angry. The committees then began their accommodation, retreating to district solutions on those parts that were still unacceptable. In preferring the district solutions, they anticipated that interest groups would generally fail due to a lack of internal consensus and integration.

A dilemma emerged because the agriculture committees provided farm groups such access.[21] Members and their staffs feared complaints of being labeled committees for only farmers and ranchers. Accordingly, a second protocol developed among agriculture committee and most House Interior and Insular Affairs Committee members. They also solicited policy proposals and solutions from other Washington lobbies. Agribusiness, rural, consumer, and environmental groups were given chances to pursue their goals through the same doors open to commodity organizations. But, just as interior committee members from the Northeast chafed at the protocol of farm groups being offered the first chance at proposing public-lands solutions, many agriculture committee members resented the open-door policy extended to nonfarm interests. Committee members had no respite from listening, though. They merely became more critical of interest-group politics. Farm and nonfarm groups bickered with one another and slowed committee deliberations by compounding the number of issues to consider.

Nonfarm groups, moreover, generally lacked a significant base of policies from which to draw proposals as well as the expertise, the technical command, and the grassroots networks comparable to that of farm interests. After the staffs scrutinized them, many nonfarm groups were felt to be so out of touch with the problems facing the accommodative committees that they lost access, particularly to committee hearings. Their lobbyists, therefore, were disadvantaged, and widely seen to be even less likely to offer workable policy solutions in committee than were commodity groups. For example, committee policymakers solicited proposals that reconciled farm, business, and environmental interests on water-quality problems in the 1990 farm bill. None were forthcoming. Members, though, were not interested in policy solutions providing for environmental regulations that lessened water problems but created intense farm or business opposition. Said one House agriculture committee member: "We quickly shut the door on that." The committees then borrowed from various home and Washington proposals. Environmental and other nonfarm groups found several of their ideas included in legislation, but they certainly never drove the solutions.

District influences affect protocol for granting access to nonfarm groups, thus further underscoring lobbyists' failures as brokers in members' eyes. Most western members of the House Interior Committee, for example, rejected the idea of increased fees and regulation of lands and water as unacceptable and, so, refused to listen to environmental interests. It made no sense to them to listen because attitudes back home were unyielding among key constituents. This attitude was rare on other issues.

But the effect of the district was generally more positive than that of western districts on environmental issues. Most of the members with committee jurisdiction over agriculture and public lands saw evidence of constituent changes in their own districts. Unlike the districts of western members, their midwestern and eastern districts included influential voters who found new directions for agriculture policy either useful or necessary. Local attitudes favored, not unexpectedly, environmental initiatives and efforts to increase area business opportunities through expanded trade. Those attitudes made it important to pay attention to farm groups, even to give them first hearing; but, they also made it necessary to appear broadly responsive to a mix of prominent national interests that reflected grassroots worries. Once again, enterprises were bringing interests together, creating the issue-mixing seen earlier and also diminishing the leadership role any single set of groups could play. An agriculture staffer concluded: "We listen to damn near anyone to keep this committee's deliberations as current and objective as possible. The sector is changing too fast for us not to."

These member enterprises made it clear that various interest groups were still part of the committee process for sorting out solutions to agricultural-policy problems. A plethora of solutions from constituents were included in policy vehicles. But interest groups won sometimes and lost other times, just as some constituent issues were found acceptable while others were rejected. But groups were always players in the agriculture committees, and they were not in those committees outside the domain that only periodically handled agricultural issues.

Attitudes of members on these committees toward groups were quite surprising. Farm groups were seen by those who served on nonagriculture committees as unusually inept. Their lobbyists, it seems, lacked knowledge of both policy content and committee processes outside their own committees. As a Budget Committee analyst observed after $13 billion was stripped away from agriculture for fiscal years 1992–95 in the Budget Reconciliation Act, "The farm groups come in here together and make excessive demands that they can't back up. We know that no one else wants these same things." In addition, members and the staff of these committees perceived the array of farm interests and programs as unfairly favoring major commodities over other farm problems. When problems of other growers came up in their nonagriculture committees or their personal initiatives, members received totally inadequate information from Washington groups: "Ask the Farm Bureau about Christmas-tree problems. You get a blank stare."

Members and staff criticized public-interest groups—especially environmentalists working on farm pollution—and organized agribusiness associations for being so exceptionally narrow in their demands that they affected the margins of policy but seldom its direction and purpose. Those groups, like farm organizations, were seen as both most interested in and knowledgeable about agriculture-committee policies. They were less aware of and comfortable with regulatory initiatives affecting agriculture in air and water legislation, however. Their lobbyists, in consequence, provided information that was of limited use on issue initiatives before these committees. As a senior staff employee explained, "We're not making agriculture policy here [House Energy and Commerce]. . . . We're making policy that *affects* agriculture. . . . Groups with a special food or farm interest have a disadvantage. Other interests define the rules." That remove obviously explains why members avoided non-domain vehicles with their agricultural issues.

But it also explains why members of these committees who were never on agriculture committees disregarded interest groups in their own agricultural-issue initiatives: "I don't even return their phone calls. They can't stop us because our office has as much leverage with the agriculture committee as they do." In short, interest groups had no veto with individual members who had their own power base, as they did on the accommodative agriculture committees. And that remove also explains why most members and their staffs felt that overlapping committee assignments, except on House agriculture and interior, seldom worked to the advantage of interest groups concerned with agriculture. "I have one job and set of expectations of me on one committee and another on agriculture. My obligation to give farm groups a hearing [in Commerce] doesn't apply." Farm groups had no historically established policy relationship there; nor did they have relevant expertise, institutional memory, or any capacity to mobilize the grassroots at the loss of a program. The net result was that, beyond the domain, agricultural interest groups offered few issues for members of Congress and had little brokerage skills for the committees.

Why, though, did interest groups get high marks for influence from members of Congress who were least likely to have observed agricultural interests operating in committee? As with district influence, familiarity played a major role, in this case by imposing familiar sanctions. These members had not seen agricultural interests helping to sort out solutions as they do before the agriculture committees; nor had they seen the same groups appear inept on related committees beyond their domain. These members had, however, initiated agricultural issues of their own, and eighteen of them found that their enterprises lacked control when they did. Their initiatives had been scrutinized closely by both farm- and public-interest lobbyists who were close to agriculture committee members. Why? As a member said, "I have no independent committee leverage with the aggies, nor do they really need my vote when they have several to spare."

Each of the eighteen members had expected such treatment, given their impressions of the agriculture committees as especially parochial. Eight of them, in fact, had chosen not to initiate one or more specific issues because they anticipated interest-group opposition; they knew that some things were unwinnable. Likely opposition had not come directly from lobbyists, however, but as a result of their networking within state or regional delegations and caucuses. "I found out through discussions among the mushroom caucus," explained a legislative director. "I couldn't help our growers then without risking a damaging news release on product health and safety from the consumer lobbies." These views confirmed the influential, if limited, role interest groups still play on agriculture committees.

But that role does not mean that the committees are impermeable to the initiatives of the rank and file. Thirteen other members without committee assignments dealing with agriculture had very different experiences from those of the eight who met opposition. They just picked more timely issues on which the agriculture committees welcomed their intervention. All had initiated issues for constituents when nationally organized interests had not been effective or had ignored a district problem. Accordingly, constituents were blaming Congress for being unresponsive. Members were faulting farm organizations, trade associations, and public-interest groups for one or more of these failures, but not as obstructionists; they were just seen as unable to offer solutions. Members mentioned farm-disaster assistance most frequently as a solution to district concerns and saw interest groups incapable of aiding local growers. In each instance, members found the agricultural committees responsive to change, yet excessively slow and unwilling to act until several members complained. As one very senior member concluded about his success: "The circumstances have been altered so dramatically in Congress in the past twenty-five years that today I work things out with a colleague. Back then I went to the cotton cooperatives and the Farm Bureau, hat in hand, for my constituents. And I usually failed. It's not my seniority that matters, it's the rapidly changing process."

Within those procedural changes, interest groups have retained their greatest influence by applying their expertise to committee solutions. Yet even that strength is less important than many assume, in light of these mixed congressional views. Groups have incurred their greatest loss in influence because organized interests no longer tie district voters to organized policy goals, even as domain brokers and technical experts. Groups, as a result, have lost considerable relevance to committee negotiations because they too often generate conflict when the committees hope to accommodate diverse views.

Reconciling with Group Theory

Criticism of interest groups was extensive in Congress. Few members and staff expected to do what lobbyists wanted. In addition, many lobbyists no longer anticipated winning on their issues when they served merely as information brokers. As more members of Congress became more involved in more issues, two things hurt group cooperation in Congress. First, incompatible issues were being brought to agricultural policy games where more easily accommodative coalitions were once the rule. Second, a wider range of interests was represented in Congress: there were more groups of each issue type, and there were widely apparent differences between group and grassroots interests.

The role of interest groups in contemporary agricultural politics, therefore, needs reassessment. Little congressional commitment exists for even the most traditional domain groups, even on the agriculture committees that depend most on their technical expertise and institutional memories. Lobbyists are given little time to find and offer solutions to pending policy problems or to build coalitions that can find and offer them. Members of Congress who depend on issue and policy information quickly turn elsewhere for ideas. For most members, including those on key committees, agricultural groups matter only when they match an already identified enterprise interest.

The reasons why organized groups mean so little seem simple. First, for most congressional members, organized agricultural interests have little competitive advantage in reaching district constituents for information and advice; members of Congress can reach them on their own. Even groups that have outlets in members' constituencies are best at arousing district interests to a threat rather than at winning converts to national policy positions. Second, when interest groups move beyond the domain with which they are traditionally identified, they face an even greater competitive disadvantage in policy deliberations; they have no policy base on which to claim technical superiority. Thus, for most congressional enterprises, organized groups do little to influence member interests in agricultural policy. At best, groups help find solutions amidst an already plentiful array of partial solutions. Overlapping policy jurisdictions between committees have exposed weaknesses in group influence that were less apparent when strong and less necessarily accommodative committees ruled the Congress. Still, however, interest group influence and committee influence are interdependent.

What does this mean for interest-group theory? Members of Congress and their staffs did not offer pressure-group explanations of power. Where E. E. Schattschneider and Earl Latham once saw a passive Congress buffeted by relentless and well-organized interests, lobbyists are now seen as representing but one type of potentially useful interest.[22] In addition, although Congress is still seen as reactive, members and staff see its present dynamics as anything but passive: members define outcomes, whereas district informants set issues in play through the policy solutions they propose.

Transactional group theory helps clarify this relationship. Raymond Bauer, Ithiel de Sola Pool, and Lewis Dexter found interest-group influence to be dependent on how intensely members of Congress needed their services.[23] Group influence varied according to the importance of the transactions, or exchanges, made between lobbyists and legislators. That interpretation seems especially relevant to the postreform Congress, where information is a variable commodity in the diverse political marketplace of any policy domain.[24] From the enterprise's perspective, resolving uncertainty is the primary good derived from information. When group resources that are tied to membership and cohesion break down, or fail to develop the principal information services for which groups were long valued, organized interests decline in importance to enterprises.

This happens because the value of a group's supporters provides it much of its policy expertise and technical capacity. When a group lacks integration and common purpose, it does not matter much that its leaders understand issues, policy, and effects better than anyone else in Washington. Grassroots interests and their competing news from the district will necessarily undermine that information, at least for congressional enterprises that focus more on positive district relationships than on accumulating Washington power.[25] Interest group information is, then, a service both less useful and more suspect in an individualistic Congress. Consequently, members of Congress more routinely talk to those from home.

BUT WHY NOT AGENCIES?

What would be the impact on agencies of the decline of the role of the interest group? Would a declining-interest group role mean that agency and department officials would matter more, even in a shared way with constituents? In the iron-triangle metaphor for providing informational services, agencies should better develop policy and technical knowledge;

planning and policy management are their jobs.[26] Interest groups offer political, more than analytical, information about how policy or alternate proposals work.[27] Although groups have begun doing more analytical tasks, isn't that evidence of the continuing value of the bureaucracy?[28]

It is—but only to an extent. Public administrators do seem less affected than interest groups by congressional and policy changes. Members and their staffs felt that agencies have retained their traditional tasks and responsibilities. But the agencies matter little to congressional issue initiators, even on the agriculture committees, because blended information, which combines information relevant to both policy and politics, has a greater value than the policy information generated by agencies. Also, members and staff questioned much about the usefulness and the validity of agency operations and analysis, and they did so for all the reasons seen in earlier chapters.

Members and staff saw USDA and other federal agencies as having resources that are integral to national agricultural policymaking. They mentioned two types of resources. First, agencies perform research, analysis, and forecasting services; members saw all these services as essential for any issues of policy change, especially in determining funding and cost levels. Agencies also contract out for data collection and studies that became part of the public policymaking information base.[29] Members acknowledged that the cumulative effect of agency efforts was to produce higher levels of expertise and knowledge in agencies than can be found elsewhere in the Washington policy community. Others, who work with Congress, from interest groups to foundations, rely heavily on agency information for their own secondary analysis of government data.

Second, and more important to congressional members, agency officials use their considerable discretion in implementing what Congress designs. Not only does the secretary of agriculture make decisions on commodity prices and support levels, but other agency officials intervene in such things as environmental and nutrition questions. No issue types are untouched. As a consequence, for example, environmental initiatives from the 1990 farm bill depended on USDA decisions for service delivery and regulation. Decisions about individual farms and their practices are made at the county USDA level for commodity-program eligibility, conservation practices, credit availability, and plant and animal disease problems. Most issue initiatives thus depend on agency cooperation.

Why, then, were administrators so little valued and rarely used in selecting and prioritizing issues? Seventy-nine office enterprises mentioned that staff had recently been in contact with one or more federal agencies to resolve a problem in implementing programs. Sixty-eight of these contacts were made on behalf of constituents and eleven, on behalf of interest groups. Agriculture committee members all made such contacts, and they did so frequently as part of the daily job, over and over. But so did other enterprises. Only 5 of the 120 sampled offices did not have a staff person doing agriculture casework.[30]

Casework, however, dealt with relatively minor problems that generally took little time and were easily handled by the agency. Enterprises easily distinguished it from issues work for the district. According to a senior Senate staffer: "It has no policy-setting purpose." Most casework, such as reviewing rejections by county USDA agencies, was referred to an administrative appeals process or simply reconsidered, with reports made back to the enterprises. Administrative discretion made this work frequent and easy. Time-consuming and priority administrative issues were quite different from casework, usually going to a department secretary, an agency administrator, or an under-secretary, and involving several enterprise staff. All of these issues were about policy changes, such as new eligibility requirements or price levels. Most also went through executive branch legislative liaisons, which made them nonroutine and universally disliked: "You're in it for a long time when you confront the Secretary's office."

Members and their staffs disliked administrative issues, as opposed to casework, because these initiatives pitted the legislative branch squarely against the executive branch. And initiators, regardless of their party, saw executive branch officials as inherently unresponsive at the secretarial level and throughout middle management. As one Republican member noted of a Reagan-era request, "It took me nearly two years to get a quite simple study done and, for the entire period, I was denied access to the USDA agency that would do the report." The typical comment was, "They don't want to aid congressional policymaking."

Frustrations did more than cause members of Congress to avoid issues of policy with ranking administrators; they also led most members and their staffs to disregard administrative agencies in selecting and formulating their own issue initiatives. Only two enterprises selected issues because of federal agencies, only three used agencies' information to decide a solution, and two of these members saw agency officials as their most trusted informants. Only four enterprises ranked agencies as their most important information sources; only thirteen others ranked them second (see Table A.14). Fourteen of these seventeen members were Republicans, benefiting from a Republican administration. Yet only eight enterprises, and six of these Republican, regularly sought out agency advice on policy.

This disregard was more than a simple problem of Congress versus the administration. Members complained specifically about trust. Most complaints, moreover, emphasized problems in policy analysis and data presentation that were seen as resulting from political changes of the late 1970s and 1980s. Committees had as many agency problems as did the rank and file.[31] Eighty-four member enterprises complained that congressional offices got very little useful information, or even what they requested, through personal contacts with agencies. Staff either lacked information about who had knowledge and expertise within each agency, or they felt that requests were unwelcome: requests were filtered through agency superiors, answered with hesitancy and a lack of candor by analysts and specialists, or simply left untended. Two comments were typical. As a senior appropriations staffer laughed: "They'll tell you what's written on paper, nothing more. It doesn't matter if you threaten to drag them to the Hill. They'll just bring a legislative liaison person with them and really clam up. It reminds me of invoking the Fifth Amendment." A junior member felt for a time that his own staff was incompetent: "They kept telling me that neither USDA or FDA would do anything more than send a published report. . . . I thought something was amiss until I talked [the problem] over with other members and found it was normal."

Problems in communication did not imply a lack of available policy information. To the contrary, each member enterprise was inundated with publications and reports, especially from USDA. Most of them were long and complex analyses and position papers on everything from important to mundane policy problems. So much appeared, in fact, that staff generally threw away most unsolicited reports: "Once a week, sometimes twice, swish, into the garbage can." More than informational overload was to blame for this flood.

Fault lay with the increased sophistication and complexity of analysis. As an agency administrator averred: "We do the best analysis ever done in this agency, and it's over fifty years old." Member enterprises saw reports, however, as unreadable or too difficult to scan for the relevant information that most congressional issue initiators wanted. Documents often compiled numerous studies and ran to hundreds of pages. Most important, data were seldom broken down by state and never by district. Congress, as a result, ignored much agency work.

Yet, a division between analytically precise agency officials and a home-style Congress did not fully account for the congressional attitude toward agency analyses. Many junior members saw agency information as largely irrelevant, but senior members blamed other factors for declining trust. Veteran members and their staffs from sixty-two enterprises cited one or more procedural problems that led them to question the reliability and validity of agency documents. Enterprises complained forty-two times of incorrect assumptions in analyses important to those enterprises: weather, economic growth, and trade effects were examples. Thirty-eight instances cited department officials who provided one set of facts while county USDA and state extension offices gave the congressional enterprise another. Twenty-nine complaints were made because of incomplete analyses from what were perceived to be censored documents. A House appropriations committee staffer said: "I saw the original data that was to be collected. Only 70 percent of it was presented." Fifteen respondents claimed that studies requested from agencies were denied by departmental officials, even in some instances after congressional inquiries were made. Those in twelve enterprises, including that of an appropriations subcommittee chairman, were unable to get data or reports they knew existed; according to his staffer: "They just lied to me over the phone." USDA was seen as no better or worse than other agencies.

When issue initiators wanted analytical information, they usually turned to the Library of Congress for help with federal data and reports. They also looked to alternate information sources that they saw as independent of administrative constraints. The Congressional Budget Office was one. Twenty-three member enterprises sought out interest groups that were thought to be especially skilled in data analysis. As one senior staffer said, "I'd have no reason to talk to the Rice Millers Association or the Milk Producers. But I made those contacts because I can get . . . answers to questions that I can't get at USDA."

The Washington policy community held no monopoly over alternative analysis. Members liked analyses from what they saw as grassroots sources. Eighteen member enterprises relied on the Food and Agricultural Policy Research Institute (FAPRI), a data collection and analysis center maintained jointly by Iowa State University and the University of Missouri. Eleven other members, from the South and from California, used land-grant university economists from their states to generate data for their issues. Agriculture committee members felt that such requests for alternative analyses were so frequent, and so often coordinated by several enterprises, that few committee decisions were made on farm issues without this added information. FAPRI was especially influential;

according to a House agriculture committee staffer: "Not a feedgrains issue is accepted in the House until FAPRI data is compared with USDA." Members were thus reaching three conclusions about the need for analysis in policymaking: it gets too extensive, much of it can be ignored, and, sources other than agencies are useful, even if administrators collectively have better skills.

The search for analysis, though, get even more local and less analytical than those conclusions suggest. For example, thirty-two offices solicited information from county USDA employees; staff relationships with county personnel were good because of years of doing casework with them. But information was more important than casework. Twenty-five of the county informants compiled county-by-county reports of district problems for the Agricultural Stabilization and Conservation Service, and they often became grassroots confidants. One typical remark provided an excellent summary as to why county personnel gained the confidence of enterprises: "ASCS county people are the best information sources we have in government about farm and agribusiness problems. They know all aspects of local producer problems. They can give us reliable cost and price data, plus information on markets and the operating conditions of district processors and manufacturers. We don't need a lot more complexity than that."

Other policy participants saw congressional perceptions as accurate. Agency administrators confirmed that questionable assumptions, department censorship, and limits on data collection were troubling. To circumvent these difficulties, some administrators occasionally allowed Washington research institutes to publish studies generated by agencies that were likely to be controversial rather than suffer embargoes and department censors.

Equally troubling to agency officials was what they saw as their gradual, two-decades-long removal from all but the most highly structured policy forums. The agency leg of the iron triangle was, to them, administered away by those focused on bureaucratic hierarchy and control. As one agency administrator said, "My predecessor talked directly to members of Congress, one-on-one, and he sent employees to their offices." Administrative liaison offices changed that kind of relationship, even in discouraging back-door contacts. "We certainly have no congressional relationships," observed one executive, "I'm allowed to testify at hearings on an approved summary of my remarks." Exceptions are rare. A few administrators whose small agency programs operated under private-sector boards were allowed contacts with Congress. Although they used interest-group influence to facilitate access to Capitol Hill, even these administrators were "forced to be careful." That same executive continued: "I have to make sure I'm responding to congressional inquiries and doing it in public. I'm not in regular staff contact, and I sure as hell don't lobby those guys." Even with such autonomy, officials had to submit reports and projects of these programs to routine scrutiny and executive control: "There are things we just can't print." Therefore, even articles for professional journals were reviewed for approval. As one official explained, "technical reviewers sign off, then the agency editor, then the assistant secretaries to whom my agency reports, and whoever else the report impacts. Next, we go to the communications office, and final approval rests with the public affairs staff, and sometimes the secretary's staff intervenes." With informality the key to cooperation within the iron triangle, the basis for such narrow and specialized interaction as occurred in the iron triangle no longer exists. "And that's the point," argued a senior official, "we just can't have program operators cutting their own deals and serving special interests. We want administrationwide policy, not agency advocacy."

Lobbyists and other group representatives found this process both inconvenient and advantageous. On the one hand, agency officials were isolated from informal policy networks where their participation would have been useful. Direct information from analysts and policy specialists was almost impossible to secure: "It's clear that such contacts are unwanted," concluded a House member. On the other hand, however, unlike members of Congress, those in the private sector found ways of identifying and reaching agency experts without always relying on political appointees. The most effective ways were professional and policy meetings where at least some agency experts could be found. Private-sector representatives exploited shared educational or work backgrounds with agency representatives as well as contacts with land-grant policy specialists who knew agency personnel through contracted services.

This contact provided interest groups and business firms with considerable materials, but not much more than Congress had. Lobbyists were frustrated by their inability to get more information than the published reports and data sets already open to the public. There were few recurring contacts with familiar bureaucrats. Groups, however, used this lack of access to their advantage in the brokering that they did in Congress, particularly by a more sophisticated use of information than congressional players employed. "The big difference between us and Congress," observed one commodity lobbyist who wanted embargoed data, "is that the agency people send information to the Hill in such large volumes that untrained staff throw it away. Plus, those kids are not very selective or farsighted in what they scan. We fight to find what's out there, get what we can, and then translate it into usable information." He continued, "The agencies, as a result, become largely irrelevant to brokering new issues and legislation. Just because they supply 50 percent of the information on which decisions are based doesn't mean they control the outcome. How can they when they're denied a voice in the process, one that answers questions and interprets findings?" He concluded that, "That leaves people like me to be the real information brokers."

None of this behavior seems related to those congressional-agency relationships suggested by the triangle metaphor or its extension into networks of competing institutional interests. Members of Congress and lobbyists saw that agencies networked with one another and produced policy only when congressional and private-sector players were disinterested. When policy games were under way, agencies exercised little influence and were often the subjects rather than the arbiters of controversy. This status may not represent a quantum change, even though administrators saw agencies affected by trends of the 1970s and 1980s.

Paul Appleby described USDA's always mixing politics and policy with great difficulty; crop reporting and price forecasts in the 1940s were "under constant fire" from Congress.[32] During the next decades Harold Seidman was struck by USDA's inability to coordinate planning between its agencies and those in related departments. Members of Congress resisted secretarial control, demonstrating the old origins of congressional-agency tensions.[33] In as late a measure as the 1973 farm bill, Congress pressured USDA to increase the role of political appointees within agencies to increase responsiveness to the Hill.[34] Members saw career officials as too isolated and of little use. Policy analysts, then as now, were subjected to specific criticism as subcommittees in Congress gained influence; analysts wanted to develop comprehensive policy, and Congress wanted a more piecemeal approach. The controversy surrounding data collection became even more pronounced than that which Appleby observed.[35] Analysts, with their penchant for collective rationalization and their preoccupation with multiple variables, were not meeting the needs of a more fragmented Congress. When Congress saw increasingly complex policy tasks, they simply divided the assignments—including oversight—among more members.[36]

Tensions between congressional fragmentation and executive control were not lost on agricultural-policy observers and the Reagan administration in the 1980s. Executive politics of that decade further broke down what remained of cozy policy networks. President Jimmy Carter had lost the support of his own agricultural officials in the 1970s when Congress responded to grassroots farm protest; as a result Reagan emphasized tighter administrative control.[37] Reagan was also moved by President Richard Nixon's preoccupation with the same problem of controlling the executive branch.[38] Because Nixon failed to achieve management restraints through his use of the Office of Management and Budget, and because Carter failed to micromanage from the White House, administrations of the 1980s relied on loyalist political appointees and heightened control of career officials to achieve their ends.[39] Members and congressional staffs were complaining of those results.[40] As a Republican agriculture committee member observed: "Suddenly, in 1981, we didn't have people in USDA who could talk agriculture and its needs. We had people there who talked conservative politics about agriculture and who just didn't play with anyone in Congress. Imposing partisan rules on what has long been bipartisan policy only disenfranchised USDA."

There were no administrative entrepreneurs in the 1980s who could cooperate with Congress.[41] Scientific advisers were out of the networking loop.[42] Another Republican congressman concluded: "No leadership or ideas came from that administration. It was as reactive as Congress. When USDA supported one idea, it was ideologically dead on arrival or a very costly special favor for a group with White House access." The administration, that is, was doing ad hoc networking. Like interest groups of the era, administrative agencies provided no useful service to Congress, and its members felt even more comfortable getting their cues, and their issues, from their home districts.

CONCLUSION: RETURNING TO
CONGRESSIONAL NETWORKING

Policy networks have been criticized as being both too fragmented and too inclusive of others for them to dominate policymaking. Other factors also help to explain their limited scope. An erosion of trust and a decline in reliance on both organized interests and federal agencies further disrupt what are generally regarded as the traditional patterns of decision making for the domain. Interest groups are suspect, and agencies operate under restrictive administrative controls. Interests, whether private or agency, are no longer effectively integrated, even as coalitions proliferate.[43]

Networks, in consequence, are not dominated by informal clusters of routine players.

This limited influence does not mean that politics is just harder than before; it is necessary to remember events over agricultural policy's stream of time.[44] Integrated networks of agricultural policy players came together in the 1920s only because interests in issues were shared, confidence that the issues would recur was established, and the mutual advantage of participants working together without others was probable. Farm-state members of Congress, as a result, provided interest groups a competitive advantage in influencing policy. USDA contributed to this advantage by its agencies' provision of plans that facilitated network agreements.[45] In the process of developing networks, congressional leaders and political parties lost the trust and reliance of members of Congress who worried about their local voters.[46] Agricultural politics thus remained tense because leaders, parties, and the White House remained on the playing field, but they were not in control.

Today, however, the representation of constituents by district appears to be a more critical policymaking variable than before. Members of Congress now find constituents with their own competitive advantage over Washington groups, and they and their staffs have a somewhat general disregard for agencies on anything more than routine matters. Advocates of unconventional or publicly unpopular policy demands are rejected as "high demanders and preference outliers."[47] At the grassroots, constituents know their interests, define their problems, and offer narrow solutions. Grassroots informants now, as they did not in the 1920s, directly and frequently communicate with members of Congress and their staffs. Members of Congress, where they can best win, follow those local interests into policymaking. Institutional knowledge, policy relationships, protocol, and cooperation with agricultural interests are less important in policymaking because neither private groups nor public agencies are expected to win very much of what they want. Agriculture committee members have no more faith in interest groups and no more hope for USDA agencies than does the rest of the Congress.

Contemporary domain politics is quite unlike what policy observers have come to expect. Networking is less stable, prone to meander beyond the traditional bounds of a domain, very individualistic and enterprise centered, issue- rather than program- or policy-specific, and far from knowledge based. Congressional issue initiators worry little about the need for detailed analysis, analytical conclusions about policy effects, and expert opinions among those with institutional memories. Congressional accommodation of numerous interests is extensive, but sweeping policy change appears to be a product of forces much larger than coalitions of organized interests, or of more capable administrative planning, or of any combination of the two. Yet one question remains. Why in the face of such a dynamic equilibrium, are members of the postreform Congress so confident in their abilities to win things for district constituents? That answer lies within the changing influence of committees.

8

The New Committees?

I like to think that modern congressional committees are new, not that they're fresh and virtuous or anything. But the old stories are of heavy-handed rule by an autocratic chair. Today's committees take into account the needs and problems of nearly each member. The chairman is reduced to equal parts boss, guidance counselor, and servant. It remains in committee that the work gets done.
— A veteran of both House and Senate, thinking out loud about congressional change.

Common interests in agriculture are disintegrating, any changes in the Washington policy community are directing members of Congress to their districts. What does this mean for agriculture committees, which in the iron-triangle metaphor govern because of strong, integrated support from interest groups and USDA? With so many members of Congress involved in more agriculture issues, and with more shared powers within the Congress, committees obviously have had to adapt to evolving circumstances. Thus, committees exclude few members, consider knowledge about constituent problems as legitimate policy information, and broaden the range of policy concerns far beyond those of farms and ranches. In light of those practices, agriculture committees have lost whatever autonomous influence they had and hang on to their remaining power because they serve much of the rest of Congress, one member at a time.

But what influence really remains to committees? They draft and assemble legislation, and their members dominate the conference committees that resolve House and Senate differences. In doing so, they control much of the governing process, at least logistically. Committee effectiveness, within that process, is as obvious as their adaptability. Committees have designed policy vehicles, particularly omnibus farm bills, that make logrolling obsolete under existing policy games. Moreover, committees have effectively maintained, even expanded agricultural policies in general, and farm policies in particular. To critics, that success alone demonstrates committee power, both prereform and postreform.[1]

Contemporary issue initiatives reflect the same farm biases that have long been criticized. Although most members of Congress successfully initiate agricultural issues, few of them fail to do farm-income favors. In addition, few members address new, or genuinely reformist issues. The originating issues that do gain considerable attention from the congressional rank and file take on a bandwagon effect, as with environmental and trade policy games of the late 1980s and the 1990s. Members flock to a small range of particularly timely types of issues.

Members also select issues that are likely to win, tend to disregard those that are not, and look extensively for cues about what to avoid. The number of issues that an enterprise can successfully initiate is limited as well. Members also seek to avoid issues that would trigger disputes between committees. All of these factors suggest that the agriculture committees offer considerable advantages to the congressional rank and file without losing their own lawmaking prerogatives.[2]

Why? Two factors keep agriculture committees influential. First, their success depends on their keeping the purposes of the committees quite simple, even as things change.[3] In this case, the committees organize around farm benefits that can be particularly well adapted to numerous member interests. The central agricultural-development principle, or the story, also matters here. Second, with the existing and very extensive agricultural policy base, the committees have gatekeeping advantages.[4] The main advantage is their considerable certainty that omnibus farm bills will pass; committee members use their consequent advantages to restrain numerous issues, ideas, and nonconforming members.

Agriculture committees, in that gatekeeping sense, do not aim at fulfilling the policy preferences of the Congress as a whole, just at the bits and pieces that win the necessary support for any vehicle.[5] It does not matter if most members rank agricultural policy very high compared to other policy domains; members need only see it as important. The committees then design vehicles that are able to provide congresswide opportunities.[6]

Other factors have some importance for sustaining committee influence. In and out of committee, not all issues are dealt with for constituent reasons. Members also pursue goals of good policy, party and presidential agendas, and influence in Washington.[7] Because different issues satisfy different congressional goals, and because many of these issues bring committee members into mainstream politics, the committees have somewhat broader importance than they often seem to.[8] Some of the committees' most recurring Washington policy-community contacts help the agriculture committees maintain that prominence by calling attention to the domain's expanding purpose.[9] These groups and agencies may lack the ability to determine policy solutions, but they still provide information about agriculture's collective national importance.

KEEPING THINGS SIMPLE—BUT NOT EASY

The four agriculture committees—the House and Senate agriculture committees and the appropriations subcommittees on agriculture—organize their members around the simple idea that farmers and ranchers come first. Members—both present and former—acknowledged this commitment in several ways: in their reasons for being on the committees, in their ranking of agricultural issue types, and in their policy assessments. These committees try hard to concentrate on a simple, integrative task rather than to make the always difficult governing process too complex.[10] This farm focus means the committees necessarily operate somewhat beyond the usual policy preferences of most of the House and Senate.[11] This also means that committee members do not relish the many issues that are brought to them by the rank and file. "Don't even think we don't see things that modify our policies as unimportant," explained a senior member. "We see how multiple issues disrupt committee goals. But we have no choice but to be conciliatory. Grin and bear it! Pass the bill!"

Being There

Why do the committees emphasize stability? The reasons why members gained their assignments are an important explanation. Members of these committees indicated that they had little choice of which assignments to seek. Since farming is fragmented by crop, production capacity, relative efficiency, and region, state and district representation of farming on agriculture committees is the only means for aggregating policy wants nationally. Their districts, in one member's words, "made us all do it. [That is, serve on committees.]" That member was a dairy representative, whereas others were advocates of cotton, wheat, dry beans, apples, and so on. Half the committee members were from districts where representatives historically gained agriculture committee assignments because of the importance of local farmers. The other half were appointed because the state delegation or regional caucuses wanted representation on the committee, sometimes because they had lacked a seat in recent years for their farmers.[12] As one member said "I was expected to do it. . . . It was my turn."

Expectations meant that most of these members sought their agriculture committee assignments when first elected. Some had won prior commitments from the leadership in order to get elected in the first place. A few agreed to take assignments temporarily, until their seats rotated to others, or they gained more prestigious positions. One member understood the assignment as a route to the Budget Committee; another, also correctly, understood it as a way and a means to Ways and Means. Members were rewarded for their farm emphasis and saw the committees as good, if not desirable, assignments: "We're given our due by the rest of the House for sitting here."[13]

It was mostly constituent reasons, however, that made the committees attractive.[14] Agriculture committees were seen as high-profile assignments back home by both local farmers and the local media. Members were subject to frequent contacts from the district, committee work was easily explained to the home folks, the local importance of agriculture was easily understood and even exaggerated, and the press regularly reported on agriculture's local economic importance. Although other committees received greater coverage from the national media, agriculture was seen as a better assignment because it was clearly linked to district problems. Members believed that they could create favorable home-style images by representing even a segment of the local economy. Other committees lacked that appeal, even major ones. Constituents and the local media failed to understand the work of tax or budget committees and were often disdainful of Congress and foreign affairs. "Agriculture," one senior staffer explained, "is just right for most of its members because it's easy to portray the committee's work as important, very basic, and an immediate good for most Americans. It's about food, about business, about local economies." After first-year Senator Ben Nighthorse Campbell thought about his banking committee assignment and compared it to the opportunities he found in the House on agriculture, he complained loudly to the leadership for a transfer to that more familiar assignment.

In view of the diversity of farm types and problems, the emphasis on food, business, and local economies rather than other agricultural issues makes sense. Thirty-two members had once been on an agriculture committee, and all but one of them sought or accepted the seats to protect the farm sector. As a member noted, "I learned right off that big cotton was my concern because few others in Congress cared." No one took these assignments to make rural, environmental, or food policy.

Why? Farmers remain the most active and, therefore, the most prized rural constituents.[15] "It's not that other purposes lack importance," emphasized one member from a moderate-size city who actively campaigned for a House agriculture committee seat, "farmers just have more pressing problems, and those are the ones that can be addressed by the policies we deal with in committee." Members also emphasized both committee deliberations and caucus leadership as reminders that farmers are important.

Those reminders explain why members with other than farm interests are excluded from agriculture committees. A committee staffer explained: "Over the years, not a lot of people want on this committee. But don't think that everyone gets on. I've watched people be excluded for being farm activists, farm critics, rural advocates, environmental zealots, and urbanites. We can't afford the luxury of wanting to accomplish too much here." Should members forget their district expectations, then, the governing process reminds them. Those with unique or extreme policy preferences about agriculture are rarely involved on agriculture committees.

Ranking Agriculture's Policies

The policy values of those on the agriculture committees make them outliers marginal to the rest of the Congress but not in ways that destroy committee effectiveness. Each of the office enterprises ranked up to three of the most important areas of agriculture policy for their members. They gave choices of fourteen policy areas: farm income/price policy, farm credit, international trade, taxes, family-farm protection, animal and plant regulation, environmental protection, energy, resource conservation, forestry, nutrition/hunger, research and development, rural development/poverty, and animal welfare.

The thirty-two members who had served on the agriculture committees made 72 selections of important agricultural-policy areas. Sixty-eight of them were farm and trade policy choices: 32 for income/price, 21 for international trade, 12 for credit, and 3 for taxes. The remaining eighty members made 171 policy choices. Only 87 of their choices were for farm or trade policies. The remaining 84 choices covered the range of other options, with the environment, food and nutrition, rural, and energy selected 68 times. Quite clearly, those without agriculture committee experience valued policy diversity far more than did those with it.

There was, however, one important convergence of opinion. Not only did all agriculture committee members select farm income/price policy, so too did those in sixty-six of the other enterprises. Only two were not in favor of some type of farm-income assistance. Most members shared in the committees' primary interest, which certainly keeps those policies from being too threatened. "That's an idea that most people accept," summarized one chairman, "they have no trouble with that." A member added: "It's why the agriculture committee exists, why it's not natural resources." Even members from largely urban districts agreed that their own experiences with farmers led them to share those opinions.

So, where do the committees have problems? Off the agriculture committees, almost all members felt it important that agricultural policy be both for farmers and for a broader social interest. This attitude, of course, gives the committees their accommodative emphasis and brings forward evolving games with the agricultural policy base. Enterprises that had no agriculture committee seats made it extremely difficult to keep policymaking limited to a simple farm purpose. But, as seen earlier, constituent interests also led committee members to initiate issues for both farm and nonfarm beneficiaries. This breadth meant that the committees easily accepted environmental and other nonfarm social issues, for reasons of both district and Washington work.

First, however, the committees did what they could to resolve farm policy demands. As a Midwest member of the House agriculture committee concluded: "We follow a two-stage process, take care of affordable farm problems first, and then move on to add what's necessary to pass the bill. Its ritual." Several committee members felt that ritualizing the process in this way was more important to committee influence than any other congressional factor. Committees had to reconsider a large number of farm policies with each farm bill and in each appropriations bill. Once members got through the complex array of farm programs and satisfied issue initiatives where they could, the committees then turned to issues of social relevance. Members who cooperated with committee preferences on farm issues gained committee cooperation on their nonfarm problems. This procedure allowed the committees to keep farm-policy outliers at bay, but it opened the committee up to particularly timely and popular issues that otherwise might have been ignored. Reforms came about, but only after farm issues had been addressed. For example, in working out farm-income problems, the Conservation Reserve Program was added to the 1985 farm bill to stabilize falling land prices. The program also reduced the costs of commodity payments, which the committees needed to do, and incidently met the demands of environmental interests.

Members emphasized the long-term stability of Congress in following this two-stage ritual, even when it seemed likely that things would change. When Washington's Thomas S. Foley replaced the caucus-deposed chairman of the House agriculture committee, W. R. Poage (D-Texas), expectations of the liberal Foley were high in the harshly critical reform climate of 1974. As one former member explained, "I thought at the time that he was agriculture's John F. Kennedy, bringing in a new era." Yet Foley, with his wheat-grower constituents, aggressively continued the committee's profarm stance.[16] Texan E. "Kika" de la Garza did the same when Foley moved on to the House leadership prior to the formulation of the 1981 farm bill. Many had expected that the unproven de la Garza, from one of the nation's poorest rural districts, would have other policy priorities. Those were the same expectations that most senators had when Vermont's Patrick Leahy gained the chairmanship of the agriculture committee in 1987. With environmentally interested constituents and a state beset by rural problems, and with few Vermont farmers, Leahy, some felt, would place reform issues first on the Senate committee's agenda. He did not, as a senator explained: "Political reality forces your hand, you realize." Leahy first sought to forge a solid partnership with the committee's ranking minority member, Indiana's Richard G. Lugar. The two skillfully passed a farm-credit bill with the House, then failed on an unpopular rural-development bill, and took on farm problems first in the 1990 farm bill.

Why did Foley, de la Garza, and Leahy act as they did? Collective expectations dictated the behavior of these committee chairs. Indeed, in the past leaders have intervened if things have gone astray. When de la Garza experienced problems with the 1981 farm bill, Foley played an active leadership role.[17] Kansas Senator Robert Dole, for all practical purposes, led the Senate agriculture committee in both 1981 and in 1985. Members claimed that Chairman Jesse Helms (R-N.C.) and his archconservative ways would poison congressional relations for the committee and lead to policy losses. With price and commodity-surplus problems severe, Congress rallied to its causal story about farm assistance.[18] No one had time for Helms's ideological battling or for de la Garza, when he claimed that no better bill for farmers was possible. Instead, members were listening to farm constituents who were concerned with losses in farm-program benefits, which was about all members could do since they had built much of their careers on serving local farmers.

Are electoral fears a compelling reason for keeping this farm focus? Committee members think so. They mentioned those agriculture committee members who openly advocated strong environmental issues in the 1990 farm bill and then faced reelection. One senior House member, George E. Brown (D-Calif.), with almost no farm presence left in his now urbanized district, was reelected: "Those were voters who were irritated with farmers. Brown could poke agriculture all he wanted." The other two House members, James Jontz (D-Ind.) and David R. Nagle (D-Iowa), were defeated: "They just scared farmers when the enviros praised their work." Senator Wyche Fowler (D-Ga.) was also defeated, even after softening his environmental stands and seeking greater farm-group support as the election approached. "What's the lesson?" asked a senior member. "It's that you learn what the central tasks of this committee are and, furthermore, you don't confuse people into thinking you don't know that farmers come first."

Assessing Agricultural Policy

Basic member opinions reveal members' primary concern for farm issues. Present and former members of the agriculture committees had one set of complaints: that there was too little time to exercise effective oversight over most agricultural programs. The complaint from fourteen enterprises was that USDA and the land-grant system were deciding to move in far too many new service directions that left inadequate resources for addressing farm problems. All other veterans of the committee noted that farm policies needed greater attention and more financing; as one of them said: "But it's impossible to allocate, given the competition." This difficulty made agriculture committee members only more committed to addressing farm problems as their first priority.

The opinions of committee veterans stood in marked contrast to those of members who had never held an agriculture committee assignment. These members criticized agricultural policy for insufficient attention to nonfarm issues, for continuing to support antiquated agricultural organizations, and for just being slow to change. Those in seventeen enterprises also questioned whether farm-assistance programs were allocated properly, or provided too little support for "needy farmers." The effect of these criticisms and questions was to direct rank-and-file attention to agriculture committees that emphasized important policies but, for most of them, in the wrong mix. That was why a legislative director found that "the 1990 farm bill gained attention from the greatest number of members that we've ever seen."

Where was there room for agreement? Despite these differences of concern, most members, regardless of committee status, were supportive of the current directions of most of agricultural policy. Most also felt that the wide range of policy was important, and why not: they won because of its presence. Members' complaints were about marginal issues: policy was not doing enough, it failed to eliminate the worst programs, and it promoted programs that had largely symbolic importance. Only seven members felt agricultural policy to be unnecessary.

As a result of this support, Congress has little congressional will for major change, but also no sense that the committees should make policy on their own. Farm-income problems are widely appreciated. Members also recognize that the agriculture committees are adaptive and flexible on nonfarm problems. Given such agreement, the committees use their logistical advantage for: (1) the constituents who matter most, (2) the issues that are their priorities, and (3) the problems that are felt to be most acute. Accommodation, in other words, works quite well as the means for retaining committee influence.

GATEKEEPING ADVANTAGES

How does accommodation work? Some say that postreform congressional committee power rests more on negative rather than on positive influence.[19] This assertion seems only partially true in agriculture. In a positive sense, committee members gain from (1) information that is more complete than that available to the rank and file, (2) the work of their staffs, and (3) their capacity for rapport with other members. Issue initiators from beyond the committee *want* that body to succeed; otherwise their own initiatives fail, and they lose opportunities. Of course, this positive influence works only because committees and rank-and-file policy beliefs are generally reconcilable.

Negative influence remains, however. As gatekeepers, House and Senate committees can keep legislation off the floor and away from a vote. Their jurisdictions over policy content are written into chamber rules, although the rules are less rigid in the Senate. Even the move to allow multiple referrals to two or more committees provides each of them increased chances to filter out unacceptable initiatives or policy ideas. Moreover, members and their staffs indicated that there were few opportunities to block agricultural issues without being on the committee. Even exclusion from conference committees meant a loss of blocking ability, as one House member explained: "You can only argue something out if you're there. . . . Conferences are looking to fill the water glass up . . . not drain it."

Member interests and their issue involvement, as a consequence, rarely involved gatekeeping, which was a committee, not an individual member endeavor. Enterprises identified only 21 time-consuming or priority losses that they were trying to block, in contrast to the 263 that they initiated. Moreover, all members used their committee assignments to lead opposition: eleven were on agriculture and eight on environmental committees.

Opposition issues, however, all facilitated farm-policy benefits, which placed them squarely within dominant policy games of the domain. Ten aimed at protecting farm-income policies and five others did the same by arguing against restrictions and increased fees on livestock use of public lands and water.[20] The remaining issues all resisted either stronger environmental or animal-welfare regulation because of their high cost problems for farm production. Members were successful on all but two gatekeeping issues. That rate of success and the limited number of times such priority efforts were necessary reveal a lot. Committee members win when they put their minds to it, but they usually win because they collectively signal that support fails to exist for change; gatekeeping is one of the ways committee members give out that signal. For example, the issue of food stamps was seen as off limits and rural policy was thought to be irrelevant to current committee problems. Said one House member: "If you bring those things up, the committee just sits there." Issue initiatives suggest the same points: some things are avoided by all but a few members.

The Farm Bill Cycle and Iterative Policymaking

The committees' refusal to act on some issues, while accommodating others, results largely from the advantages of farm bills and the twenty-year avoidance of partisan logrolling. On less contentious issues, the committees can be negative. Mostly, though, they use their positive influence to control the farm-bill life cycle.[21] Over a four- to five-year period, the agriculture committees adjust the last bill in year one, work on other vehicles the next year or two, move into farm bill planning the next, and then pass what seems possible at the end. Throughout the process, the committees make annual adjustments to change appropriations and budget decisions.

There are three very specific advantages to having an omnibus-farm-bill cycle. First, it makes professional committee staffs indispensable over time, not just in the short period for markup. Second, it allows for a slow-paced opportunity for committee members and staff to read the mood of their respective chambers and later, in the rush of committee work, finalize an acceptable bill. Third, it sets a commonly understood deadline, far in advance, to complete tasks and to mobilize a winning coalition, unlike the 1991 Clean Air Act, which required ten years of machinations to write. This clarity rallies issue initiators behind the agriculture committees and their efforts to pass a bill on time. The downside of the cycle is that some uncertainty exists over which members will be players in the next bill, particularly if they refuse to commit themselves early to positions on issues.

The result, of the cycle, nonetheless, is the iterative construction of the legislative vehicle over a two-year period, with ample involvement of committees, subcommittees, and whichever rank-and-file members choose to participate. Issues and policies are constantly revisited. The weaknesses of the previous bill are considered. Changing economic, political, and social conditions of the domain are scrutinized. Efforts are made to estimate congressional and administration budget targets that limit costs.[22] The most extreme demands of the executive branch, private agricultural interests, agricultural service institutions, and other congressional members are estimated as well. As one member explained, "We return to existing policy, propose alterations, and scale back change as you confront reality."

Simultaneously, committee members and their staffs work to galvanize support for a new bill. They collectively address criticisms, either by acknowledging their legitimacy or refuting them. One House agriculture committee member said: "It's hard to ignore the evidence that 25 percent of existing soil and water pollution in the U.S. comes from farming." That evidence led the committees to open up the 1990 farm bill to expand efforts to improve environmental safeguards in production practices. By the time issue initiatives were under way, the committees were signaling that some policy changes were needed.

Committee members also mobilize likely supporters, both through direct contact and through use of the media. Both Washington-based and district interests generate momentum for the bill.[23] Emphasis is always on pending problems in passing legislation, as one agriculture committee staffer explained: "The best pitch is that an urban majority might make the previous farm bill the last one. That brings out all the passive beneficiaries." Accordingly, each farm-bill cycle sees the committees inviting commodity groups, agribusinesses, professional associations from the land grants, and some public-interest groups to explain their policy needs. All are then encouraged to secure widespread congressional support. The result in Congress is an unsequenced round of meetings as committees, subcommittees, commodity interests within subcommittees, and regional and state delegations mull over increasingly evident problems. Opponents of the committees do the same.

But what makes gatekeeping effective, other than compatible issue interests between rank-and-file members and accommodative committees? Three things are responsible, all tied to the iterative nature of decision-making. First, the committees revisit early assumptions in light of constantly available new evidence. As one committee veteran allowed, "You find out there can be real garbage in a bill that some people really like . . . and protect. Then it's not a policy flaw after all!" This ability always to adjust gives the committees the advantage over farm-bill opponents as they design provisions that encompass multiple solutions to member problems.

Second, the revisiting of problems and proposed solutions, combined with the mobilization of more interests, gives the committee the chance to distinguish between the issues that just have Washington appeal and those that also matter at the grassroots. Committee members use that knowledge to advise rank-and-file issue initiators of the likely consequences of their actions. In the early 1990s, for example, committee members redirected the demands of several environmentally concerned colleagues by explaining how sensitive the public seemed to be to violations of private-property rights in proposed regulations. This tactic allowed the committees to take the initiative in defining regulatory strategies.

Third, committee members just get started earlier in filling out the bill. Eighty percent of the issues of committee members were laid out the year before the bill was passed. Noncommittee members, worried about their issues being preempted, brought only 12 percent of their issues forward by that time. The advantage for the committees was a considerable head start in defining key issues, and making many other things extraneous.

The result of this gatekeeping is that the committees oversee a constantly changing legislative vehicle right through the final months of each farm-bill cycle. Even committee members are uncertain of content: "I'm always surprised. In 1981, my first farm bill, it appeared that farm-district demands for a generous bill would win. It turned out there were no hidden supporters out there [in Congress] and Tom Foley led the charge to narrowly pass an austere bill for farmers." Prior to exercising that leadership, Foley announced that he might oppose the bill on the floor.[24] The next two farm bills provided similar surprises, deviating from widely held expectations.

In 1983, congressional planners saw a market-oriented 1985 bill emerging with strong support from prominent agricultural economists and agribusinesses. But farm protest and a well-publicized farm-debt crisis led instead to extraordinarily high price-support payments and a costly bill in a year otherwise given by Congress to budget deficit problems.[25] "The grassroots," as one member explained the change, "went in revolt, even the moderates. The committees then ratcheted up demands." Changing events in 1990 led to a more gradual erosion of support for what most members saw in 1988 and 1989 as the likelihood of a strong environmental bill. Other reforms were felt to be likely as well. Interests in world trade took over, however, numerous demands from environmental interests were ignored, and reformist family-farm and rural-development policy goals were all but deleted from the bill during the late months of active debate on it. The committees found which reforms were most timely, accommodated those they needed, and left the rest alone.

These committee advantages, however, clearly rest on staff resources.[26] The long months of the cycle leave most members personally disinterested and active in other policy domains. Even in the last days of legislation, interested staff first meet on each new problem, then generate as much agreement as possible, and then let their members finalize negations. Member meetings are often very brief. In the Senate, where members have two to three other competing committee assignments of importance, the staff is relied upon even more than it is in the House.

The greatest edge of the committee members is the expertise and collective knowledge of their staffs. Only twenty-two of the eighty-three members who were not on the agriculture committees had personal staff who held their agriculture assignments for three or more years. All but three of those assistants also covered issues other than agriculture. Twelve of twenty agriculture-committee enterprises employed three-year veterans as legislative assistants.[27] And all but one were assigned only agricultural responsibilities. Also, each of the member's administrative assistants, who serve as their personal adjuncts, had routine agricultural responsibilities. Fifteen of these members were assigned additional agriculture-committee staff, most of whom, unlike rank-and-file staff, had educational or occupational backgrounds in agriculture.

This resource provided committee members advantages in dealing with committee leaders as well as with the rank and file. "Those are our political slots," explained a staff director. "I work hard to keep a balance of half analytical and half political staff. But even that makes the [committee] staff as loyal to individual members as they are to committee leadership." As several political staffers emphasized, their committee appointments brought them daily access to data analysis and information that other staffers lacked. "I'm right there," emphasized one economist, "and that means that the interests of the senator from my state are considered as routinely in committee as are the interests of technical proficiency or a nationally produced commodity or industry." He also might have added that this personal representation also muted partisanship on the committees, since few staff saw themselves dependent on the caucuses.

What does this mode of committee operation mean for policymaking? Although issue initiators often note that the process operates on the basis of precious few facts, and although they try hard to impose their demands at the most tactically opportune times, noncommittee members operate at an informational disadvantage that seems unresolvable. Often mobilized by others to become part of farm-bill coalitions, these members are never as secure about what they can actually win in a farm bill as committee members are. Committee members, who serve there to protect farm incomes, can more easily sell the idea that some issues are unwinnable. Their selective use of negative gatekeeping reinforces that view. "There is," as one veteran member concluded, "a great deal of bluffing when it comes to the committee versus the rest of the House. They never know what we know and so assume the worst about their chances. Their uncertainty and lack of involvement in the day-after-day proceedings of the farm bill or any other major bill keeps demands from outside the committee far more temperate than most members would appear to want if they could win on anything."

Policymaking Implications

It is worthwhile to ask here whether the committees and their members are in control of agricultural policies. Members and their staffs were divided on this question. Those in seventy enterprises saw the committees as still being in control within the Congress, two were uncertain, and thirty-nine rejected the notion of committee control. Almost everyone had some reservations about their opinions, but it was differences between those held by agriculture committees and those held by noncommittee members that said the most about committee influence.

Agriculture committee members, sixteen to four, felt that they no longer controlled the continued evolution of policy. Not surprisingly, many of the reasons they gave for the lack of committee control were about the inability to keep some issues out of agricultural policy. Eighteen members saw the committees' inability to derail the momentum of timely issues as a problem. Yet there were other problems, too. Twenty members felt that budget targets made it impossible to allocate resources appropriate to agricultural needs. A House leader said: "Why start anything new, or move in a new direction, when there is no new money and everyone on the Hill is protective of their favored programs for the sector. It's a prescription for impotency." Fifteen of these members explained that budget problems were made more severe because Congress was unable to prioritize the importance of its many agricultural programs.[28] Committee members, therefore, were divided against themselves as well as the rank and file. This was why information provided limited advantage, according to a veteran Senate staffer: "These people really don't know what goes on in agriculture. And they don't care. Then they can't recognize that we could make much more good policy if the committees were allowed greater flexibility in creating change."

The involvement of other committees in agricultural issues was mentioned by those in twelve agriculture-committee enterprises. At the same time, issues of banking, commerce, the environment, health, and foreign trade were seen as often beyond agriculture's influence. Agriculture-committee enterprises, particularly in the House interior committee, saw public-lands grazing as a problem. Western and eastern members split badly on those issues, refused to compromise, and saddled production agriculture with a reputation for belligerence. That conflict, in turn, spilled over to the committees. Committee members felt that shared influence: (1) inhibited the agriculture committees from addressing the most important policy, (2) eroded some financial resources from the agriculture budget because of unnecessary conflict, and, most important, (3) reinforced views in Congress that agricultural institutions could not effectively address their own problems. As a midwestern member explained: "Each proposed policy change, from seafood inspection to food labeling to support for new products, was a challenge to agriculture's capability and, more significantly, its integrity. . . . The committee suffers."

One place the agriculture committees suffered was in yielding their claims to multiple referrals. By emphasizing accommodation on the committees as a goal, the chairs and members felt it best to be consistent and challenged other committees only infrequently.[29] They also felt it wise not to harangue the leadership. Challenges, they feared, would only lead to retaliation against agriculture's expanding agenda. As de la Garza explained, "We really don't want to get into a fight with anyone. There are too few farmers, and we are too vulnerable."

Members and congressional staff who had never been part of the agriculture committees saw things from a different perspective.[30] Because these members wanted broader and more socially responsible agricultural legislation and only got parts of their wishes, most believed that these committees generally controlled policy. They emphasized two points: first, that numerous programs seemed extraneous to the wants of most congressional members; and, second, that the concerns of their own enterprise were made very difficult because of the complex and often arcane language in the volumes of agriculture policies that they confronted. Issue initiatives, thus, were seen as very committee dependent, even though the committees were accommodative. A House member said: "Eventually you're at the mercy of the damned committee. They have to incorporate what you want in *their* language and programs." Another member warned, "Don't influence what you can't understand." Over one-half of these enterprises had dropped initiatives that they found hard to sell in committee or to other congressional sounding boards who felt that the committees would resist them.

What, on the basis of these statements, can be concluded about agriculture committee influence? The committees accommodate most members, but still retain their authority by excluding or modifying numerous issue initiatives. This practice allows members of the committees to use their personal experiences and gain reputations for influence about which they feel skeptical, given their own accommodative ways. It should be noted that nearly one fourth of the rank and file, all on committees that overlap on agricultural issues, shared the view that agriculture committees lacked policy control.

Nonetheless, agricultural bills and appropriations bills, despite the skepticism about committee influence, are expected to pass rather than fail because majorities can be won. Committee members may not like all the content of a bill, but they have used their strategies to keep farm income policies generally in place. This attitude toward the bottom line has proven successful. De la Garza in particular, because of the depth of House Democratic reforms, has had to engage in agriculture committee leadership under the most precarious conditions of anyone ever in his position: spokesperson, in an urban and a suspicious Congress, for farm residents who make up less than 2 percent of the nation's population.

This representation of a small minority meant, noncommittee members confirmed, that de la Garza and his Senate counterparts have had to condition their committee cohorts to lose gracefully on many issues. Sometimes, the committees roll over easily; on other issues they resist, and, frequently, members help colleagues or allow them to find other sources of issue satisfaction. The net result is that agriculture committees gain more supporters, who find their conciliatory ways welcome and helpful. If committee members have a problem with this strategy, they may be reminded that they do the same thing back in their districts, offering initiatives for nonfarm constituents with the same frequency as noncommittee members (70 percent). Like the rest of Congress, committee members value their own opportunities in agriculture more than they value the collective interests of the committees. As a staffer concluded, "In many ways we work harder at making the members look more open-minded and multi-interested in the states than we do in Washington."

OTHER COMMITTEE GOALS

Agricultural policy has been described as "fragmented and meandering."[31] An iterative means of analysis and decision making accommodates whatever diversity of member interests is necessary to pass a farm bill. Politics matters more than rational considerations to the establishment of policy, which is complicated by the use of multiple policy vehicles and interdomain influences. Further complicating committee influence are goals other than constituent service. Agriculture committee members are fully involved in Washington power games, some partisan politics, and even dialogues about better policymaking.[32] All this participation tends to strengthen the committees' influence and, to an extent, the influence of those rank and file who want something from agriculture.

Bipartisanship

For the agriculture committees, meeting multiple member goals means being generally nonpartisan. USDA became more partisan in the 1980s and early 1990s, but the committees experienced no resurgence of partisanship. Therefore, the agriculture committees resisted the partisan trends associated with the postreform Congress.[33] Why? Members were better off protecting their flexibility in the service of their own districts. Quite simply, they felt that agricultural policies would not pass if they were seen as partisan, particularly since they were always subject to the criticism that they were of limited social relevance. In the Senate, the move by Leahy and Lugar to work together reinforced party cooperation. De la Garza always insisted on it: House committee norms advocate bipartisan district visits by members, not campaigning against committee cohorts, and committeewide responsiveness to multiple interests in order to avoid party fights.[34]

Although issues of the environment have become more of a Democratic concern and those of expanding international trade more of a Republican one, particularly as these issues extend beyond agriculture, members of both parties nonetheless initiated issues of each type; district considerations are more significant than partisan ones. The same balance was struck by prairie-state Democrats who worked closely with farm-protest groups from 1977 to 1987. Their districts were among those with high production costs and they favored production controls.[35] Republicans from similar districts advocated production controls as well. As a veteran House agriculture committee member explained: "Issues are going to be imposed on agricultural policy like it or not. It only makes sense for those from both parties to put aside differences and get on with it." Caucus leaders on both sides of the aisle have agreed with this member, and they have supported the committees in being accommodative to timely issues, such as the environment, and rejecting outlier demands, such as those from the prairie populists.

None of that unity means an immunity from partisan pressure.[36] It means only that the accommodated issues and policies are generally nonpartisan. Members do other things to keep that partisan reputation. In the interviews forty-four members, including four Democrats and three Republicans on the committees, felt that the White House affected their agricultural issue initiatives. Eighteen members, three of whom were committee Democrats and two of whom were Republicans, indicated that caucus leaders also had a partisan influence. Partisanship effected setting budget targets or specific appropriations requests in major ways. Twenty members reacted to the White House, and four members reacted to caucus leaders. Whereas thirteen of these members found their initiatives cut, eleven enterprises used the White House or the leadership to help fund their issues.[37] The influence of partisans, therefore, was not in proposing policy, but in advancing their own nonpartisan issues. As veteran legislators explained, each White House farm-bill proposal since 1970 was "dead on arrival in Congress." In contrast, however, Vice-President Dan Quayle went out of his way to derail a wetlands agreement negotiated by USDA and endorsed by the committees.

Why was there this emphasis on issues rather than on policy leadership? In all eleven cases, members had cooperated with party leaders on other issues, all but two of which were nonagricultural policies. In exchange, partisan pressures were applied to the advantage of issue initiators in budget and appropriations policy. Other evidence indicates that such intervention is hardly rare. Members and staff, for example, credited House Speaker Foley and Senate Minority Leader Dole with routine involvement in support of agricultural policies, in no small part because of their own district farm constituencies. Both party leaders were instrumental in avoiding even sharper cuts for agriculture as these cuts were made in the five-year reduction plan budgeted in 1990. Staff from their offices, as well as from those of House Minority Leader Robert H. Michel (R-Ill.) and Senate Majority Leader George Mitchell (D-Mass.), acknowledged the leaderships' roles in affecting both the policy domain and the policy interests of rank-and-file congressional members: "We get involved because leadership provides us those opportunities. While Foley seems to want a great deal, don't think that Mitchell doesn't leverage far more than just for his potato farmers. He does, however, want those producers provided for too."

There were also other partisan effects. Twenty-five members had traded support on agricultural issues with the White House for support on those in more partisan domains. Fourteen members had done the same with House or Senate party leaders; according to a leadership staffer: "They hold us hostage on farm policies, we hold them hostage on the major issues of the day." The quid pro quo for agricultural policy on these exchanges was always the same for members: either supporting or breaking with their own party on major issues that divided Democrats and Republicans.[38] Members, even those not on the committees, did both to win in agriculture. White House and party leaders traded agricultural issues for high visibility ones such as foreign affairs but never for low visibility ones like education or transportation.[39] A member explained administration support for his sugar and fruit growers: "I win more frequently than my colleagues because the leadership feels I have a good future. This also gives me unusual access to the leadership. But, really, I know that they assess me first and foremost on whether I toe the line on the big votes."

As a result, partisan involvement paid dividends, even in a generally nonpartisan congressional committee. In an increasingly partisan Congress, on nonpartisan problems, this involvement is probably unavoidable. Members, on and off the agriculture committees, saw their opportunities for succeeding with constituents being enhanced—at least on the margins—by following party and presidential agendas, but not on agricultural matters. This distinction, of course, further distanced Congress from the ever more partisan USDA: "And the same thing will happen to the Clinton Administration, even with a Democratic Congress," according to a veteran Democratic agriculture committee staffer. It also allowed several members to circumvent budget-imposed limits by otherwise being good party soldiers, as long as they did not embroil partisan leaders in controversial reforms. "It's an irony," concluded one Republican committee member, "tacit presidential and congressional leadership influences let us prosper."

Good Policy and Washington Influence

The prevailing emphasis thus far has been on issues that serve the district, even in explaining partisan ventures that affect the agricultural policy domain. But, why maintain those policies that constituents seem to neglect? Those are not necessarily the ones noncommittee members see as extraneous, or that stretch agriculture's credibility. Policy problems as varied as USDA operations, land-grant services, rural poverty, animal welfare, and new product research were at most topics of miscellaneous interest. Nonetheless, issues such as these either continue to command agriculture committee attention as they have for decades or find new places on the committees' agendas. What, in an individualistic postreform Congress, accounts for the paradox of persistent committee interest in some issues and their simultaneous neglect by issue initiators?

Members and their staffs emphasized the notion that competing personal goals came into play for the committees.[40] Specifically, some people had to worry long-term about good national policy, and they had to do so with information and budget uncertainty. In almost the same breaths, several ambitious members emphasized that they hoped to leverage their agriculture-committee assignments into positions of congressional power, "Which won't happen if I look like only a hack." Accordingly, with so much at stake in the domestic economy, some members could not help but turn their attention, at least occasionally, to the sustained productivity of the agricultural sector.

This ambitious attention led to members' interest in maintaining the domain's service, or outreach, institutions—local USDA offices, land-grant colleges, experiment stations, and the extension service. It also led, with some obvious reluctance, to encouraging those who operate these institutions to expand agriculture's policy jurisdiction and address wide-spread concerns about its social relevance; that approach was seen as the only way to save farm policy. Given committee member attitudes about too many policies, there was obvious irony in that encouragement. The overriding concern of members was the uncertainty of what would take place in the farm sector if research, analysis, education, and extension services were curtailed, or if they were not adjusted to reflect the needs of a twenty-first-century agriculture. A midwestern member explained, "There exists great skepticism about what farm-service agencies still provide for U.S. agriculture. We have even greater fears, though, about what effects we'd find if those services are lost."

Members are caught in another causal story of agriculture:[41] the U.S. fostered the world's most economic and efficient farm sector; those gains were made because of technology and development; farm service providers were the essential players in development who brought technologies on line; therefore, to ensure continued productivity, agricultural outreach requires protection. Members also noted that U.S. agricultural-development institutions had been exported internationally, leading to worldwide modernization in production. Because this institutional expansion encouraged competition in world trade, it was felt especially vital that domestic institutions be able to contribute to the farm sector. As a senior staffer observed: "For many reasons, we're never certain what the so-called agricultural establishment contributes, and we're always reluctant supporters, given the sector's greater dependency on private enterprise, but we have no choice on this committee other than preserve things as much as budget choices allow.[42] A trained and educated farm population remains the key to the successful farm business practices needed today."[43]

Local politics, though, encouraged even that view. With USDA county offices in nearly every congressional district and the land-grant colleges and experiment stations in every state, the committees and rank and file had a common concern. On institutional service and outreach issues, agricultural politics shifted somewhat from its piecemeal and highly personal emphasis on farm-sector and nonfarm district diversity; for fear of undermining the economy of an always precarious farm sector, committee attentions turned—in far more detached and impersonal fashion—to protecting, cutting, and suggesting reforms for the institutions that serviced farming and ranching. This led to such efforts as Senators Leahy and Lugar's leadership in proposing reorganization of USDA and a reassessment by House appropriations leaders of federal grants for the experiment stations. Good policy considerations also led to the Senate's and then the House's reorganization of their subcommittee structures, leading, in turn, to greater coordination of major commodity reviews. Those in seventeen of twenty agriculture committee office enterprises concluded that such efforts were vital to committee work, even though only three of these members expressed any personal involvement. One commented, "Most of us are just listeners in the hearings process, waiting for inconsistencies. . . . It's long hours of good citizenship."

How does this review process affect committee influence? First, responsibilities fell to committee and subcommittee leaders. Second, the work was possible only because of committee staff.[44] Summarized one House committee member: "We just let the staff play the lead role in evaluating these problems. The committee lets it be known that changes are in order but that we want to minimize their disruptive impact." Most committee members saw the staff exercising broad discretion, but one senator warned, "They don't have marching orders to change the system, so staff review becomes a cautious and inherently conservative process." Staff agreed that while they challenged committee leaders with new ideas, they were equally careful not to get too far ahead of the leadership: "This is advice and counsel only, soldier work." So, even with staff dependency, the leadership maintained control and secured information necessary to rally Congress around institutional protection.

Committee influence is enhanced by a third factor in this review, the routine informants. Since only major projects activated district interests, and since farm-commodity groups were only passive supporters of agricultural services and their farm focus, some otherwise minor interests took on major responsibilities. In the words of a staff director, "You'd be surprised how much we rely on bit players to conduct the review." Recurring contact, with familiar budget complaints, come from USDA, most often by way of Agricultural Stabilization and Conservation Service (ASCS) and Soil Conservation Service (SCS) personnel who deliver most of their benefits through county offices. Other routine informants included the Experiment Stations Committee on Policy (ESCOP), the Extension Committee on Policy (ECOP), and the National Association of State

Universities and Land Grant Colleges (NASULGC).[45] State memberships sustained them all. Together, these five organizations address the wide gamut of agricultural domain services with the greatest available expertise—and, of course, their personnel have the added advantage of always understanding the local basis of agriculture policymaking.

As John Wright emphasizes, those who most routinely interact on the issues most affect the outcomes.[46] Members and their staffs, in this case, agreed, but they did not see the iron-triangle metaphor as an apt description of these deliberations. Said an agriculture committee staffer: "We put agriculture [service providers] on the bubble as they help us sort through program and funding priorities. They get marching orders. First, serve the sector. Second, help Congress adjust to the competing budget and social pressures that the agriculture committees face. With those competing expectations, we throw SCS, ECOP, and the others into a state of panic which they convey back home. Hopefully, from that condition, we gain the information to make useful policy recommendations." A staff colleague added, "It's a crapshoot conditioned by fear; that . . . farm interests will abandon . . . and that the enviros, animal-welfare types, and other reformers will get them."[47] In that fearful atmosphere, by fostering good national public policies under budget duress, the committees provide themselves with informants who can, in turn, activate local pressures on members of Congress from throughout the nation.

The agriculture committees, therefore, benefit and get their way because, on these issues, they emphasize an important distinction between district issues and goals, on the one hand, and good policy issues and goals, on the other.[48] In the notoriously constituent-directed agriculture committees, the large base of public policies and their encapsulation in omnibus policy vehicles allow members to emphasize good national policies, but only when district pressures are not salient and only if budget pressures allow. Other than under those conditions, good policy gets defined locally. In the words of a member: "Even in determining experiment-station policy, all the rules were tossed out on [House Appropriations Committee chair, Democrat Jamie] Whitten's Mississippi issues and [subcommittee chair, Democrat Robert] Traxler's Michigan pork. Other than that, we developed some excellent policy for both setting funding priorities and establishing evaluation criteria." To that extent, the spirit of W. R. Poage, a prereform chair of the House agriculture committee, lives at least a little in a domain committee system that has otherwise changed greatly. The member's remark is a reminder that numerous members, from Dole to Foley, use their personal successes in agricultural policymaking to demonstrate their capacity for Washington-wide influence.[49]

CONCLUSION

Why do so many issue initiatives win? Because the agriculture committees have no choice but to let them. Power and influence are widely dispersed in Congress, and the agriculture committees retain influence by recognizing that fact and adjusting to it.[50] Agricultural politics has again been remarkably adaptive to change; party leaders, committee chairs, subcommittee chairs, informal issue caucuses, state delegations, and the rank and file share power and influence. Iron triangles, as exclusionary networks of a few influentials, exist on only the most mundane issues because congressional interests and resources are so effectively divided; agriculture committees manage their policy processes, but they rarely control them. The chairman of the House agriculture committee is in no position to negotiate personally preferred policy positions with private interests and USDA;[51] in the more free-wheeling Senate, where members have long exerted more independence, the chair is even more constrained.

Yet that dispersal of power over a large and fragmented base of agricultural programs does not mean that the committees no longer organize the domain's policy goals. Although no forum or caucus exists for all interested congressional players, the agriculture committees still serve as adequate substitutes.[52] But they engage in seemingly contradictory actions: holding to a central focus on farm programs, yet acknowledging that policies of the agricultural domain have no coordinated purposes; expanding agricultural programs to accommodate an ever divergent range of issues and seldom challenging the rest of the House and Senate, yet still occasionally being punitive in gatekeeping; diligently keeping their own policies bipartisan, yet interjecting committee members into other partisan politics; and relying sometimes on the White House and congressional leadership, yet relying mostly on their own professional staff resources. Historically, agricultural policymaking and politics have always been hard, and now, they seem harder. Nonetheless, making agricultural policy still seems very possible, given the large number of enterprises and interests who not only win, but also win from, its decisions. That inclusiveness allows Congress to remain the primary cornerstone for structuring and determining federal agricultural-policy decisions.[53]

That congressional role also brings up a second answer about winners and what they mean for committee influence. Both the committees and Congress have shown a nearly singular preoccupation for satisfying district and state constituencies. As R. Douglas Arnold suggests, citizens choose their congressional representatives by their connections to policy. Of course, members act in anticipation of citizen wants.[54] Rank-and-file and committee members, as issue initiators, win in such large numbers because they have no choice but to let the moderate and cautious agriculture committees succeed, if farm and nonfarm constituent wants are to be met. That situation remains possible only because the committees and the rank and file both worry about farm incomes and the sector economy. Of no less importance, the committees understand that policies must take on broader social relevance than just doing farm favors.

Other factors matter. Committee members also trade their partisan behavior for support on constituent-enhancing issues. They worry as well about making good policy because of the manner in which disappointed constituents and, therefore, fellow congressional interests might react to failure. And a few members see congressional leadership opportunities inherent in future reactions to a changing agricultural sector. The interaction of these factors leads to a truly fragmented Congress, but one that nonetheless integrates its diverse members into a politically functional domain. So, why do members win and the committees have influence? Members are necessarily inclined to look for winning circumstances. They are also inclined to yield personal policy preferences to find those circumstances. In the end, the domain and its policy base are more important than committee influence.

This scale of importance, of course, also bring an equally fragmented set of agricultural policies that meander toward disparate purposes as the strategic needs of individual members and committees dictate. Even committee members, as seen earlier, are not inclined to be proactive in the search for good national policy; nor do they think about coordinated programs or comprehensive policy.[55] But, because of constituent interests, policies are at least generally predictable in a Congress where members play on behalf of extremely predictable motives and interests. In the future, perhaps even more than the past, this mode of operation will probably lead to both extensive policy change and a continuation of the prevailing equilibrium among agriculture's beneficiaries. At least members and their staffs see the politics of the domain moving policy in both of those directions.

9

Change and Stability in Agricultural Policy

Farmers are important because they're always underfoot, and they're intelligent stakeholders in public policy. That's not true of most people.
—A southern member of the House interested in agricultural policy change.

An urbanized national majority has not destroyed the influence of a small farm population, and it will probably not destroy that influence in the future. The way district politics is organized around numerous local interests means that few policies aim at the majority.[1] Farmers, as a consequence, still matter a great deal in national policymaking because a representative democracy provides a reactive Congress chosen by home folks. Within that Congress farmers are important to much of the congressional rank-and-file, to committees, and, at least to some extent, to party leaders—indeed, to all the centers of influence.

Members, their personal staffs, and committee staffs explained three major reasons for the persistence of farm influence in congressional agricultural policy. Given its large-farm bias, they explain how agriculture policy responds to its most resourceful interests.[2] First, farmers are thought to be incredibly well-organized and vocal, from the grassroots up to Washington circles. Farmers are not only organized into interest groups, though. The groups and single producers are deeply integrated into the entire range of discussion points in national politics. This integration is more than organized lobbies exercising power. Farmers as individ-

186

uals are active in local communities, in congressional events at the district level, in the local operation of USDA programs, in personal discussions with congressional offices in Washington, and in almost all policy deliberations that take place on the broad range of farm and related issues. Moreover, farmers divide between activist local leaders and passive supporters.[3] As Chapter 6 showed, farmers, with their local problems, are not dependent on Washington lobbyists to mobilize their views.[4] Local opinion leaders do it best. Members of Congress frequently noted that this integration of effort and the accompanying local focus of opinions made farmers, and not just their lobbyists, a de facto part of the legislative process. A veteran House agriculture committee member said: "I can't and won't decide without a dialogue with farmers, no way."

Second, farmers as a well-organized and vocal minority cannot be ignored without most members assuming high risks in the next election, even in districts that appear safe. When ignored, farm interests create considerable noise, at both the local and the national level, that members fear will be unfavorably received by the public in their districts. When those connected to other interests hear clamor from respected sources, they perceive it as a response to irresponsible congressional action against some vital component of the district and the national economy.[5] "Don't just think about how the national public rallied to protesting farmers in 1978 and 1985," warned a congressional member, "think way beyond those organized events to how Main Street opinions are shaped daily as farmers bitch about prices and policy failure. The problem is that farm programs do affect local economies, and people have always seen that impact, at least on an anecdotal basis."[6]

Neglecting farm noise runs the risk of a backlash that affects a member's home-style image, even if farmers are only a small constituency. Noise costs votes in elections, and not just farm votes. In short, these are not just matters of numbers of farmers, but rather historic ones of organization and perceived socioeconomic importance.[7] Because of this long-term institutionalization of farmers into national public policymaking, explicit trades and logrolls are seldom necessary for members of Congress who want to initiate farm-benefit issues. A member need not go into the details of trading before doing a favor for the Tennessee Walking Horse industry. To serve the farm sector broadly, and keep farm bills popular, the agriculture committees accommodate supportive members and their industries.

Institutionalization is also tied to the third reason that farmers receive the bulk of attention under existing policy games. Members emphasized the ease with which farmers are served through legislative procedures and those of agency oversight. The farm-income portion of the policy base is both extensive and malleable, even though it represents less than 20 percent of agriculture's budget. Moreover, that policy base also serves numerous agribusinesses that benefit from farm production. In contrast, interests seeking reforms win with much greater difficulty because they need to add to or even challenge the domain's policy base.[8] Other established nonfarm beneficiaries, such as those of food stamps, with its budget exceeding that of all commodity programs, are less easily provided for by marginal adjustments in law. But although the budget is extensive, the food-stamp policy base is smaller and service delivery far less subject to manipulation for local reasons. A larger and more complex policy base means that members of Congress and their staffs essentially need to be creative in order to take care of their district farmers. They search for the most fitting among numerous programs, such as disaster aid or grain standards, and adjust the benefits without changing the essence of farm-policy distribution; according to a Senate staffer: "Since entitlements are often involved, or because the transfer is a no-cost one, you rarely need to worry about budgets and appropriations in rolling things in."

These three factors—extensive integration of farmers into the political process, the electoral impact of their clamor as policy interests, and their easy use of a large policy base—provide a framework for looking at future agricultural policies. If constituent characteristics and the malleability of the agricultural policy base have affected recent congressional actions on farm policies, they should continue to do so. Similar factors for nonfarm constituents of agriculture should affect other major policies of the domain. Constituents and their relationships to policy bases, along with the effects of policy complaints of congressional members and their staffs, will help to determine current trends in agriculture policy. Of course, continuing uncertainty of the conditions that prevail for current policy games seems to be the greatest certainty of the entire policymaking process.[9] One cross-section of data, even though it has been examined in a historical context, cannot predict everything. But, because uncertainty appears to have led members to their home bases in the first place, the following analysis of quite a stable domain at least identifies likely pressure points where future policy change may occur.

THE FUTURE OF FARM PROGRAMS

The cumulative effects of farmer organization, clamor, and the policy base make it likely that commodity programs, as only one form of farm-income support, will disappear in the span of the next two to three omnibus farm bills. International agreements under the General Agreement on Tariffs and Trade (GATT) will not be solely responsible for their disappearance. Because more members of Congress are active on behalf of more farmers, many of whom fail to benefit from commodity programs, farm policy will evolve. Congress will not *want* to keep existing programs. Rather, its members will be better served by underwriting the production risks of all producers. Changes in the 103rd Congress that further reduced commodity subcommittees reflect those attitudes and will foster these changes.

Commodity programs were a means of selectively allocating federal dollars to those depression-era farmers who volunteered to comply with federal supply-control mandates. Farmers, not surprisingly, liked getting their own federal checks. The emphasis of the programs has always been on the incentives, to promote voluntary participation, rather than on the regulation, to enforce mandatory participation, with the government realizing that useful benefits to farmers brought cooperation only if the costs of compliance were comparatively low.[10] Despite retaining that voluntary emphasis and keeping supplements to farm income, commodity programs have undergone important changes since their inception in 1933, showing a congressional willingness to be adaptive.[11] Supply management gave way to "target pricing" in the 1970s, with the effect of gearing farm payments to market prices. In the 1990 farm bill, "triple basing" with "flex acres" provided producers reduced acreage payments but gave them greater flexibility in making planting decisions. Maximum payment limitations per farm have also been imposed, though never very effectively.

Still, all crops are not covered. Commodity programs are for major crops, but exclude livestock. Not all commodity programs follow target pricing and triple-basing practices. For example, the dairy industry receives support from federal purchasing through a complex form of price supports and a market order program. Other programs, like tobacco, employ unique means, such as keeping prices high through quotas rather than direct payments. Program costs go to consumers through higher prices. Nor do all commodity programs with target prices reward growers of different crops equitably. Variable regional production characteristics and costs also lead to less benefits for some growers of a commodity than for others growing the same commodity elsewhere. Of course, inequity is important to congressional members because it fuels policy complaints from local stakeholders.

Local complaints bring surging rounds of proposals and changes as enterprises consider farm-income needs under their constituents' varying production conditions. Nearly any change or issue initiative in a commodity program, even one that does not take away direct benefits to others, still affects the income of producers of another commodity or alters costs or prices among growers of the same commodity. This system of effects explains why field-crop producers found livestock interests reacting harshly to the 1983 Payment-in-Kind (PIK) plan to retire land in return for stored surplus crops: Feed costs would increase.[12] It also explains why cotton growers, who felt a sudden market disadvantage because of drought, were given a second opportunity to supply their commodities to meet PIK demands. A shortfall, and a farmer irritant, was created.

These factors explain much about why diverse members of Congress gain opportunities to serve their districts by addressing farm income. These are not just midwestern and southern crop issues; commodity problems affect ornamental-tree growers and western grazing rights, too. That broad impact explains why production issues are salient to so many districts and why policy demands are so intense. Those factors are the political pluses for current policy. But, in addition, the same factors explain why the ever changing dynamics of the policy process are an irritant to farmers; they may create short-term goodwill for local members who work for the district, but they lead as well to a negative evaluation of Congress as a whole.[13] Continued tinkering with policy, when financial assistance is limited, creates general frustration with income support.

There are other negative effects for current policy. Farmers know from experience that unpleasant commodity-program provisions will be forthcoming even though they generally like receiving federal dollars. In the late 1980s and early 1990s, farmers learned that program benefits decreased as commodity payment levels were cut under budgetary pressures. Average-per-farm government payments for all farms fell, in 1991, to 51.3 percent of the 1987 average amounts. Payments to farms with sales of $100,000 or more fell to 40.6 percent of 1987 levels.[14] Farmers also learned, as more environmental regulations were mandated, that the costs of voluntarily participating in commodity programs increased. All this change intensifies the political minuses of commodity programs. Instability, less income assistance, and increased associated costs lead many recipients and members to wonder, as one Midwest House member did, if the programs really have merit: "There are as many of my growers who hate the programs as there are those who insist on them."[15] The same factors limit the goodwill constituents feel toward otherwise successful congressional issue initiators, as one House staffer noted: "They know, long term, they're losing."

Other farmers see even more negative elements that point to change. Being left out is a major farm-policy complaint, one that takes on greater significance when more members of Congress who represent more diverse types of farmers are issue initiators. As more members of Congress, particularly those from beyond the regionally organized agriculture committees, intervene on behalf of their farmers and ranchers, perceptions that inequality and basic unfairness are important grow in Congress. Those who represent livestock, specialty crop, and fruit and vegetable regions find the farm programs that they and their constituents use to their advantage, such as disaster assistance, are more limited than those for major commodities. One Senator said : "Some other [members of Congress] do business in a regular farm policy department store."

This problem grows in importance because of already existing fragmentation among farm-sector representatives in Congress. Over the past four farm bills, members of the agriculture committees have found it difficult to allocate available budget dollars by commodity program.[16] With subcommittees divided by commodity from 1977 to 1990, and budget targets set, internal committee discipline and coalition building slipped. As one party leader observed to his staff in 1990: "It's been dog-eat-dog for several years. Now the dogs are sharpening their teeth."

Tensions between members have also increased when regionally based livestock interests disagreed on the questions of grazing on public lands. This was a particularly nonaccommodative issue in agriculture, even beyond the idea of regional fairness. Those outside the West, particularly in the Corn Belt and Great Plains, failed to sympathize with westerners who were generating even more than normal conflict with environmental interests. Why, under those conditions, they asked, is unqualified mutual support among farmers still a good idea? The conflict between advocates of greater flexibility of public land use, as in the Sagebrush Rebellion, and proponents of intense environmental protection convinced many in Congress that such disputes would lead to solutions determined by third parties. These conflicts could set dangerous national precedents.[17] "At some point," a member concluded, "we probably will pull the rug out from under the grazing guys just to save our nonfarm alliances."

Negative attitudes among farmers about current policies and resulting tensions among congressional members increasingly make many in Congress look to extensive changes in farm programs to solve problems that are essentially ones of process. Members wonder whether uncoordinated commodity programs and associated trade-offs with nonprogram crop farmers and ranchers can keep the farm sector sufficiently unified to continue accommodating nonfarm interests.

This uncertainty leads to a pending policy game, the search for farm-policy alternatives in Congress. Members, in the search for balance between the rank and file and the committees, want a farm policy that meets six criteria that relate to long-term farm problems with price policy: (1) the new policy must still try to stabilize the farm sector from economic disruptions; (2) it cannot appear to abandon those who planned their farm practices on price programs; (3) it must be less subject to incessant tinkering and hostile reactions from adversely affected farmers than current programs; (4) it must cover all farmers regardless of crop; (5) it has to continue to address, with flexibility, the problems of regional and commodity variation within the sector; and, (6) the new policy should also address recurring problems in other farm programs, such as crop insurance, disaster assistance, and trade intervention. The replacement must also, to satisfy congressional members who want social relevance in agriculture, be intended for farmers who need financial support. In summary, members of Congress want to retain a flexible and place-specific farm policy base that will be acceptable to the always influential farm sector and to a sympathetic public. Although that base must address multiple problems, members do not want to continue the existing pattern of uncoordinated programs that, when adjusted, always leads to politically troublesome farm reactions.

Policymakers, eventually, will likely replace commodity benefits with a mandatory-insurance and price-intervention policy that provides periodic benefits to producers affected by weather, natural disaster, and trade dislocations.[18] Although such policy will lack the high payments associated with present programs, and will thus save scarce federal dollars, policymakers can argue that it appears more acceptable to the farm sector than currently uneven programs beset by inevitable budget-deficit problems and cost-cutting. Such policy can bolster the always tenuous relationships between congressional members and farmers back home because it will keep decisions about distribution and need at the local level and open to member initiatives.

THE ENVIRONMENT AND FOOD PROTECTION

Members of Congress and their staffs find problems in addressing the environment and food protection, two closely related public-interest issues that are quite unlike those for farm-income policy; the constituency is different from that of farmers, public-policy rhetoric produces a distinctly different citizen interest, and the base of existing policies is less important to those who matter most to Congress on these issues. Nonetheless, these merging agricultural policies of health and ecological sustainability have a generalized public popularity that keeps them alive. The farm sector, though, does not face unbridled congressional enthusiasm for either an untarnished environment or a notably safer food supply— unless, however, a not improbable public crisis creates new policy games and new interests. Public-interest lobbies, for one thing, are not as strong as farmers in effectively influencing policy. Public-interest and farm issues are not represented in the same way. In contrast to the relative clarity of farm policy, unaccommodated fragmentation among reform activists, variable issue salience to the public, and an absence of clear cues to Congress plague public-interest efforts: "Those who express concern about the environment don't know what they want. How can we?" asked a House Interior and Insular Affairs member.

The organizations that represent public-interest issues have several divisions. Washington groups are split by ideology as well as by their differences over which issues should prevail and by the levels of government they prefer to respond to those issues. Unlike the very pragmatic commodity and general farm lobbies, environmental and food organizations find that their alliances suffer from more than just divisive budget pressures.[19] Agreement on public-policy goals, particularly in defining winnable ends, is hard for environmentalists because their work aims toward setting social standards with potentially severe economic consequences: "We all feel really driven by our own personal senses of being correct," observed one environmental lobbyist.

A more pronounced split among advocates is that between national associations and grassroots locals, even when groups like the Sierra Club have local affiliates.[20] Locals are moved by issues of their own places and time, often without regard for the usefulness of a national policy base. As a sympathetic member of Congress described the locals, "They have a pat response, 'ban it'." Other local organizations find many degrading practices acceptable, but only if the "NIMBY" principle—Not in My Backyard—works to their advantage.[21]

Other splits, as NIMBY suggests, reflect the relative salience of issues. Leaders sustain most environmental groups through their own intense commitment. Yet the public at large, from which group memberships build, sees environmental issues as far less personally important than do activists. Issues of national defense, the economy, and morality have ranked as more important problems to Americans in the 1990s.[22] Salience increases when a specific concern, such as clean air, gains sustained media attention over time by focusing on a legislative controversy. Support for and membership in environmental groups fluctuates considerably, and they frequently need to appeal to financial patrons rather than to the public for survival.[23] With these problems, public interest groups often make questionable, even outrageous claims to generate attention and support.[24]

Members and their staffs understand these dynamics and are especially suspect and cautious: "There seems to be a great sense of theatrics taking place among many environmentalists and their fellow travelers. Their public positions are not just intended to inform, but rather to intimidate." Other suspicions exist. Unlike farmers, the environmental public seems not to be in politics for the long haul, even while their leaders try hard to intensify the electorate's interest. The use of district informants shows this problem: members find few informants and confidants on the environment who can seriously and with experience discuss district problems, except about NIMBY issues; no local bridge exists between environmental group leaders and the public. Grassroots environmental demands generally are either too directed to projects and small places or too abstract as generalized public fears to take back to Washington as district views.

Congressional responses to environmental issues, as a consequence, are neither as predictable nor as conducive to coalition building as they are for farm policy. Environmental supporters in Congress tend to be Democrats.[25] This lessens the prospects for broad member interest: "I often need to take an environmental position because of my reputation as a liberal Democrat. Not doing so would seem inconsistent of me for those who vote on my behalf." Interparty splits compound that problem for many members. Most disputes, as with that over the Clean Air Act's automobile emissions standards, are influenced by district and state economies.[26] This local influence lessens the prospects for Democratic caucus influence in exercising environmental leadership.

Other policy disagreements persist. Without clear caucus or district direction, many members see only competing district interests.[27] Conflict leads to issue avoidance and limited member commitment when, unlike for farm-income problems, there is no security in responding to public clamor that galvanizes the district. Members therefore respond slowly to environmental issues, as opposed to their responding steadily to farm interests.[28]

What does this kind of congressional response mean for agroenvironmental issues? Unless an environmental crisis temporarily heightens the salience of an issue to the public, farm interests, with their recurring problems of price and income, have a competitive advantage over environmental interests that want to restrain farmers. Farmers keep coming back to the members.[29] A crisis gives the advantage to environmentalists in the short run because the public's general environmental concerns, prompted by media attention, cover all congressional districts. Legislation often passes quickly when it is driven by emotions spurred by a crisis.

Relative advantage over the long term, however, is likely to be most important in determining regulations on health and sustainability. There are meaningful choices in how regulatory rules are written.[30] Each of those choices, moreover, remains embedded in existing institutions that were created at specific times. For agriculture, three regulatory choices apply to food and environmental issues. Soil- and water-conservation efforts, like farm-income policy, owe their existence to an era in the 1920s and 1930s when regulation usually consisted of voluntary compliance with rules established through industry cooperation. Much of USDA regulation still occurs in the same way, including the regulation of environmental provisions from the 1985 and 1990 farm bills.

The regulatory era that followed the 1920s and 1930s, though, gave strong impetus to preventing and minimizing health and environmental hazards. Social-advocacy interests, reacting strongly to the previous emphasis on the participation of regulated industries, determined much of the regulatory agenda and many of the procedures for new policies.[31] Those policies that encourage litigation to enforce regulation are the best example of the change.[31] The Delaney Clause of the 1958 Food Safety Amendment, which sets automatic bans on any additives that have more than zero carcinogenic risks, and the creation of the Environmental

Protection Agency in 1970, both emphasize litigation. Since both Delaney and EPA significantly affect agricultural policy, future regulations could be designed in ways consistent with strategies of litigation. Delaney and EPA remain agricultural precedents for environmental policymaking. But, in contrast, a third choice emerged later in the 1970s that dominates more recent regulatory efforts. Its practices are to weigh social benefits of regulation against incurred industry costs. Efficiency, not industry convenience or minimizing hazards, becomes the prime goal.[32]

Should issues of food production and the agricultural environment follow this latest regulatory policy game, costs to the farm sector and associated agribusinesses would gain principal attention. Such a shift could even lead, because of newly emphasized inefficiencies, to a legislative reversal of Delaney. Should USDA regulatory mechanisms continue to govern under rules from the 1930s, even under the efficiency game, agricultural industries would have an influential voice in determining costs, benefits, and policy direction. Farmers and agribusinesses would have a leading role in the policy game if they developed new products and practices that played on the public's general concerns for health and a quality environment. Accordingly, such a shift would not put agriculture, or probably the agriculture committees, at a terrible disadvantage.

But, if farm and agribusiness interests resist regulatory efforts that impose costs on production, as they usually have, health and environmental battles will, without a crisis, go on for a long time. Indecision and agricultural protectionism, though, will give way when the first sustained and publicly prominent crisis calls into question the safety of either the food supply or farming resources. Members of Congress will then listen to the most intense environmental interests, whose representatives will be busily alarming the public.[33] Forget efficiency and industry costs; ignore what moderate consumer groups say about the price and availability of food.[34] Zero-risk practices, like those of Delaney, would become the regulatory norm.

Thus, in light of the interplay of constituent interests and existing policies, one of two scenarios will dominate issues of the environment and food protection. The most likely scenario, driven by recent policy games, favors traditional agricultural policy approaches to the issues and only marginally increases costs to existing beneficiaries. The other scenario, driven by crisis and emotions, challenges traditional approaches as well as existing beneficiaries. Avoiding real disruption depends on farm and agribusiness interests preemptively addressing issues that they typically consider secondary, unimportant, or merely problems for their opposition.

POLICIES FOR AGRICULTURAL
SERVICE INSTITUTIONS

It seems, at least in a world ordered by rational policy analysis, that agricultural service institutions will be highly valued under policies that aim both to stabilize the farm sector and to move it forward in protecting health and sustainability. Daniel Bromley points out, though, that policy analysis seldom determines policy outcomes unless it focuses on what influential and affected individuals and groups really want.[35] Constituency interests, therefore, will have the greatest impact on the outreach problems of agricultural service delivery, education, research, and extension.

With budget-deficit concerns an unavoidable part of the next two to three farm bill cycles, existing policy games are likely to be unkind to USDA and various parts of the land-grant system. What their organized interests want to maintain will be less valued by players in those policy games, as four observations from earlier chapters explain. First, even on the agricultural committees, issue initiators largely ignore these policy topics. The exceptions are those few members of Congress who want to deliver highly specific facilities or research institutes to their districts. Second, for their policy role, agricultural service and outreach institutions generate considerable hostility throughout the Congress. Institutional analysis is suspect, policy planning is viewed as more political than objective, and, in general, responsiveness is criticized. Members see organizations as overly bureaucraticized and failing to adjust to new policy needs. Members hold little faith in the capacity of these institutions to contribute to the farm sector and to the resolution of its problems. As one congressional member observed, "The bureaucratic inertia characteristic of traditional organizations explains [congressional] interest in moving away from competitive grants and putting an emphasis on a new generation of newly designed units such as [Iowa State University's] FAPRI. We want involvement, not the allocation of funds that get sucked up in keeping old programs and projects alive."

Third, congressional committees have absorbed the responsibility for maintaining these institutions with little direct or personal member interest; the committees do maintain them primarily because of uncertainty as to what their decline would bring to U.S. agriculture's competitiveness, and because they provide an uneasy accommodation of farm and nonfarm interests in the domain's policy base. This committee responsibility provides little reservoir of support among those most involved in agricultural policymaking. Fourth, there appears to be little commitment to these institutions from either highly valued farm interests or newly accommodated nonfarm interests. Since direct price supports and other income assistance to farmers gained dominance after World War II, no one sees service providers as very salient.

Farm and nonfarm interests have other policy priorities, and they make demands on USDA and the land grants because these organizations happen to be part of the complexity of existing agricultural policy. Since so much policy depends on successful implementation, various interests need to be at least nominally worried about service delivery. But, because both farm and nonfarm interests question organizational responsiveness, no one would be too averse to changes and extensive budget cuts that spared their personal priorities, in good part because agricultural service providers extend their benefits as collective goods, open to all potential users, as opposed to through selective allocation to designated beneficiaries.[36] Even extension users, who receive some of agriculture's most tailored services, complain about the farm sector sharing resources with nonfarm users. As a congressional member observed, "No one feels any longer that the Extension Service is there to meet unique and personal farm needs."

This complaint suggests that, as budget pressures intensify and domain policies evolve, both administration and outreach will be subject to extensive cuts. The federal share of land-grant budgets has already declined in the past two decades in comparison to other sources of revenue. Moreover, Senate leaders, as well as both the Bush and Clinton administrations, advocated reorganization and a consolidation of service providers. These changes range from moving food inspection efforts to the Food and Drug Administration to combining and closing numerous county USDA offices. These proposals have in common their advocates' insistence that farm, health, and sustainability issues are not dependent on current organizational arrangements. Policy needs, not the maintenance of organizations, are what matter. Even the most ardent district proponents in Congress have a difficult time rallying support for one or more USDA offices in every county. As a member noted: "We understand that those arrangements are from a horse-and-buggy era and so will constituents."

Flexible congressional opinions indicate that a downsized agricultural establishment will have more specific federal expectations. First, programs that are central to farm, health, and sustainability concerns will be targeted for support because they relate to major policy interests. Second, caucus and committee leaders will emphasize the accommodation of member interests in these issues but in few others. Given the rank and file's propensity to favor popular and winnable issues and to argue for increased social relevance for agricultural policy, that accommodation will be relatively easy to achieve. Comparatively few issue initiatives aim at the margins of the domain, as opposed to the central policy games, anyway. Third, with agriculture committees and the rank and file restricting their interests, proliferating nonfarm issues of other types will largely stop. Fourth, USDA budgets and personnel will be reduced regardless of whether environmental and food-protection issues stay within the department. If farm and business interests fail to exercise leadership on those issues, even less of USDA will remain intact. Fifth, the effect on the land-grant system and on extension will be similar to that on the other programs. To the extent that issues remain beyond farm-income maintenance, public health, and resource sustainability, funding will have to be raised from the states, private grants, and user fees. Programs like community assistance and rural-economic development will have to be reshaped with a farm or environmental focus to gain support, unless the budget-pressed states provide assistance. Sixth, to ensure compliance and to address congressional beliefs that agricultural service organizations avoid oversight, accountability will be mandated. The agriculture committees and the General Accounting Office will spend more time determining whether a smaller set of policy goals are actually being met. When committee interests favored nearly all policies to expand political support for agriculture, oversight was seldom possible or useful.

These expectations constitute more than budget and resource cuts. They mean a considerable reversal of congressional and agricultural reliance on bureaucracy. The future will bring less administrative flexibility in reacting both to the wide range of policy problems and to those who identify them. Elected officials and a smaller number of interests will define more, if not most, service rules; that will mean less administrative and professional autonomy in deciding the future, particularly in providing what Vernon Ruttan calls a "more sophisticated perception" of balanced policy needs.[37] Cooperative relationships between members and program managers and key clientele will be more essential than ever. What is now ambiguous congressional interest achieving a good public-policy goal by preserving agricultural organizations will shift to the more predominant emphasis on district interests and reelection. With less to focus on, congressional enterprises will be better able to tell if administrative units satisfy district and state interests.

RURAL POLICY

Rural policy, as one of the most talked about but ignored agricultural-policy areas, provides an excellent example of how and why place-specific policy initiatives will work to the disadvantage of professional ones. Four findings from earlier chapters are particularly relevant to this example. First, issue initiators in Congress give rural problems little attention, despite the fact that most rural residents are nonfarmers. Second, rural issues come primarily from members who represent high farm-population districts with numerous small towns. They do not come from those nonfarm areas where manufacturing, tourism, or government services dominate local economies.

Third, rural topics are not of much concern for agriculture committee members. Congressional interests in rural topics escalated because of opportunities provided by Senator Leahy's unsuccessful rural-development bill. Members and their staffs, however, predicted a subsequent decline for this marginal policy game after successful consideration of some rural issues in the 1990 farm bill. That prediction and the low issue salience it suggests seem accurate, given that the committees did not direct ongoing staff concern to rural policy, as they did to agricultural service institutions. Fourth, there are few district advocates for rural initiatives. When informants and confidants are mentioned on those issues, they are nearly all career-minded local government officials—city managers, county administrators, and development personnel whose jobs often relocate them from district to district. Community residents show little interest in rural public policy.

None of those points should be surprising. Since the 1909 Report of the Country Life Commission, questions about the quality of rural life have been part of a more general concern for farm development.[38] The commission concluded that a healthy rural society depended on a healthy, technologically progressive farm sector. As an understanding of the bounded interests of the agricultural policy domain evolved, the environment in which the farm sector did business was necessarily included in the prescription.[39] Conservation, credit, electrification, phone service, and transportation were made available to farmers and, by way of inclusion, to many other rural residents and businesses. What was important, though, was the constant primacy of modernizing the farm sector.

By 1909, development and modernization had formed a causal story for resolving farm problems through public policy. The events of the next twenty-five years intensified commitment to its message. But it was events that began in 1862 that brought the development and modernization story forward in agriculture. The creation of USDA as a scientific agency, of land-grant education, of experiment stations for research, and of extension services for disseminating knowledge was intended to break patterns of subsistence agriculture among what were usually price-plagued farmers.[40] The emerging agricultural establishment set in motion a cycle characteristic of the farm sector: more production information made for better-informed farmers who used continuing technological innovation for ever greater production of more food and fiber; this process created oversupply, chronic surplus, excess capacity and means of production, recurring price and income problems, continuing farm-population losses through exit from the sector, and left larger farms among the survivors. To farm larger units, and to bring greater public consumption, information and technology demands increased. The sector became capital intensive rather than labor intensive, operating more and more on what Willard Cochrane called a "technological treadmill."[41] Farm-income support programs, with voluntary production restraints, emerged as a response. Farm interests failed to support mandatory production controls to limit farm growth, and they refused to attack production gains made from past and future advances in technology. Farmers themselves, facing non-exclusive markets and competition within their own economically strapped ranks, could not work out privately organized collective actions for effectively reducing production.[42]

When other problems of rural America, such as employment and poverty, were brought to their attention policymakers asserted that only the continued pursuit of the agricultural development story would make a difference.[43] "A sound farm economy," as one typical House member opinioned, "is the best, really the only possible rural policy." Of course, stories developed within the central story, such as the committees' defense of price supports.[44] Experiences supplemented the stories. Price supports, as selectively distributed incentives for voluntary farm-program participants, created intensely active interests within the sector,[45] including the commodity interest groups that came to increased prominence and, of course, the individual beneficiaries. Farmers gained highly personal property rights from programs that provided them additional income for their businesses.[46] They protected those rights and used politics to keep the agricultural-development paradigm alive and to kill any alternative stories. To acknowledge the need for rural policies as an alternative would only have been politically self-defeating: "Why argue that the whole direction of farm policy doesn't stabilize anything?" Thus, as a senator noted, "Every farmer you see claims that farm programs are rural programs and that rural programs are farm programs. That remains orthodoxy within the industry."

The results of stories and their politics are not surprising. USDA and other agricultural economists and policy professionals have argued consistently that farm-income programs do little to improve the conditions of most rural economies.[47] Other agricultural policy analysts have emphasized the fact that economic gains for rural areas, as for urban areas, have resulted mostly from social-service income transfers and other benefits, such as health care and welfare.[48] Nonetheless, USDA, with congressional urging and its policy jurisdictions in mind, has retained administrationwide coordinating responsibilities for all departments and agencies that provide programs for rural communities.[49] Although much of that effort leads to little significant policy review or coordination, USDA still maintains the policy domain's identity as the caretaker for rural issues.

Within this context, few rural interests organized and created any clamor for action. As William Nagle insists, in an analysis for Congress, no constituency exists for rural policy.[50] Few rural interest groups are active, and none pay comprehensive attention to the multiple needs of rural regions. Major interests represent businesses such as electic cooperatives that depend on the small base of consolidated farm/rural programs. Others are local government associations with only some rural members. As a former congressional member explained, "Rural interest groups are nearly nonexistent."

There are other problems of representation, too. Rural communities and regions have lost many of their local institutions and their capacity to mobilize the public.[51] As rural communities have lost population and businesses, few service clubs and churches address their problems of place. The exception is farm groups. Thus, the lack of organized interests and the decline of rural communities leaves other rural residents at a great competitive disadvantage to farmers.

What does this mean for the future of federal rural policy, and probably for that of most states, as well? The answer is: nothing of promise. With a downsizing of resources for domain service institutions, fewer professionals will be available to address rural communities. Remaining analysts will confront two problems: how to promote interest in community development when the benefits go collectively to the community and not to direct recipients; and how to ensure that funds are spent on communities that can successfully use development expenditures. Congressional staff ask, "What do you do with the SLTs—the shitty little towns that will gobble up resources?" Accordingly, rural-development advocates have a great competitive disadvantage, unless their initiatives assist with farm-income problems, use farm products, address food-safety and nutrition issues, or help identify the necessary balance between farm and environmental use.

For those reasons, the agriculture committees will fight to retain their jurisdiction over things rural. This fight for continued jurisdiction will produce spillover effects on some types of policy. Programs such as those that search for new farm-commodity-product uses and those that introduce more environmentally friendly commodities, such as USDA's Alternative Agricultural Research and Commercialization Center (AARC), have unique advantages. They can arguably bring new, safe, farm-dependent industries to designated local communities and districts. Because of their farm and environmental focus, though, initiatives such as AARC will be rural policy in only the most symbolic ways. Beyond that symbolism, the problems of most rural residents will continue to be dealt with through the raft of nondomain policies—for example, education, health, social services, transportation, and welfare. Agriculture's rural policy will be inexpensive, a byproduct of other interests, and supported skeptically in Congress.

CONCLUSION: INSTITUTIONS AND THE AGRICULTURAL POLICY DOMAIN

Only projections of developments within agriculture's domain are possible because policy games are always evolving. Trade policies, in particular, have been ignored because they depend largely on exogenous circumstances within the international arena, such as resolution of the GATT conflicts and changes in availability in international food and fiber crops.[52] All that can really be said under this cloud of uncertainty is that

Congress will continue to promote exports, particularly of value-added rather than raw commodities. The four policy types considered here each link issues, interests, and home places to existing policy bases in forecasting the future of the domain. Whether they are accurate or whether crises will render them inaccurate, the projections explain much about the present and future conditions of agricultural policy institutions and their politics.

What seems of paramount importance in understanding that future is the existence and meaning of the policy domain. Four factors are critical to domain development: previous political activity over time, the establishment of public and private organizations participating across governmental boundaries, the framing of issues that serve these organizations, and the capacity of these organizations to mediate the wide scope of public concerns about policies and policy problems.[53] The policy domain, as understood by its players, provides a rational mechanism for easing the difficult politics of competing claims; it provides an effective institutional base for the integration and accommodation of diverse demands, even those that champion budget reduction. As Kenneth Shepsle points out, structures induce equilibrium, but even the most robustly institutionalized ones are not immune to renegotiation.[54]

The domain, therefore, is more than the analytical assignment of public policies to different categories by those trying to understand policymaking. The domain is both real and dynamic. The entire policy base that was established over time matters, for it both stabilizes politics and allows for change. That significance in its dual aspect is of central importance to this study and to the development of domain theory. The policy base, for example, provides the only means to analyze what interest groups do and to what effect.[55] For a domain such as agriculture, where the struggle for stability is formidable, interest groups will develop niches from which they can focus on clearly identifiable goals and also avoid conflict with competing organizations.[56] Multiple and diverse players can win on an extensive policy base, even when the policy games surrounding them are intense and controversial. This phenomenon can only be observed by examining issues, not policy vehicles, as the units of the established and evolving policy base. Farm interests win in large part because of their advantages in relating their numerous issues to that base.

The agricultural policy domain has been described here in precisely the following terms: it is organized around a central principle—or story—of agricultural development, it commonly meets its participants' interests; it is institutionally bounded as a gatekeeper for policy matters, yet it is still elastic and permeable for even old domain insiders sometimes pursue agricultural interests in nondomain institutions.

These terms have important and very practical policy consequences. Only certain issues and interests define the substantive problems that constitute domain boundaries and the reasons why the domain exists. If the most central issues and interests fail to win, however, the raison d'être of the domain vanishes and the domain itself collapses. Should that happen, though, members of Congress would simply go on to find another conceptual framework for dealing with what they can of the constituent pressures they face. There is no necessity for an agricultural policy domain in the future, even though influential institutional forces currently maintain it and probably will be successful using it.. More immediately, there is certainly no need for a domainwide commitment from all the domain players to all of its current policies and organizations. As a member of Congress explained: "When a part to the puzzle of passing farm bills becomes extraneous, it gets dropped."

What does this indeterminacy mean for the future governance of agriculture? First, no one should think that all or even most parts of the old establishment will share the same fate. Agricultural policy lacks cohesion, shows no effective integration of its players, and is remarkably adjustable; accommodation of interests does not mean their perpetual acceptance. Traditional and reform interest groups, current USDA agencies, and service providers from the land-grant system are all politically vulnerable as institutions.

Second, no one should think of the agricultural policy domain and its organized players as autonomously self-governing.[57] The stabilizing politics of closed policy networks are gone, if indeed they ever truly settled the myriad of agricultural disputes. The reliance on agricultural professionals is in considerable decline. Policy games that led to substantial autonomy, self-governance, and professionalism have been changed by budgetary pressures and by a growing congressional emphasis on what selected and important district constituents want. Some of the future agriculture policy results nonetheless seem quite predictable, given agriculture's ever-dynamic equilibrium, with its historic avoidance of significant budget and program cuts for most of its beneficiaries.

10

Understanding the Dynamics of Congressional Networking

The devil is in the details, but so, too, is much of the virtue of the process. It's in the details that workable policy satisfies a wide variety of people. That's what representative government is all about. What must be considered, however, is the need for the committee to somehow integrate divergent details.
> —A high-profile caucus leader expressing his mixed views on policy-making.

Any member of Congress who speaks of bedevilment and virtue may seem involved more in a drama than in policymaking. Yet the member quoted above was neither campaigning nor pontificating. His comments were intended to clarify his vision of the postreform Congress. This member saw Congress and its policy processes both accommodating of rank-and-file individualism and still institutionally strong. Much of the details of legislation are left to members and their enterprises as individual interests. At the same time, however, the need to accommodate these diverse interests in policy vehicles brings continuing importance to committees, organized interest groups, and federal agencies. Someone needs to provide an institutional framework for the details, and these vestiges of the triangle metaphor for policymaking still provide it through extraordinarily weak network relationships. This balanced view of Congress and its behavior must be remembered, even as it must be acknowledged that constituents come first.

Roger Davidson's 1992 comments about the postreform Congress parallel that view. As a former Congressional Research Service staffer, he notes the uneasiness he felt when "terms like 'fragmented,' 'atomistic,' and 'centrifugal' were tossed around with abandon" by those describing that Congress.[1] How, he asked, could an incoherent and noncohesive Congress such as this survive? The Congress he knew was certainly individualistic and decentralized but still "elaborately structured and routinized." The "'big bang' explosion" of rampant participatory rights, as expressed in the reform era of the 1970s, was settling away.[2]

Davidson seems more correct than those who view Congress as chaotic. Congress, at least in its handling of the complexities of agricultural policy, indeed seems to be adjusting quite well to the competing tensions of increasing individualism and reliance on old institutions. As Kenneth Shepsle argues, "full service members of Congress . . . are incredibly competent at . . . geographic representation."[3] But, he worries, can they pass bills and mobilize alliances? The answer, it appears, is yes, but in ways that are far more ad hoc than those of the past. The modern Congress, for this policy domain at least, passes its bills and mobilizes its supporters on the basis of geographic considerations. There are, however, costs: district issues, rather than rationally determined national needs, have become the building blocks for policy. Thus, although the institutional vestiges of triangle networks remain, their relationships with one another are so different that they can no longer collectively set policy. Policy is accommodative and distributed widely within a domain, but only as coordinated and comprehensive political bargains, rather than as social and economic consistency require. There are several reasons for these characteristics.

POSTREFORM CONGRESSIONAL NETWORKING: PLACES

Accommodation of diverse members means that Congress maintains a dynamic equilibrium. Extensive congressional networking explains the decline in traditional Washington alliances as well as the corresponding increase in district and state relationships. This networking merges Washington and home-style work.[4] Contemporary congressional behavior follows Arthur Bentley's simple argument that interested policy players find one another and operate as decision-making groups for as long as they need to.[5] Nothing about either Bentley's argument or Congress implies either that relationships among players are permanent or that all players regard networks as equally relevant. Neither inference would be true.

Members and their staffs revealed and other policymakers confirmed that congressional institutions and the domains in which they do business have changed considerably since reform but not in unrecognizable ways. The Congress is quite different from that of the prereform, strong-committee era. Specialization by topics of interest and jurisdiction, autonomy over policy, and aloofness from the congressional rank and file are no longer strongly associated with those who write agricultural policy. However, some elements of each trait necessarily persist within the committees because someone in Congress must in the end be responsible for crafting final farm bills and other policy vehicles.[6] The unattractive alternative to working with the committees would be yielding institutional control and associated policymaking opportunities to those outside Congress.

Protecting committee influence, though, is of secondary interest to congressional members, and perhaps it always has been. The primary interest of members of Congress, both on and off the agriculture committees, is their care for home districts through the use of an extensive and malleable policy base. Congress has organized the agriculture committees to give regional balance to the most farm-dependent—yet competitive—places for at least seventy-five years.[7] Members of the committees worried about their own places, their own farmers, and their home districts' regional production problems, just as members do today. The other guys were important only for passing legislation.

Conditions in the postreform Congress only, if quite significantly, extend that preoccupation with home districts to a much broader range of congressional members. Congress, except for its extreme outliers, allows nearly everyone who wants to serve his or her district interests to initiate successful agricultural issues. An extremely broad range of the rank and file take that opportunity. Although many different players are attracted by agriculture's diverse policy base and wide range of issues in ways that were impossible as late as the early 1970s, providing for farm constituents remains the single most important agricultural interest of congressional member enterprises. Although constituent reasons help determine that interest in farm constituents, the committees' institutional interests in farm policy as a first priority influence those choices. Under existing policy games, there is little room within the individualistic postreform Congress for rank-and-file reformers who want to reform domain policies from outside the committees. Issues of environmental quality are the major exception, which seems to ensure them a permanent place in the domain. However, the biggest institutional shift is the evolving policy game of extending some farm-policy benefits to producers of crops and livestock not covered by traditional commodity programs.[8]

The Congress has not changed alone. Indeed, changes attributed to postreform congressional effects may more likely be products of other changes among those in policy networks identified with the domain. Other institutions and institutional arrangements have been altered in ways that matter to a changing Congress. Interest groups have proliferated and presented problems for decision making; determining which group wants what and how to reconcile more numerous demands have become difficult. Federal agency involvement is more extensive, more partisan, and less cooperative with congressional interests than in the prereform era. As a result, congressional committee members do not find or expect much agricultural policy leadership from the administration—no matter the party in control of the executive branch. Nor do members make unquestioned use of agency analysis and data. Issue initiators from outside the agriculture committees fail to care about these omissions in analysis and evidence. All this institutional change has further destabilized those policy networks that were once seen metaphorically as integrated iron triangles. As a Senator explained: "More member demands have been accompanied by more lobbying demands and a plethora of hostile agency voices. The combination translates into an inherently weak alliance of those concerned about agriculture."

Under such conditions, and with the ease of district communications increasing, constituents have filled a void in a policy domain long noted for its representation of geographic diversity. Familiarity with people, rather than a principle of geography, has become the key variable. Accordingly, members valued district informants, found reliable confidants, settled disputes within interests in favor of home folks, initiated issues that reflected district characteristics, and turned to state congressional delegation members to help determine what can realistically be pursued with committee members and staffs. The district, as a highly personalized source of information, has a competitive advantage over the Washington policy community.[9] With a greater capacity in the postreform domain for individual members of Congress to get involved, more do so with greater purpose for those back home. There were few if any reasons for committee members to insist that their noncommittee rank-and-file colleagues listen to interest-group leaders or USDA administrators: "If I write dairy policy for those in central California, it's fair that Andrews push farm-policy protection for New Jersey apple growers. How can I seriously tell him to protect the integrity of national policy?"

Thus, the more open congressional networking of the postreform era has implications of real consequence to policymaking even though Congress maintains much of the order that was found in a prereform era. An "ad hocracy" of networking can be seen in Congress for this domain with members interacting mostly in the short-term and only on the basis of interest-based needs. Only commonly understood views of the agricultural domain's policy base and an associated awareness of what opportunities lie within that base give order and prevent institutional chaos. The process is extraordinarily wide open, yet quite capable of gatekeeping against extreme outliers, because of an interest in the policy base. Those members who initiate issues that challenge either the central principle of agricultural development or Congress's general willingness to accept that institutionalized principle have not found room in domain policy games.

In congressional networking, several factors are at work in maintaining and ordering this ad hocracy. First, the rise of truly omnibus farm bills transformed the agricultural policy process after 1973, while still allowing for choices of other policy vehicles when the need arises. As the vehicle of strategic choice for most issue initiators, though, routinized farm bills are the most likely to provide numerous opportunities to serve districts. Differences in localities can be meaningfully expressed in policy through politics and, more importantly, through the institutional structures of governmental authority.[10] Logrolls are no longer necessary for passing farm bills.[11] Filled with celebrating the pomp and ceremony of agriculture's extensive domain institutions, and consuming large amounts of congressional time over a multiyear period, omnibus farm bills allow the legislative process to be broadly accommodative and subject to extensive congressional networking.[12] Members expect new networks and new policy games within the domain. One clever Senate member drew a historical parallel to farm bills, which are "not unlike medieval jousting tournaments, where the colorful conflict attracts everyone. Since the battles are largely over personal glory, there is no real warfare to drive the casually involved to cover."

This elaborate process transpiring in a postreform setting brings much of the agenda setting of Congress to the rank and file and their frontloading of assorted policy vehicles. Committees and their chairs, weakened by postreform rules, do what they can to pass a necessarily fragmented bill. Nonetheless, this push of rank-and-file members combines with the resistance of the committees to provide the basic structure of agricultural policy. Presidents and party leaders find the combined forces of members and committees too formidable to challenge, given the few incentives they have for doing so. Within this context, district voices win, networks based on institutional specialization continue to lose, and the committees take on far more modest gatekeeping responsibilities than in the prereform congressional era, when the triangle metaphor was widely thought to appropriately describe politics. Kika de la Garza could never behave as W. R. Poage did.

Congress therefore targets agricultural policy for change and modification, based primarily on the problems members see in representing their interests within the domain. Although preserving a policy base for various constituents is extremely important to assess desirable changes, maintaining all traditional domain institutions and organizations is not. As a member concluded: "You change enough of the details, then you get a truly significant and irreversible prescription for policy reform. It just isn't planned." What that member meant was simple: as policy games change, a considerable number of members moving together in a new policy direction exhibit nonincremental influence that significantly alters the domain. Through the work of numerous enterprises on individual parts of a collective policy puzzle, issue-initiating behavior produces major reform, like that likely to develop in the next few years with basic farm supports.

PURSUING MEMBER OPPORTUNITIES: INTERESTS

Prescriptions for policy reform emerge because interests in agricultural policymaking shift. Fully staffed congressional enterprises organized as interests in their own right. Members of Congress, buttressed by good organizations of their own, need not have any critical or compelling reasons to participate as agricultural policy players. They can just do so, with a minimal investment of personal time, because they can identify some opportunities. In a Bentleyan sense, then, enterprises occupy the political intersection between private concerns and their placement in public policy. As a commodity lobbyist complained, "If only my office had the resources of Charles Stenholm [D-Texas] or Dan Glickman [D-Kans.], who you remember need only worry about a small chunk of the countryside."

The emergence of members of Congress as interests should hardly be surprising. The scope of interested players extends not just to organized groups but to all active units in the making of public policy.[13] Also, as I find in my own earlier work on influence in agriculture, concentrating on only the organized associations that are usually thought of as interest groups examines far too little.[14] Professors, think tanks, consultants, multiclient lobbyists, and business firms also matter as interests. Interest behavior creates an intense focus on the pursuit of opportunities for congressional members and enterprises: "You might as well keep your staff busy and, to keep them occupied, you need to reward them"; as this analysis confirms, better opportunities in an uncertain political world are found by turning to the more manageable home district. The inverse is also true, namely, fewer opportunities are found in the Washington policy community than expected. Accordingly, the relationships between member enterprises and at least some district constituents are well cultivated by listening to trusted local opinion leaders, or confidants, who are thought to have a sound sense of their home places. These relationships form relevant policy networks.

Congressional personnel appear to understand that the local electorate responds favorably not only to those members with whom they agree, but also to those who generally seem to work for the district.[15] "You win with nearly everyone," concluded a House member, "when you get a local reputation as involved with visible or respected district groups. Even if they don't like farmers, local voters respect you for caring." For such reasons, most members of Congress spend considerable resources taking care of constituents, even if they dislike the "time and energy" it takes.[16]

Steven Rosenstone and John Mark Hansen explain why when they argue convincingly that the behavior of political leaders does somewhat more to mobilize political participation at the grassroots than do their initial preconceptions.[17] Thus, when a member of Congress, assisted by staff, behaves knowingly as a political interest, the enterprise maximizes the opportunity for favorable treatment back home. This behavior transfers considerable influence from the member enterprise to local social and economic minorities that are well-organized, clamor for action, and gain the most from existing policy bases. Mobilization by office enterprises, with attendant explanations of what, in a member's words, "your congressman has done for you," reveals why members are able to select among several issues, identify the most winnable ones, and then initiate their priorities with some certainty.

Members and their enterprises, while remaining reactive, are therefore more than users of interest-based policy demands. They, along with organized Washington lobbies and subsets of district constituents, compete for public-policy influence. They are—to risk some confusion in terminology—political interests. Certainly the purpose of these types of interests vary—which is precisely why members of Congress can turn to organized lobbies for information on national and local policy needs and balance that information with knowledge of what constituents want back home.

This interest-based congressional behavior is by no means restricted to the agricultural policy domain. It may just be somewhat easier there and in other domains, such as health, with sizable policy bases that are under recurring review. Agriculture committees, by reputation, are driven more by constituents than motivated by good policy.[18] Moreover, local informants who understand both policy and its effects can propose solutions to local problems as well as identify them. Agriculture is only a more consensual and less partisan and ideological policy domain than others.[19] Modern farmers are only marginally more politically involved than others, sustaining their participation more over time and overcoming a historical reputation as nonactive voters.[20] Because of greater committee integration and easier and more desirable accommodation of farmers, members of Congress and their staffs may find greater strategic latitude in behaving as interests in the agriculture domain rather than in others. But all that matters in only a relative way.[21]

The same sense of district representation and individual interest was particularly evident in major nonagricultural issues in 1993. Two prominent Democratic members of Congress, on separate matters, publicly broke ranks with the Clinton administration. David Bonior, while House majority whip, served as the de facto leader of the attack in Congress on the North American Free Trade Agreement (NAFTA). His southeastern Michigan district, with its heavy United Auto Workers (UAW) constituency, certainly provided him the chance and the reason to mount that challenge. With leaders of the UAW also mobilizing against NAFTA, Bonior had the perfect opportunity to appear locally responsive. Senator David Boren, from the oil state of Oklahoma, behaved similarly in fighting the administration's proposed energy tax in the budget bill.[22] He, too, as another Senate issue initiator, noted that his own work in agriculture "accomplished that all-important goal of looking real good at home."

POLICY CONSEQUENCES: ISSUES

The shifting meaning of interest politics alone cannot explain congressional networking. To understand the preoccupation members have with their districts in policy work, it is also necessary to think carefully about issues, not policy vehicles, as the exact topics of political concern.[23] That is not easy to accomplish. The whole of issue adjustments are more intriguing than a myriad of small and generally non-newsworthy deals. Academics tend not to muck about in these often technical details, frequently because they do not understand their importance.

Any policy vehicle, though, may be the target of those who advocate numerous and often noncompeting issues. Farm bills, as single vehicles or events, accommodate and are built on a base of multiple policies and issues that are nearly too numerous to inventory. Some of the issues are dramatic; others are mundane to all but the beneficiaries. Thus, to identify where opportunities for members of Congress and other interests lie in policymaking, vehicles and events should be subjected to extensive disaggregation of their issues; what, it must be asked, lies within what? For other types of analysis, such as looking at the potential for group conflict, disaggregation need not be so extensive.[24]

This type of disaggregation of issues from policy vehicles, or from political events, seems particularly important in the years of postreform congressional adjustment and proliferating political interests. At the beginning of the postreform era in the early 1970s, over 15,000 bills and resolutions were introduced in some years. By the 1980s, annual introductions fell to as few as 2,700 items.[25] Within that period, the reliance on omnibus bills increased throughout the Congress.[26] This shift, too, altered congressional behavior.

Opportunities for amendments decreased as time factors limited debates at the end of the legislative process.[27] But the data in this analysis indicates that this change also put a new value on issue initiation and its emphasis on front-loading vehicles. The effect was to focus, congresswide, on units of policymaking that constituents and, of course, narrow Washington interests could work with effectively. That is, they could both identify problems and offer solutions on issues of importance. Also, members of Congress could be active and successful on particularly popular types of national issues, such as environmental quality, but on the basis of uniquely local points of view.

These conditions provided members another advantage. They no longer needed to go through the complex actions of drafting amendments, then building winning coalitions for each one. Coalition building on amendments entails the creation of a quite general demand for policy. In issue initiation, members need to generate only a core of strong supporters, most often through state congressional delegations, who can then help influence what are prone to be accommodative committees. This issue-focused behavior was evident on NAFTA. Several congressional interests in agriculture supported NAFTA's passage only at the last moment, even though trade policies are more subject to international circumstances than domestic ones. The Florida and Louisiana delegations responded to President Clinton's leadership only when, respectively, citrus and sugar protections were added; Oklahoma members gained further negotiations for wheat growers; Southeastern members won support for peanut producers. For these members of Congress, the issues determined their support or opposition to the trade agreement.

INSTITUTIONS, TRANSACTIONS, AND DOMAIN POLICYMAKING

What members of Congress and their staffs have described of their operating environment is a dense interest structure, where domains necessarily have "porous boundaries and shifting coalitions."[28] That the number of interests in a domain are far larger, however, than the 215 organized private interests I found concerned with the 1985 farm bill became obvious to me.[29] Accordingly, the scope of my analysis of interests has expanded in this book.

With that expanded scope, it seems necessary at least to comment on why the domain concept is useful. It becomes the core of a general theory of interest politics in a densely structured situation.[30] Institutions and Roger Davidson's plea to consider Congress as orderly in both its rules and its policymaking relationships are central to such a theory. But the focus on institutions and interests must be broad. Economists, by leaving unspecified much of the meaning of interests and organizations in their models of group politics, have simply failed to provide a sufficiently broad focus on what moves politics.[31] Political scientists are worse than economists, with no disciplinary agreement either on the definition of interest groups or on whether organized interest groups—as voluntary associations—are indeed the appropriate unit of analysis for group theory. These scholars end up, institutionally, with a plethora of partially specified models. Both economists and political scientists should reflect carefully on Stephen Lee Skowronek's state-building study, in which he argues that over time, politics produces changes both in public policy and in the sum total of organizations that determine policy.[32] This current analysis of interests and their networks in an evolving domain has been influenced only slightly less by Skowronek than by Bentley's emphasis on political grouping.

Although the ideal goal would be to formulate a general theory of interest politics operating in a densely populated domain, theorizing here has been restricted to agriculture and its large base of diverse policies. But that theorizing seems applicable within other domains. Agriculture, therefore, provides an excellent chance to ask a question central to a general theory: What takes place in driving an institutionally dynamic equilibrium for a policy domain under complex and densely structured conditions?

To answer the question we must begin by noting that the institutions of the state are, as with the agricultural establishment, more matters of inheritance than purposeful choice.[33] For that reason, the politics of the agricultural policy domain proceed largely from its extensive policy base. The capacity of that base to accommodate and expand is what exercises causal influence. Thus, different policy games—from developing an agricultural establishment, to reconciling farm diversity, to logrolls between rural and urban legislators, to structured conflict over omnibus bills—have characterized the domain over time, even as the principle of agricultural development retained its primacy and led to spin-off causal stories. Indeed, the data described cross-sectionally in this book represent only one stage of agriculture's changing policy games. Yet that cross-section makes an important point. Density of interests emerged because of—indeed from—this base. Multiple interests only expanded the base, they did not create it. Inheritance, therefore, is of especially great consequence in determining interests in agriculture.

That premise leads me to explain change and stability—that is, the dynamic equilibrium of agricultural politics and policy—in terms of transaction costs. As Douglass North explains, "Transaction costs are the costs of measuring and enforcing agreement."[34] Interests—whether an organized group or a social movement or a congressional office enterprise—determine those costs, in highly selective terms. Interests make their cost determinations after assessing three factors: the value of their property rights as embedded in current policy, the relative degree to which their assets are fixed in existing versus modified policy, and the likelihood of using particular political issues and associated initiatives to improve the status of personal property rights while coping with the limited flexibility induced by asset fixity.[35] Transaction-cost analysis, in that sense, is a decided extension of the view of politics as merely a series of exchanges of benefits. It asks the costs of obtaining those benefits in light of institutional givens in politics. Issue initiatives are particularly important because, in negotiating transactions, they exist as low-cost options to either holistic policy change or new legislation.

This transaction-cost approach seems personally useful in developing a general theory of interests operating within a densely structured domain because it has previously helped me to understand the politics of modern American agriculture. The first instance of my using the approach involved applying it to the study of the adjustment of numerous organized private interests to one another in a common context.[36] The second instance involved applying it to the study of the failure of the agriculture domain to integrate the demands of modern-era farm protest in agriculture, despite more than seven years of conspicuous activity.

In these empirical studies, the universe of organized private interests was found to be filled with groups, associations, and firms that were compelled to develop widely identifiable political identities. These identities were based on a combination of their issue interests and the manner in which they represented those issues. Most groups had narrow issue interests that they followed where needed; others, such as the American Farm Bureau Federation and National Wildlife Federation, had broad ones that they pursued through old allies in national politics. Still others, like the American Agriculture Movement, had a base of narrow issue interests but found an advantage in commenting on a wider variety of policy problems, almost always from vociferously antagonistic positions. Nonetheless, broad or narrow and mainstream or protest, groups in agriculture were known by their exact works, both among policymakers and among those likely to join.

This confluence of group identity and interest directed attention to some among numerous policy decisions and neglected others, even when some degree of an interest's property rights in an issue could be seen. With the extensive array of interests active in agriculture, and with greater competition for attention among them, groups had incentives to cling to their niches. Each of them fixed their assets in their political identities and in what the groups stood for politically. In a domain with extensive policies but considerably fewer players and issues, there would have been more willingness to lobby for a greater share of what was potentially negotiable. Groups could have become policy gadflies. Assets would not necessarily have been fixed on so narrow a range of political property rights, nor would the focus on issues rather than the sum of policy have been so important.

Within agricultural domain politics, and in other domains when circumstances created movement elsewhere, organized private interests avoided conflict whenever they could—even in a domain potentially laden with a controversy and with a congressional interest in emphasizing basic disagreements. Newly involved interests had entry problems in mounting an effective challenge. Old ones had maintenance problems with their fixed issues and allies in considering escalated involvement. The domain, despite its contentiousness, was less full of competing demands than was expected. Most interest groups, especially the smaller ones that gained the greatest reputations for influence, mastered the art of including their issues in the policy vehicles of others. As a result, they were accommodated by policymakers who were happy to see neither excessive demands nor a great escalation of congressional problems to overcome to pass cumbersome policy vehicles. After all, the creation of place-specific tensions over policy in Congress made it all the more necessary that actions be taken to mute them in finalizing legislative agreements.

None of this accommodation and conflict avoidance applied to farm protest groups, however. These organized interests, in effect, waged war against the existing policy base and all of the many interests gaining from it. They were attacking the political and policy property rights of every mainstream agricultural interest, including those in Congress, by fixing their assets in the incompatible and unobtainable issue of parity pricing. With their own assets fixed in other, more easily attained policy, few opponents would yield.

Over time, as protesters continued to avoid accommodative politics and negotiated inclusion, they faced outright rejection and repudiation, even by other interests on the margins of domain politics, such as environmentalists and rural advocates. Even members of Congress who found pockets of intense protest activism in their own districts stopped trying to appease them. Members, for example, no longer tried to add commodity-supply controls to farm programs. By fixing their political assets in unattainable goals, protest leaders had no choice but to move further to the fringes of agricultural policymaking. Accordingly, other policy players who aspired to affect the domain seriously isolated the protesters so that the conflict they created would not immobilize decisionmaking. As a perplexed protest leader explained, "Over the years I found myself talking for no purpose to a congressman to finally walking down the street with Jesse Jackson's Rainbow Coalition. That did me even less than no good."

Congressional enterprises/interests face those same problems of avoiding high transaction costs in selecting issues and getting involved in policymaking. No one in Congress wants to walk in the margins of anonymity, especially in the sight of constituents at home. Members take credit for real things with real people who know. The lesson of this analysis shows that a large and diverse array of members find useful political property rights—or vested opportunities—institutionalized within the same policy base that successful interest groups relate to intently. Postreform rules of Congress make this institutionalized integration possible, but so too does the clamor of more numerous private interests that have helped provide the momentum for moving agriculture from a farm focus to its multipurpose emphasis. Members, as a result, fix their personal assets in what best meets the wants of other interests—for the most part, those within their districts. They find it much harder to work with and appreciate the contribution of either an expansive universe of interest groups or more politically polarized public agencies.

In politics, however, congressional interests have an advantage over other interests. Members of Congress have the latitude and luxury of fixing assets over a shorter term than do interest groups or constituents; they can pick and choose, looking for the most winnable issues. This advantage means they usually have greater flexibility than do those to whom they react in selecting issues; it led to the unusual loss of the honey, the wool, and the mohair programs between the 1990 and 1995 farm bills. With their primary congressional defenders visibly committed to budget-deficit and USDA-reorganization initiatives, these often-criticized programs were targeted in the appropriations process; Representative Stenholm and Senator Lugar had fixed their political assets elsewhere than on these minor programs.

Those members who serve on agriculture committees have broader responsibilities than the congressional rank and file. They need do what they can to salvage private group and administrative agency interests that help maintain the committees' policy base. Thus, committee members have longer term and more severe asset-fixity problems. Yet they are also adaptive. Whereas committee members might have little interest in meeting demands from the National Association of Wheat Growers or in following analysis from the U.S. Department of Agriculture, they certainly have an interest in preserving those diverse organizations that have continuing importance to the protection of the agricultural policy base. But they seldom extend that interest so far as to go against the district, unless, as with bees and mohair, they have no choices. "Now let's clarify," said a member of the House agriculture committee, "I don't use lobbyists as much for what I want. But I do find their existence useful to the big picture."[37] Congressional members appreciate the momentum provided by the many interest groups of the domain, even if their enterprises often ignore specific group proposals.

No one has any interest, though, in using the scarce resources of either congressional time and energy or public policy appropriations to maintain institutions that fail to contribute to the preservation of the policy base. For that reason, in the long run, nothing is immune to renegotiation within the domain—even the existence of the domain itself, in light of the work of overlapping domains. Noncontributing rules and organizations are no longer fixed within the equilibrium of agricultural policy. To the contrary, institutions that fail to contribute actively to resolving representational dilemmas or to meeting some multiple-district concept of good public policy encounter a dynamic—and for them, negative—situation. Those institutions are not unlike farm protesters who outlived their usefulness to the domain, and they can be advantageously dismantled or their resources redirected.[38] Few transaction costs intervene within Congress in such instances. This political utilitarianism, of course, contravenes principles of open democracy or those of analytically determined policy decisions. Undoubtedly, many observers of the policy process will find such institutional circumstances as objectionable as the bias members of Congress exhibit in their selection of confidants. Nonetheless, that utilitarianism appears to be the irreversible factor that makes dismantlement one of only two viable means for policy change. And it is particularly important to Congress in periods of budgetary shortfalls and declining revenues like those seen in the 1980s and early 1990s.

For those intent on democratic values, however, there is some solace in the way new policies originate as another means of policy change. Some types of policy that impose high transaction costs on congressional enterprises and other interests in agriculture will be brought into the domain as new policy games develop. Environmental policy stands out as an example, even though the mechanisms for its regulation of the farm sector remain unresolved. The periodic shifts in domain policy games also serve as historical precedents. What such future policies and their entry into the domain require is sustained national public commitment and the accompanying creation of supportive interests that cannot be safely rejected by domain gatekeepers.

Congress, just as its members do in serving their districts, avoids uncertainty by incorporating such policy changes. Even farm protest groups, for example, gained congressional access for years because of the prevailing fear among members of Congress that the public was somewhat responsive to farmers' well-publicized economic plight.[39] Thus, when the public and the institutions that public responses inspire create intense demands for new policy rather than for simply incremental issue inclusion, previously high transaction costs go lower. Congress, acutely attuned to representational concerns, seems in the postreform era to have the institutionwide and well-staffed capacity to respond to those concerns. When its members flock together to a newly popular type of issue, their individual actions can easily create what is for the domain a disjointed policy response. What seems difficult within the existing structure of interests is to create the intense and sustained public demand that produces a new type of issue.[40] Public opinions are so often fleeting; decisions about what new institutions to impose on the domain, therefore, may well be harder and rarer than the still always difficult decisions of what to delete.[41]

What should be emphasized here is that a general theory of interest politics should not focus on individual groups but rather on accommodative and often short-term political groupings. The same focus should be directed on Congress. The effects of procedural reforms in Congress cannot be understood as distinct from changes in the Washington policy community and from the reasons congressional members gravitate to the home folks. Three things, for example, could change much about the central role of congressional enterprises and constituents in influencing agricultural policy: if group coalitions were more disciplined, if farm and environmental interests would jointly seek more win-win policies, or if the administration would adopt a framework of cooperative leadership, all network relationships would be affected. It would therefore be inaccurate to claim that work on those relationships is now complete.

We need to understand more about what generates shared interests in politics and how these relationships are shaped. Broader policy networks of ad hoc interests must be analyzed in their various domains. Scholars must examine the exact public policies that create multiple interests as well as the interests that create policy. What is of interest to those in politics must be fully determined and specified: Why are values important? How important are they? Only then, when the causal arrow of representation is seen to go in two directions, can scholars turn their attention to the interests that create and recreate both new policy and redefined institutions. Understanding property rights (who controls what), asset fixity (who cannot yield), and fixity within recurring types of issues and policies (the inability to yield on specific things) are all vital parts of such analysis. Each element, of course, helps explain why public policy-making is such an inherently conservative and slow-moving process, even when conflicts that are always escalating are effectively incorporated into the process sufficiently to legislate.[42]

APPENDIX

Most of this book is based on a series of interviews with randomly selected members of Congress and their staffs. Although the interview data provide much of the information used in the book, other data are employed as well. Additional data on the leadership and partisan status, committee and subcommittee involvement, and district/state characteristics of each sampled member were integral to the analysis. Along with that information, other demographic data were collected that might reveal characteristics that influence the issue interests of individual members. Data on congressional tenure, race, and other assorted characteristics on which a congressional career is built were collected.[1] Similar characteristics of each staff respondent were also gathered.

Methodological considerations meant that conceptualizing the study design for data collection brought an easy part to the research project followed by a hard part. Planning for data needs was generally straightforward and easily decided. Background data on members and their districts is plentiful and available. Given the focus of the study, the essential format of the questionnaire to be used in the interviews was simple to construct.[2] That questionnaire is reprinted at the end of the appendix.

In the first stage of the sampled interview, respondents were asked to identify specific issues that had recently consumed extensive amounts of staff time and those that held high personal priority with the initiating member. This information was collected after ensuring that respondents understood the complex array of issues that constitute the agricultural policy domain. The intent was to avoid a listing of all issues dealt with in agriculture or even all bills tossed in the hopper. Most bills and issues are not followed diligently by members and their staffs. They constitute posturing in that members often introduce things they have no intention of championing but still talk about to those with an interest. In some cases, as explained in Chapter 4, respondents were asked to compare recent office priorities with those from 1985 legislation. Thus, the study design probes intensively for issues that are the most salient to the member, at least within this policy area. Follow-up attention and member commitment are key concerns. Personal feelings about the value of the issues and positive and negative views of the policies of which each issue are a part were tapped as well to gain insights into member motivation.

The second stage of the sampled interviews turned to an assessment of information sources external to Congress, specifically as these create demands on the members and staff on each of the priority issues. Respondents were asked to judge the relative importance of constituents, interest groups/lobbyists, policy professionals/consultants, agency officials, and various media representatives both in determining the member's selection of individual issues and in deciding specific positions to take on each one. That is, they were asked both about which issues they pursued and about how they fleshed out the substantive content of these issue positions. Respondents were asked to identify specific people and organizations as principal information sources.

The third stage of the sampled interview involved a similar assessment of demands and information from inside the Congress, ranging from the leadership to those from other member offices. Once again, in getting data about congressional interaction and institutional relationships affecting issue selection and prioritization, interviewers asked respondents to note when possible specific individuals who were important to their decision making.[3] Finally, they asked respondents to make open-ended observations about their attention to issues, the demands they faced, the information they used, and how all of these were prioritized in their offices.

The logic of this outline of what sorts of data to collect and what questions to ask obscures the practical problems inherent in such a study. One neither walks gingerly into congressional offices to chat nor, once there, finds members who can make comparisons among all the issue types that they confront. The hard part of this study design was twofold: identifying a reason for respondents to talk to the interviewer and ascertaining a means by which they would talk more than superficially about what were comparable issues, policies, and information.[4]

After a pretest, the option of highly focused interviews about a single policy domain was selected rather than an option preferred earlier of examining four domains and then assessing their potential influence on U.S. agriculture and rural America. This alternative would have provided considerable data beyond that useful for this particular book. There were two reasons why that option was abandoned. First, sample respondents were overburdened by the questions when they were asked to go into detail about the politics of more than a single domain. Inevitably, and surprisingly, almost all member offices have issue priorities in at least three of the four domains under discussion. In the limited time allocated for interviews, respondents could not recall sufficient information quickly enough to cover comprehensively the events that had taken place in several domains. Moreover, despite their widespread understanding of institutional and practical domain boundaries, their involvement in an issue within one domain inevitably affected their involvement in that of another. Responses, as a result, lacked focus and meandered from one context to another. Accordingly, the interviewer missed many of the issues that respondents thought important. Second, the amount of issue and policy knowledge an interviewer required to ask, probe, and follow through on questions about more than one domain proved overwhelming. Quite frankly, as key findings indicate, this study was not based on the expectation that so many members would be so involved in each domain. Interviewers found that to follow the flow of answers intelligently and to record them was impossible for multiple domains.

Selection of the single policy domain, agriculture, marginally affected both the originally determined sample technique and the initial questionnaire in ways that enhanced rather than weakened the final study. Since the test was of members who varied with their attachment to this domain's politics, the sample was stratified by committee assignment in order to measure the impact of those positions by keeping percentages of each type constant. Twenty members of the agriculture committees and agriculture subcommittees of the appropriations committees were sampled, 60 were sampled from the nine House and six Senate committees most likely to significantly effect agricultural policies, and the remaining 40 were sampled from members who lacked any of the above assignments. It is important to note that the sampling technique did not oversample those with agricultural assignments or undersample those without such positions. Although the Senate was slightly oversampled to include a sufficient number from which to generalize, at 30 percent of membership compared to 21 percent of the House's, committee-based samples were very comparable. The agriculture category was sampled at 24 percent (20 of 82 members in what was 15 percent of Congress). Related committees, not including those on agriculture, were sampled at 22 percent (61 of 277 in 52 percent of Congress), and the final category was sampled at a 23 percent rate (39 of 172 in 32 percent of Congress). Of the samples, respondents from 113 (20, 56, and 37 of the above groupings) member offices were interviewed after promises of complete anonymity and confidentiality.[5] Nonattribution proved particularly useful since, to further establish the importance of the interviews in the minds of respondents, the survey instrument was modified so that each interview began by asking for a candid assessment of agricultural domain policies, their importance, and the member's relative degree of support. This allowed respondents, the pretest showed, to better recall with less prodding the wide range of issues they had initiated and advanced or, alternately, defended against within their respective chambers. It also allowed respondents to move on more casually and logically to explain the reasons for their choices of issues, interests, and information sources.

Congressional staff and other respondents with Capitol Hill experience helped select the committees seen as most closely linked to agriculture.[6] Agriculture-related committees (as they then were called) included: in the Senate, standing committees on Budget; Commerce, Science and Transportation; Energy and Natural Resources; Environment and Public Works; Finance; and Small Business. In the House, they included the standing committees on Budget; Energy and Commerce; Interior and Insular Affairs; Merchant Marine and Fisheries; Rules; Science, Space and Technology; Small Business; Ways and Means; and the Select Committee on Hunger. Because of domain characteristics, the intent was to ensure a large sample of members tied to committees having jurisdictions over issues of the environment, public lands, energy, and commerce. Respondents represented their respective houses well (within 10 percent) in partisan identification, leadership status, seniority characteristics, region, and race.

Interviews were all conducted personally and almost all by the author/ project director in 1991. Some follow-up interviews were done in 1992 and early 1993, but not from any new offices. The interviews followed the logic of the congressional enterprise, in which all office participants were seen to be working collectively toward a unified end.[7] Legislators, because of time constraints, were allowed to offer staff surrogates as respondents as long as the surrogates were involved directly in issue selection, prioritization, and information gathering and assessment for the members on these issues. Since offices are run as small and very personal enterprises—and because no questions were asked about the private involvement of the members—this practice still provided the comparable data needed for the study. Multiple respondents were included in several offices: 54 respondents were members, 133 were staff personnel with responsibility for one or more parts of agricultural and rural policy.

Several of these interviews, including those of a few members, were completed after three other study papers were written to secure explanatory information. None of those interviews changed data from those papers, however. Because of specialized assignments and the limits of what members knew about staff efforts, it was sometimes necessary to interview two and even three respondents in each office to get complete interviews, that is, to get through all the questions. Complete interviews were held with 112 offices, one partial interview was done. Four of the missing interviews resulted because members and their staff had left Congress and could not be found. Most such missing former Hill people were found, however. Only three requests for interviews were denied. It was agreed that no list of respondents would be released. For that reason, the text develops around numerous unattributed quotes.

Other parts of the book depend on less systematic background interviews, such as those I did when I sought out members who sponsored alternative farm bills. This dependence on less systematic interviews is particularly true of the last four chapters. Many of the 187 survey respondents spent additional time covering a wide range of topics they saw to be important to agricultural policymaking. In addition, 267 other respondents were sought out for background information or volunteered to provide it. These interviews were completed between January 1989 and March 1993. These respondents include members of Congress, former members, congressional staff, officials from several federal agencies, and numerous private-sector individuals. The latter include lobbyists, corporate executives, grassroots activists, and consultants. The contribution of these individuals to the second part of the book, especially, is invaluable. Particularly helpful is information and interview data from the offices of the four legislative leaders: Mr. Dole, Mr. Foley, Mr. Michels, and Mr. Mitchell.

CONGRESSIONAL SURVEY

1. At the onset would you share with me some of your perceptions about agricultural policy? Probe for three.
   a. personal attachment:
      1. strongly supportive _____
      2. supportive   _____
      3. mixed   _____
      4. opposed   _____

      5. strongly opposed   _____

      6. no real feelings   _____
        (push choice)

    b. overall perception:

      1. seen as complex   _____

      2. seen as farm only   _____

      3. seen as scam   _____

      4. seen as confusing   _____

      5. other _____
        (force selection)

    c. comparatively ranked:

      1. very important   _____

      2. important   _____

      3. don't know   _____

      4. unimportant   _____

      5. very unimportant   _____
        (force selection)

2. Could you rank for me what you personally feel are the three most important areas of agriculture policy? Present list.

    a. farm income/price policy   _____

    b. farm credit   _____

    c. international trade and
       world food   _____

    d. farm and food taxes   _____

    e. family farm protection   _____

    f. animal/plant regulation   _____

    g. environmental protection   _____

    h. energy   _____

    i. resource conservation   _____

    j. forestry   _____

    k. nutrition/hunger   _____

    l. research and development   _____

    m. rural development/poverty   _____

    n. animal welfare   _____

    o. other _____   _____

3. Do you feel any of the above are out of place or inappropriate to agriculture policy? yes _____ no _____
Which? _____ _____ _____ _____ _____

4. Could you briefly explain how the internationalizing of markets and

the GATT affects your own decision-making? Probe, select best choice.
greatly _____, somewhat _____, not at all _____.

5. Are there any other areas of agricultural policy that concern you and your office? yes _____ no _____
Which? _____

6. Which specific issues in these various policy areas, if any, do you consider to have been especially time consuming or to have involved your staff at great length?

_____, _____, _____,
_____, _____, _____,
_____, _____.

7. Which ones, if any, do you consider to have the highest priority with (the member)?

_____, _____, _____, _____,
_____, _____, _____, _____.

Why? How? What did your office do on these issues? _____

_____
_____.

8. Why was it difficult for our project team to learn from printed sources of your involvement on some of these issues? a. no publicity value _____, b. unimportant to district _____, c. too touchy to publicize _____, d. promised others to be discrete _____, e. other, explain

_____
_____.

9. On the issues that your office initiated, which source of information is most responsible for your issue selection? Present list. a. constituents _____, b. interest groups/lobbyists _____, c. agricultural professionals _____, d. USDA _____, e. other government agencies _____, f. news media _____, g. professional/technical media _____.

10. How about in determining your position on these issues?
a. _____, b. _____, c. _____, d. _____, e. _____,
f. _____, g. _____.

11. I want you to evaluate the overall importance of each of those sources for me. But first could you rank them? a. _____, b. _____, c. _____, d. _____, e. _____, f. _____, g. _____.

12. Now let's talk about why each is important, or alternatively not. Just give me your thoughts. Probe for: a. who they talk to, b. why they do

so, c. what information (political intelligence, policy analysis, public opinion) is used, and, d. what problems they see in being responsive to each. (Hold out list of choices, then probe for others.)

District/state influence?

Interest groups/lobbyists?

Agricultural experts?

Agency officials and reports?

Media? Probe for local/state versus national press distinctions. Probe for professional versus general media distinctions.

13. Given your comments, how do you feel about the often expressed view that Washington interest groups drive the agricultural policy process? Strongly agree _____, agree _____, don't know _____, disagree _____, strongly disagree _____.

14. Do you rely on other legislators to help you select issues and prioritize them? Always _____, frequently _____, sometimes _____, never _____. Probe as to why.

15. Given your position and home state, are any of the following legislators helpful in issue selection for you? (Identify short list here.) Can you name a few others that are particularly important? _____, _____, _____, _____, _____.
Why? _____

16. Could you explain to me how congressional committees affect one another if indeed you believe they do? Probe for two.
   a. 1. consider similar problems   _____
      2. issues overlap   _____
      3. legislative solutions overlap   _____
      4. interpersonal contacts responsible _____
      5. leadership involvement   _____
      6. rarely happens   _____
   b. 1. very important   _____
      2. important   _____
      3. can't judge   _____
      4. unimportant   _____
      5. very unimportant   _____

17. (If relevant) Could you describe for me how your work on (list committees) affects your work on (list other committees)?
Does _____, does not _____. Probe. _____

18. Is the leadership playing a particularly important role in modern agricultural policy? Yes _____, no _____. Probe for:

specific issues   _____
broad policy goals   _____
partisan gains   _____
White House initiatives _____
interest group gains   _____
leadership goals   _____

19. Tell me briefly about the influence of the White House on your priority issues. Very important _____, important _____, don't know _____, unimportant _____, very unimportant _____. Probe as to why.

20. Given your comments, how do you feel about the often expressed view that the agricultural committees control Congress on agricultural policy? Strongly agree _____, agree _____, don't know _____, disagree _____, strongly disagree.

21. Is there anything about the operation of Congress that I've missed that is important to your agricultural policy priorities or agricultural policy in general? Probe as to what and why. Probe as to whether this is a change. _____

LA background (repeated for each staff surrogate)

22. From state: yes _____, no _____.

23. Years in Congress: 1–2 _____, 3–5 _____, 6–10 _____, 11 or more _____.

24. Previous agriculture background: yes _____, no _____. Explain.

Table A.1.   Legislative Activity on Behalf of Agricultural Domain Issues

Chamber	Number of Respondents	Number of Members Active in Domain (percentage of total)[a]	Number of Members with Priority Attention (percentage of total)	Average Number of Issues[a]	
				Given Time (n)	Prioritized (n)
House	84	77 (92%)	72 (86%)	2.2 (187)	1.7 (144)
Senate	29	27 (93%)	27 (93%)	2.4 (69)	2.0 (57)
Total	113	104 (92%)	99 (88%)	2.3 (256)	1.8 (201)

[a]equals all issues/all legislators

Table A.2.   Agricultural Issues Attached to Particular Policy Vehicles, in and outside the Domain[a]

Vehicle Types and Tactics	Time-Consuming Issues			Priority Issues		
	All Issues	Wins	Winning %	All Issues	Wins	Winning %
Domain Vehicles (with column totals)[b]	(229)	(163)	(71)	(187)	(137)	(73)
Farm bill language, modify services/regulations	135	102	76	114	83	73
Farm bill floor amendments	7	1	14	3	1	33
Farm bill sections, determine principal content	16	12	75	16	12	75
Language in other bills, modify services/regulations	15	9	60	11	6	55
Amendments to other bills	2	0	0	0	0	
Sections of other bills, determine principal content	4	4	100	4	4	100
Appropriations language	23	18	78	19	17	89
Budget language	4	1	25	2	1	50
USDA regulatory decisions	17	12	71	14	10	71
USDA oversight actions	3	1	33	2	1	50
GAO investigations	3	3	100	2	2	100
Nondomain vehicles (with column totals)	(27)	(14)	(52)	(14)	(9)	(64)
Other omnibus bills, any provisions	10	5	50	5	3	60
Single-purpose bills, any provision	7	5	71	4	3	75
Other agency regulatory decisions	7	3	43	5	3	60
Other agency oversight actions	3	1	33	0	0	
Total	256	177	69	201	146	73

[a]Where last attached; numerous issues were attached earlier to other vehicles.
[b]Although some domain overlaps occurs, all authorizing bills and agency operations are at least concurrently under the jurisdiction of the agriculture committees.

Table A.3. Winning on Time-consuming and Member-priority Issues

Types of Issues	All Issues	Wins	Winning Percentage
Time-consuming Issues	256	177	69.1
Member-priority Issues[a]	201	146	72.6
Issues that members did not prioritize	58	34	58.6
All Issues	263	183	69.6

[a]Seven of these issues did not consume extensive staff time.

Table A.4. Maintaining and Originating Behavior, by Issues and by Members

Types of Behavior	Number of Issues		Number of Members		Number of Issue Wins	
	Time-Consuming Issues	Priority Issues	Time-Consuming Issues	Priority Issues	Time-Consuming Issues	Priority Issues
Maintaining behavior only	162 (63%)	123 (61%)	35 (31%)	28 (25%)	109 (62%)	87 (60%)
Originating behavior only	94 (37%)	78 (39%)	14 (12%)	18 (16%)	68 (38%)	59 (40%)
Both			55 (49%)	41 (36%)		
Neither			9 (8%)	14 (12%)		
Total	256 (100%)	201 (100%)	113 (100%)	113 (99%)	177 (100%)	146 (100%)

Table A.5. Differences in Initiating Behavior, by Congressional Chamber

Type of Behavior	House of Representatives[a]		Senate[a]		Total[a]	
	Time-Consuming Issues	Priority Issues	Time-Consuming Issues	Priority Issues	Time-Consuming Issues	Priority Issues
Number of active members	77.00	72.00	27.00	27.00	104.00	99.00
Average number of issues per member[b]	2.43	2.00	2.56	2.11	2.46	2.03
Average number of wins per member	1.70	1.44	1.78	1.55	1.72	1.47
Average number of maintaining issues per member	1.53	1.19	1.62	1.37	1.58	1.24
Average number of maintaining wins	1.03	0.83	1.15	1.00	1.04	0.87
Average number of originating issues per member	0.90	0.81	0.92	0.74	0.90	0.79
Average number of originating wins	0.66	0.61	0.63	0.56	0.65	0.60
Average number of farm bill issues per member	1.49	1.29	1.59	1.48	1.52	1.34
Average number of issues in other bills per member	0.32	0.22	0.48	0.30	0.37	0.24
Average number of appropriations/budget issues per member	0.27	0.24	0.22	0.15	0.26	0.21
Average number of administrative and GAO issues per member	0.34	0.25	0.26	0.19	0.32	0.23

[a] n = 84, 29, and 113, respectively in the House, the Senate, and in total.
[b] Includes only active members.

Table A.6. Types of Agricultural Issues Initiated by Individual Members of Congress, by Chamber

Chamber of Initiator	Farm Benefit		Rural		Environmental		Nutrition		Trade		Miscellaneous		Total	
	Time-Consuming	Priority	Time-Consuming	Priority	Time-Consuming	Priority	Time-Consuming	Priority	Time-Consuming	Priority	Time-Consuming	Priority	Time-Consuming	Priority
House of Representatives	85	70	11	8	33	23	7	6	23	17	27	21	186	145
Senate	27	24	2	1	13	11	0	0	12	12	16	8	70	56
Total	112	94	13	9	46	34	7	6	35	29	43	29	256	201

Table A.7. Originating and Maintaining Issues Initiated by Individual Members of Congress, by Chamber

Chamber of Initiator	Farm Benefit		Rural		Environmental		Nutrition		Trade		Miscellaneous		Total	
	Origi-nating	Main-taining	Origi-nating	Main-taining	Origi-nating	Main-taining	Origi-nating	Main-taining	Origi-nating	Main-taining	Origi-nating	Main-taining	Origi-nating	Main-taining
House of Representatives	4	81	0	11	33	0	7	0	18	5	6	21	68	118
Senate	3	24	0	2	13	0	0	0	9	3	1	15	26	44
Total	7	105	0	13	46	0	7	0	27	8	7	36	94	162

Note: Typed by time-consuming issues. If priority issues are used instead, total originating issue-type numbers would be, respectively, 5, 0, 34, 6, 23, 3, and 73. Maintaining ones would be 89, 9, 0, 0, 6, 27, and 128.

Table A.8. Members Who Initiated Different Types of Agricultural Issues, by Chamber

Chamber of Initiator	Farm Benefit		Rural		Environmental		Nutrition		Trade		Miscellaneous		Total	
	Time-Consuming	Priority	Time-Consuming	Priority	Time-Consuming	Priority	Time-Consuming	Priority	Time-Consuming	Priority	Time-Consuming	Priority	Time-Consuming	Priority
House of Representatives	60	56	8	7	20	15	5	5	18	13	18	13	77	72
Senate	24	22	2	1	6	6	0	0	10	10	9	6	27	27
Total	84	78	10	8	26	21	5	5	28	23	27	19	104	99

Table A.9. Members Who Initiated Farm Issues, by Other Issue Involvement

Types of Issues	Time-Consuming Issues	Priority Issues
Farm-benefit issues only	26	25
Farm-benefit and any other issue	58	53
Other issues only	20	21
Farm-benefit and trade issues	25	19
Trade issues only	3	3
Farm-benefit and environmental issues	6	7
Environmental issues only	12	9
Farm-benefit and rural, nutrition, or miscellaneous issues	37	29
Rural/nutrition/miscellaneous issues only	5	3

Table A.10. Winning Issues, by Beneficiaries and Purpose

Type of Beneficiary/Purpose	Number of Issues (winning percentage)	
	Time-Consuming	Member-Priority
Farm-benefit	78 (70)	68 (72)
Rural	7 (54)	6 (67)
Environmental	32 (70)	25 (74)
Nutrition	5 (71)	4 (67)
Trade	25 (71)	22 (76)
Miscellaneous	30 (69)	21 (72)
Total	177 (69)	146 (73)

Table A.11.   Likelihood of Congressional District Characteristics Predicting Issue Involvement by Issue Type, Logit Results

Type of Issue	Constant	Determinant Variables			X^2	Percent Predicted Correctly
		Farm Population	Population Density	White-Collar Population		
Farm benefits	.219	.153[a]	.000	.004	7.0	74
	(1.206)	(.067)	(.000)	(.033)	(p<.1)	
Rural	-.835	.115[b]	-.000	-.060	7.8	90
	(1.695)	(.059)	(.000)	(.049)	(p<.05)	
Environmental	-1.892	-.132[a]	-.000	.040	7.4	75
	(1.327)	(.066)	(.000)	(.035)	(p<.1)	
Nutrition	-9.849	.080	.0002[c]	.167[b]	9.9	95
	(3.716)	(.110)	(.000)	(.086)	(p<.05)	
Trade	-1.387	.011	-.001	.020	9.6	73
	(1.408)	(.048)	(.000)	(.039)	(p<.05)	

[a]Significant at a = .05
[b]Significant at a = .1
[c]Significant at a = .001

Table A.12. Members Who Initiate Commodity Specific Farm-Benefit Issues, by State Interest[a]

| Commodity Interest | Number of Members According to State Ranking in Commodity Cash Receipts | | |
	Top Ten States	Next Ten Ranked States	Lowest Ranked Thirty States
Northern Cash Crops			
Corn	3	0	0
Soybeans	2	1	0
Wheat	7	1	1
Southern Cash Crops			
Cotton	5	0	0
Rice	3	0	0
Peanuts	2	0	0
Tobacco	3	0	0
Other Commodities			
Cattle and calves	6	1	0
Hogs and pigs	2	1	0
Sheep and lambs	2	0	0
Broilers	2	0	0
Fruits and vegetables[b]	11	1	2
Dairy	8	2	1
Sugar	4	0	0
Miscellaneous	5	0	0
Total	65	6	4

[a]Time-consuming issues only.
[b]Includes wine. Top ten ranking in this and the final category is by individual commodity, not the entire grouping of crops and livestock.

Source: U.S. Department of Agriculture, National Agricultural Statistics Service for year ending November 30, 1991.

Table A.13. Likelihood of Production Cost Index Predicting Issue Involvement on Market-Oriented Versus Production Control Issues, Logit Results

Type of Issue	Constant	Production Cost Variable	X^2	Percent Predicted Correctly
Marketed-oriented issues	−1.218 (.248)	−.573 (.671)	.80	79
Production control issues	−3.390 (.587)	2.474[a] (.760)	11.2 ($p<.01$)	92

[a]Significant at a = .001

Table A.14. Congressional Use and Evaluation of Information Sources, by Member[a]

Type of Information Source	Most Important for Issue Selection	Most Important for Determining Position	Most Trusted Information Source	Overall Ranking as Most Important	Overall Ranking as Next Most Important	Offices that Seek this Type of Information for Routine Issue Selection Advice
Constituent[b]	85	65	55	87	18	71
Organized interests[b]	8	22	13	17	60	58
Both of the above[c]	12	15	NA	NA	NA	NA
USDA	1	1	1	2	12	8
Other agencies	1	2	1	2	1	1
Other domain professionals	1	2	3	2	13	16
News media	2	1	1	1	1	1
Pro-technical media	0	0	1	1	6	1
Total[d]	110	108	75	112	111	103

[a] Includes all issues, time-consuming plus the few remaining priority ones.
[b] Constituents were typed as those who lived or worked in the district. Interest group representatives were typed as lobbyists and other activists who did business in Washington. The clear distinction was between the politics of places and the politics of organizations from the Washington community.
[c] The only multiple answers per office, for different issues, mentioned both constituents and lobbyist, none of the others.
[d] Includes other decision making where selection and position taking were irrelevant; some referred to issues older than those considered recent.

Table A.15. Organizational Characteristics of Primary Constituent Informants, by Issue Type for Each Member

Issue Type	Percentage
Farm-benefit (n = 84)	
Farm group activists[a]	11
Nonactivist farmers[b]	81
USDA employees	6
Land-grant employees	2
Multipublic discussions[c]	0
Rural (n = 11)	
Local government officials	91
Business leaders	9
Multipublic discussions[c]	0
Trade (n = 31)	
Agribusiness leaders	84
Other business leaders	6
Farm group leaders	10
Multipublic discussions[c]	0
Nutrition (n = 6)	
Local government officials	16
Community activists	83
Multipublic discussions[c]	0
Environmental (n = 28)	
Community activists	32
Local government officials	7
Business leaders	4
Individual farmers	7
Multipublic discussions[c]	50

[a]Farm group activists were subtyped as those farmers who were acknowledged by respondents for their group affiliation but local, non-Washington leadership.
[b]Nonactivist farmers were subtyped as those who might be group members but were seen by respondents as having independent positions in their advice and counsel.
[c]Includes opinions expressed in public forums as opposed to specific views of known constituents.

Table A.16. Types of Agricultural Policy Domain Issues Initiated by Committee Assignment, by Number of Initiating Members

Members' Committee Assignment	Farm Benefit	Rural	Trade	Nutrition	Environment	Miscellaneous
Agriculture (n = 20)	16[a]	1	7	1	3	1
Environment and Interior (n = 20)	13	7	7	0	3[a]	2
Energy and Commerce[b] (n = 17)	12	3	5	0	7[a]	1
Foreign Affairs and Relations (n = 9)	6	0	1[a]	1	2	1
House Hunger (Select) (n = 8)	5	1	4	1[a]	1	1
Other (n = 56)	47	3	12	4	15	4
Total (104)	84	11	31	6	28	10

Note: Figure may not total 100 because of overlapping or multiple committee assignments.
[a] These issues or issue have been central to the traditional jurisdiction of committee in question.
[b] Includes three committees, two House and one Senate.

Table A.17.   Committee Member Reliance on Collegial Advice for Agricultural Issue Selection and Prioritization

Members' Committee Assignment	Number Who Always Rely on Collegial Advice	Number Who Use State Delegation Advice	Number Who Use Agriculture or Interior Committee Advice	Number Who Use Partisan Advice[a]	Number Who Use Regional, Urban, or Ethnic Advice[a]
Agriculture (n=20)	11	7	5	3	4
Environment and Interior (n=20)	14	8	3	2	4
Energy and Commerce (n=17)	12	10	1	1	2
Foreign Affairs and Relations (n=9)	7	3	1	0	0
House Hunger (select) (n=8)	7	1	5	2	0
Other (n=56)	32	41	2	3	7
Total (n=104)	71	69	11[b]	9	15

[a]Refers to use by a member of any committee if the respondent saw that use as being relevant to agricultural issues (their choice and identification).
[b]Ten of these emphasized subcommittee-level contact.

Table A.18.   Members Who Initiated Issues, by Electoral Margins and Beneficiaries Served

Winning Electoral Margin of Issue Initiators[a]	No Initiatives	Single Beneficiary Initiatives	Multiple Beneficiary Initiatives	Total
50–54.9 percent	1	4	4	9
55–59.9 percent	1	11	13	25
Greater than 60 percent	7	29	43	79
Total	9	44	60	113

[a]Includes last two congressional elections except where member has run only once, major party vote only; mean average.

NOTES

PREFACE

1. Kenneth A. Shepsle, "The Changing Textbook Congress," in *Can the Government Govern?* ed. John E. Chubb and Paul E. Peterson (Washington, D.C.: Brookings, 1989), pp. 238–266.

2. For a discussion of the politics of places, see Robert H. Salisbury, "The Politics of Geography in America," in *The Idea of Place*, ed. Milica Banjanin (St. Louis: Washington University, 1983), pp. 1–10. The concept of place occupies the core of Salisbury's work in the mid-1990s. William S. White also wrote of the House as dominated by places, *Home Place: The Story of the U.S. House of Representatives* (Boston: Houghton-Mifflin, 1965); a related work is Michael B. Berkman, *The State Roots of National Politics: Congress and the Tax Agenda, 1978–1986* (Pittsburgh: University of Pittsburgh Press, 1993).

3. William P. Browne, *Private Interests, Public Policy, and American Agriculture* (Lawrence: University Press of Kansas, 1988).

4. Niches are developed at length in William P. Browne, "Organized Interests and Their Issue Niches: A Search for Pluralism in a Policy Domain," *Journal of Politics* 52 (May 1990): 477–509, and his "Issue Niches and the Limits of Interest Group Influence," in *Interest Group Politics*, 3d ed., ed. Allan J. Cigler and Burdett A. Loomis (Washington, D.C.: Congressional Quarterly Press, 1991), pp. 345–370.

5. For a review of the knowledge base, see Bruce L. Gardner, "Changing Economic Perspectives on the Farm Problem," *Journal of Economic Literature* 30 (March 1992): 62–101.

6. This can be seen in the widespread adherence to what can be called the Cochrane/Hathaway prediction of majority rule and attendant agricultural policy decline; see Willard J. Cochrane, *Farm Prices: Myth and Reality* (Minneapolis: University of Minnesota Press, 1958), and Dale E. Hathaway, "The Implications of Changing Political Power in Agriculture," in *Agricultural Policy in an Affluent Society*, ed. Vernon W. Ruttan et al. (New York: Norton, 1969), pp. 63–68.

7. Public choice agricultural economists often are distinguished within their discipline from institutional agricultural economists by their adherence to a rent-seeking, economics-of-politics paradigm. Those who study policy rather than constitutional economics tend to follow three University of Chicago scholars: Becker, Peltzman, and Stigler. See, for example, George J. Stigler, "Free Riders and Collective Action," *Bell Journal of Economics and Management Science* 2 (Autumn 1974): 359–365; Sam Peltzman, "Toward a More General Theory of

Regulation," *Journal of Law and Economics* 19 (August 1976): 211–240, and his "Constituent Interests and Congressional Voting," *Journal of Law and Economics* 27 (April 1984): 181–200; Gary S. Becker, "A Theory of Competition among Pressure Groups for Political Influence," *Quarterly Journal of Economics* 98 (August 1983): 371–400, and his "Public Policies, Pressure Groups, and Dead Weight Costs," *Journal of Public Economics* 28 (December 1985): 330–347. For an enlightening exception to this type of analysis, see Gordon C. Rausser, "Predatory versus Productive Government: The Case of U.S. Agricultural Policies," *Journal of Economic Perspectives* 6 (Summer 1992): 133–157.

8. Joel Solkoff, *The Politics of Food: The Decline of Agriculture and the Rise of Agribusiness in America* (San Francisco: Sierra Club, 1985); Marty Strange, *Family Farming: A New Economic Vision* (Lincoln: University of Nebraska Press, 1988).

9. Much of that effort has taken place under preliminary authorization of a Rural Development Administration within the U.S. Department of Agriculture, but other networks exist. On rural poverty, see Rural Sociological Society Task Force, ed., *Persistent Poverty in Rural America* (Boulder, Colo.: Westview, 1993).

CHAPTER 1. CONGRESS IN A POSTREFORM ERA

1. Roger H. Davidson, "The Emergence of the Postreform Congress," in *The Postreform Congress*, ed. Roger H. Davidson (New York: St. Martins Press, 1992), pp. 3–23.

2. Richard F. Fenno, Jr., *Home Style* (Boston: Little, Brown, 1978). There is ample evidence that this change has been coming for some time. Julius Turner, *Party and Constituency: Pressures on Congress* (Baltimore: Johns Hopkins University Press, 1950) which is revised by the coauthorship of Edward V. Scheier, Jr., in 1970; Charles L. Clapp, *The Congressman: His Work as He Sees It* (Washington, D.C.: The Brookings Institution, 1963), especially chap. 8.

3. Kenneth A. Shepsle, "The Changing Textbook Congress," in *Can the Government Govern?* ed. John E. Chubb and Paul E. Peterson (Washington, D.C.: Brookings, 1989), pp. 252–256.

4. See comments by Richard F. Fenno, Jr., *When Incumbency Fails: The Senate Career of Mark Andrews* (Washington, D.C.: Congressional Quarterly Press, 1992), p. x.

5. Richard F. Fenno, Jr., "The House Appropriations Committee as a Political System: The Problem of Integration," *American Political Science Review* 66 (June 1962): 310–324; and his *The Power of the Purse* (Boston: Little, Brown, 1966).

6. Richard F. Fenno, Jr., "The House of Representatives and Federal Aid to Education," in *New Perspectives on the House of Representatives*, ed. Robert L. Peabody and Nelson W. Polsby (Chicago: Rand McNally, 1963), pp. 237–270, and his *Congressmen in Committees* (Boston: Little, Brown, 1973).

7. Fenno, *Congressmen in Committees*, p. 276.

8. Barbara Sinclair, *The Transformation of the U.S. Senate* (Baltimore: Johns

Hopkins University Press, 1989); David W. Rohde, *Parties and Leaders in The Postreform Congress* (Chicago: University of Chicago Press, 1991). On individualistic senators, see Fred R. Harris, *Deadlock or Decision: The U.S. Senate and the Rise of National Politics* (New York: Oxford University Press, 1993).

9. Rohde, *Parties and Leaders in the Postreform House*, pp. 17–39, his "Committee Reform in the House of Representatives and the Subcommittee Bill of Rights," in *Changing Congress: The Committee System*, ed. Norman J. Ornstein (Philadelphia: American Academy of Political and Social Science, 1974), pp. 39–47; Davidson, *The Postreform Congress*. For more on reform, see Leroy N. Rieselbach, *Congressional Reform: The Changing Modern Congress* (Washington, D.C.: Congressional Quarterly Press, 1993).

10. For an extraordinarily well-integrated review that contributed heavily to the following pages, see Shepsle, "The Changing Textbook Congress," p. 248.

11. Ibid., p. 253; William P. Browne, "The Fragmented and Meandering Politics of Agriculture," in *U.S. Agriculture in a Global Setting: An Agenda for the Future*, ed. M. Ann Tutwiler (Washington, D.C.: Resources for the Future, 1988), p. 141.

12. Steven S. Smith, *Call to Order: Floor Politics in the House and Senate* (Washington, D.C.: Brookings, 1989), esp. p. 250. On early action, see Smith and Christopher J. Deering, *Committees in Congress*, 2d ed. (Washington, D.C.: Congressional Quarterly Press, 1990).

13. Roger H. Davidson, "The New Centralization on Capitol Hill," *Review of Politics* 50 (Summer 1988): 345–364; Shepsle, "The Changing Textbook Congress," pp. 254–256. For a study of how these powers were applied by Speaker Jim Wright, see John M. Barry, *The Ambition and the Power: A True Story of Washington* (New York: Viking, 1989). Special Rules in the House changed as well. See Stanley Bach and Steven S. Smith, *Managing Uncertainty in the House of Representatives: Adaptation and Innovation in Special Rules* (Washington, D.C.: Brookings, 1988).

14. Barbara Sinclair, "The Speaker's Task Force in the Post-Reform House of Representatives," *American Political Science Review* 75 (June 1981): 397–410.

15. Shepsle, "The Changing Textbook Congress," p. 255; Daniel J. Palazzolo, "From Decentralization to Centralization: Members' Changing Expectations for House Leaders," in *The Postreform Congress*, pp. 112–126.

16. Sinclair, *The Transformation of the U.S. Senate*, and her "The Transformation of the U.S. Senate: Toward a Rational Choice Explanation of Institutional Change," in *Home Style and Washington Work: Studies of Congressional Politics*, ed. Morris P. Fiorina and David W. Rohde (Ann Arbor: University of Michigan Press, 1989), pp. 113–136; Steven S. Smith, "The Senate in the Postreform Era," in *The Postreform Congress*, pp. 169–192. The "old Senate" can be seen in Donald R. Matthews, *U.S. Senators and Their World* (Chapel Hill: University of North Carolina Press, 1960).

17. Sinclair, "The Transformation of the U.S. Senate," p. 128.

18. Burdett A. Loomis, "The Congressional Office as a Small Business: New Members Set Up Shop," *Publius* 9 (Summer 1979): 35–55; Robert H. Salisbury and Kenneth A. Shepsle, "U.S. Congressman as Enterprise," *Legislative Studies Quarterly* 6 (November 1981): 559–576. See also Salisbury and Shepsle,

"Congressional Staff Turnover and the Ties-That-Bind," *American Political Science Review* 75 (June 1981): 381–425. For numbers of congressional staff over time see Norman J. Ornstein, Thomas E. Mann, and Michael J. Malbin, *Vital Statistics on Congress, 1991–1992* (Washington, D.C.: Congressional Quarterly, 1992), p. 127.

19. These are 1989 figures, with the current House somewhat lower. See Ornstein, Mann, and Malbin, *Vital Statistics on Congress, 1991–1992*, pp. 124–129.

20. Fenno, *Home Style*, pp. 31–170; see also Morris P. Fiorina and David W. Rohde, "Richard Fenno's Research Agenda and the Study of Congress," in Fiorina and Rohde, *Home Style and Washington Work*, p. 9.

21. John Kingdon, *Congressmen's Voting Decisions* (New York: Harper and Row, 1973), pp. 46–53; Fenno, *Home Style*, pp. 141–157.

22. Harris, *Deadlock or Decision*, pp. 33–34. Other studies note how difficult it is to get national airtime. See Stephen Hess, *The Government-Press Connection: Press Officers and Their Offices* (Washington, D.C.: Brookings, 1984); Timothy Cook, "Press Secretaries and Media Strategies in the House of Representatives: Deciding Whom to Pursue," *American Journal of Political Science* 32 (November 1988): 1047–1069.

23. Among the raft of materials discussing this, the most interesting and current are by House member and political scientist David E. Price, *The Congressional Experience: A View From the Hill* (Boulder, Colo.: Westview, 1992), pp. 73–90; and an edited yet well-integrated volume by Allen D. Hertzke and Ronald M. Peters, Jr., ed., *The Atomistic Congress: An Interpretation of Congressional Change* (Armonk, N.Y.: M. E. Sharpe, 1992). see also Alan Ehrenhalt, *The United States of Ambition: Politicians, Power, and the Pursuit of Office* (New York: Random House, 1991). The White House perspective on congressional individualism can be seen in Samuel Kernell, *Going Public: New Strategies of Presidential Leadership*, 2d ed. (Washington, D.C.: Congressional Quarterly Press, 1993). He sees "atomistic individualism," a term apparently coined in the first edition.

24. David R. Mayhew, *Congress: The Electoral Connection* (New Haven, Conn.: Yale University Press, 1974), p. 73. For an analysis that shows considerable constituent activity on the 1990 Clean Air Act, see Richard E. Cohen, *Washington At Work: Back Rooms and Clean Air* (New York: Macmillan, 1992); for excellent examples pertaining to agriculture see Fenno, *When Incumbency Fails*, pp. 8–9.

25. Barbara Sinclair, *Congressional Realignment, 1925–1978* (Austin: University of Texas Press, 1982); her *The Transformation of the U.S. Senate*, pp. 51–70.

26. William Riordan, *Plunkitt of Tammany Hall* (New York: Dutton, 1963). For a contrasting perspective, see James Sterling Young, *The Washington Community, 1800–1828* (New York: Columbia University Press, 1966).

27. Harris, *Deadlock or Decision*, p. 64. The term was used first by Jeffrey M. Berry, *The Interest Group Society*, 2d ed. (Glenview, Ill.: Scott, Foresman/Little, Brown, 1989), p. 16.

28. Or, perhaps, the myth expresses how it is feared society is organized, as is

the trepidation associated with many myths of authority. Myths, used as such, have policy importance. William P. Browne, Jerry R. Skees, Louis E. Swanson, Paul B. Thompson, and Laurian J. Unnevehr, *Sacred Cows and Hot Potatoes: Agrarian Myths in Agricultural Policy* (Boulder, Colo.: Westview, 1992), p. 5.

29. For two conceptual reviews of the institutional network approach see Keith E. Hamm, "Patterns of Influence Among Committees, Agencies, and Interest Groups," *Legislative Studies Quarterly* 8 (August 1983): 379–426; William P. Browne, "Policymaking in the American States: Examining Institutional Variables from a Subsystems Perspective," *American Politics Quarterly* 15 (January 1987): 47–86.

30. Hedrick Smith, *The Power Game: How Washington Works* (New York: Random House, 1988). The book served as the basis for a TV docudrama available through PBS Video, *The Power Game* (New York: Phillip Barton Productions, 1989).

31. Robert H. Salisbury, John P. Heinz, Robert L. Nelson, and Edward O. Laumann, "Triangles, Networks, and Hollow Cores: The Complex Geometry of Washington Interest Representation," in *The Politics of Interests: Interest Groups Transformed*, ed. Mark P. Petracca (Boulder, Colo.: Westview, 1992), p. 131.

32. For "the classics" see Ernest S. Griffith, *The Impasse of Democracy* (New York: Harrison-Wilton, 1939); Douglass Cater, *Power in Washington* (New York: Random House, 1964); J. Leiper Freeman, *The Political Process: Executive Bureau-Legislative Committee Relations*, rev. ed. (Orig. ed., 1955; New York: Random House, 1965); A. Lee Fritschler, *Smoking and Politics: Policymaking and the Federal Bureaucracy* (Englewood Cliffs, N.J.: Prentice-Hall, 1969), revised in three later editions; John A. Ferejohn, *Pork Barrel Politics: Rivers and Harbors Legislation, 1947–1968* (Stanford: Stanford University Press, 1974).

33. E. E. Schattschneider also saw interest groups as the dominant players. See *Politics, Pressures, and the Tariff: A Study of Free Enterprise in Pressure Politics as Shown in the 1929–1930 Revision of the Tariff* (New York: Prentice-Hall, 1935), and *The Semi-Sovereign People: A Realist's View of Democracy in America* (New York: Holt, Rinehart and Winston, 1960). An interesting article that shows changes in "iron triangles" that are determined by what Schattschneider describes as a fight is William G. Johnson, "Housing Policy Under the Reagan Presidency: The Demise of an Iron-Triangle," *Policy Studies Review* 10 (Winter 1991–1992): 69–87.

34. For cozy, see Roger H. Davidson, "Breaking Up Those 'Cozy Triangles': An Impossible Dream?" in *Legislative Reform and Public Policy*, ed. Susan Welch and John G. Peters (New York: Praeger, 1977), pp. 30–53, and his "Subcommittee Government: New Channels for Policy Making," in *The New Congress*, ed. Thomas E. Mann and Norman J. Ornstein (Washington, D.C.: American Enterprise Institute, 1981), pp. 99–133.

35. Each of the classics cited in note 32 represents that negative view of closed networks. Fritschler, for example, sees most change possible "while the subsystem is in a state of disarray." See *Smoking and Politics*, 4th ed., 1989, p. 5.

36. A quite useful book serves as an example of tinkering. See Randall B. Ripley and Grace A. Franklin, *Congress, the Bureaucracy, and Public Policy,*

5th ed. (Pacific Grove, Calif.: Brooks/Cole, 1991). So does Martin J. Smith, *Pressure, Power and Policy: State Autonomy and Policy Networks in Britain and the United States* (Pittsburgh: University of Pittsburgh Press, 1993).

37. Grant McConnell, *Private Power and American Democracy* (New York: Alfred A. Knopf, 1966); Arnold M. Rose, *The Power Structure: Political Process in American Society* (London: Oxford University Press, 1967).

38. John P. Heinz, Edward O. Laumann, Robert H. Salisbury, and Robert L. Nelson, "Inner Circles or Hollow Cores? Elite Networks in National Policy Systems," *Journal of Politics* 52 (May 1990): 356–390. For more see Heinz, Laumann, Nelson, and Salisbury, *The Hollow Core: Private Interests in National Policy Making* (Cambridge, Mass.: Harvard University Press, 1993).

39. Thomas L. Gais, Mark A. Peterson, and Jack L. Walker, "Interest Groups, Iron Triangles, and Representative Institutions in American National Government," *British Journal of Political Science* 14 (April 1984): 161–185; Salisbury et al., "Triangles, Networks, and Hollow Cores, p. 147; Heinz et al., *The Hollow Core*.

40. Hugh Heclo, "Issue Networks and the Executive Establishment," in *The New American Political System*, ed. Anthony King (Washington D.C.: American Enterprise Institute, 1978), pp. 87–124.

41. Charles O. Jones, "American Politics and the Organization of Energy Decision Making," *Annual Review of Energy* 4 (1979): 99–121; A. Grant Jordan, "Iron Triangles, Woolly Corporatism and Elastic Nets: Images of the Policy Process," *Journal of Public Policy* 1 (February 1981): 95–123; Edward O. Laumann and David Knoke, *The Organizational State: Social Choice in National Policy Domains* (Madison: University of Wisconsin Press, 1987); William T. Gormley, Jr., "Regulatory Issue Networks in a Federal System," *Polity* 18 (Summer 1986): 595–620; Jeffrey M. Berry, "Subgovernments, Issue Networks, and Political Conflict," in *Remaking American Politics*, ed. Richard Harris and Sidney Milkus (Boulder, Colo.: Westview, 1989), pp. 239–260; David Knoke, *Political Networks: The Structural Perspective* (New York: Cambridge University Press, 1990); James A. Thurber, "Dynamics of Policy Subsystems in American Politics," in *Interest Group Politics*, 3d ed., ed. Allan J. Cigler and Burdett A. Loomis (Washington, D.C.: Congressional Quarterly Press, 1991), pp. 319–343.

42. Jeffrey M. Berry touches on these strategies in "Beyond Citizen Participation: Effective Advocacy Before Administrative Agencies," *Journal of Applied Behavioral Sciences* 17 (October 1981): 463–477; and his *Feeding Hungry People: Rulemaking in the Food Stamp Program* (New Brunswick, N.J.: Rutgers University Press, 1985). Christopher J. Bosso is far more explicit in *Pesticides and Politics: The Life Cycle of a Public Issue* (Pittsburgh, Pa.: University of Pittsburgh Press, 1987); for changes in the environmental lobby, see his "Adaptation and Change in the Environmental Movement," in *Interest Group Politics*, 3d ed., pp. 151–176.

43. Don F. Hadwiger's analysis remains the seminal work on public sector response on what can be seen as issues of a closed network. See *The Politics of Agricultural Research* (Lincoln: University of Nebraska Press, 1982). For follow up, see William P. Browne, *Private Interests, Public Policy, and American*

Agriculture (Lawrence: University Press of Kansas, 1988), pp. 130–149. Fritschler's four editions of *Smoking and Politics* show this change remarkably well. Andrew S. McFarland shows negotiated differences between competing interests in *Cooperative Pluralism: The National Coal Policy Experiment* (Lawrence: University Press of Kansas, 1993).

44. Browne first explored niches in *Private Interests, Public Policy, and American Agriculture;* "Organized Interests and Their Issue Niches;" and "Issue Niches and the Limits of Interest Group Influence." See comments by Allan J. Cigler about the use of niche theory in his "Interest Groups: A Subfield in Search of an Identity," in *Political Science: Looking to Its Future*, vol. 4, ed. William Crotty (Evanston, Ill.: Northwestern University Press, 1991), p. 123; Diana M. Evans makes good use of niches in "Lobbying the Committee: Interest Groups and the House Public Works and Transportation Committee," in *Interest Group Politics*, 3d ed., pp. 257–276; Heinz et al. go to greater analytical lengths in *The Hollow Core*. A must-read, related work that shows interest evolution is by Frank R. Baumgartner and Bryan D. Jones, "Agenda Dynamics and Policy Subsystems," *Journal of Politics* 53 (November 1991): 1044–1074.

45. Edward O. Laumann, John P. Heinz with Robert L. Nelson and Robert H. Salisbury, "Organizations in Political Action: Representing Interests in National Policy Making," in *Policy Networks: Empirical Evidence and Theoretical Considerations*, ed. Bernd Marin and Renate Maynatz (Frankfurt, Germany, and Boulder, Colo.: Campus Verlag and Westview Press, 1991), pp. 63–95.

46. Browne, *Private Interests, Public Policy, and American Agriculture*, pp. 150–166. A useful popular account is by Susan B. Trento, *The Power House: Robert Keith Gray and the Selling of Access and Influence in Washington* (New York: St. Martin's Press, 1992). Another is Jeffrey H. Birnbaum, *The Lobbyists: How Influence Peddlers Get Their Way in Washington* (New York: Random House, 1992).

47. Robert H. Salisbury, "Interest Representation: The Dominance of Institutions," *American Political Science Review* 77 (March 1984): 64–76.

48. Jack L. Walker, "The Origins and Maintenance of Interest Groups in America," *American Political Science Review* 77 (June 1983): 390–406; Kay Lehman Scholzman and John T. Tierney, *Organized Interests and American Democracy* (New York: Harper and Row, 1986).

49. Berry, *The Interest Group Society*, pp. 16–43. See also Salisbury, "Interest Representation," and Browne, *Private Interests, Public Policy, and American Agriculture* on specifics of diversity.

50. Walker, "The Origins and Maintenance of Interest Groups in America." See his work posthumously completed by his former associates and students, *Mobilizing Interest Groups in America: Patrons, Professions, and Social Movements* (Ann Arbor: University of Michigan Press, 1991).

51. Laumann and Knoke, *The Organizational State;* Heinz et al., *The Hollow Core;* Browne, *Private Interests, Public Policy, and American Agriculture*.

52. Ibid.

53. For an insightful essay on where agency operations have been, see James Q. Wilson, "On Predicting the Bureaucratization of American Government," in *The State of Public Bureaucracy*, ed. Larry B. Hill (Armonk, N.Y.: M. E.

Sharpe, 1992), pp. 209–215. Three very useful examples can be seen in Morris P. Fiorina, "Bureaucratic (?) Failures: Causes and Cures," Formal Publication No. 43 (St. Louis: Washington University, October 1981); Barry R. Weingast and Mark J. Moran, "Bureaucratic Discretion or Congressional Control: Regulatory Policymaking by the Federal Trade Commission," Working Paper No. 72 (St. Louis: Center for the Study of American Business, Washington University, January 1982); Barry R. Weingast and Mark J. Moran, "The Myth of Runaway Bureaucracy: The Case of the FTC," *Regulation* 6 (May/June 1982): 33–38.

54. As Shepsle notes in "The Changing Textbook Congress," p. 260, this topic is an "academic light industry." But for two among many useful treatments that touch on Congress, see Allen Schick, *Congress and Money* (Washington, D.C.: Urban Institute, 1980); and, for its updating, Howard E. Shuman, *Politics and the Budget: The Struggle Between the President and Congress*, 3d ed. (Englewood Cliffs, N.J.: Prentice-Hall, 1992).

55. Terry M. Moe, "The Politics of Bureaucratic Structure," in Chubb and Peterson, *Can the Government Govern?* especially pp. 289–323. On the need for coordination, see Allen Schick, "The Coordination Option," in *Federal Reorganization: What Have We Learned*, ed. Peter Szanton (Chatham, N.J.: Chatham House, 1981), pp. 85–113.

56. Walter Williams, *Mismanaging America: The Rise of the Anti-Analytic Presidency* (Lawrence: University Press of Kansas, 1990), especially pp. 41–63. See also Arnold J. Meltsner, *Policy Analysts in the Bureaucracy* (Berkeley and Los Angeles: University of California Press, 1986).

57. Content explains why. Paul C. Light, *The President's Agenda: Domestic Policy Choice from Kennedy to Carter* (Baltimore: Johns Hopkins Press, 1982); for a conceptual and empirical analysis of the reasons, see Mark A. Peterson, *Legislating Together: The White House and Capitol Hill from Eisenhower to Reagan* (Cambridge, Mass.: Harvard University Press, 1990).

58. As quoted in Richard P. Nathan, *The Administrative Presidency* (New York: Wiley, 1983), p. 30. Erlichman was writing only of political appointees at the time, but his sentiments fit.

59. Williams, *Mismanaging America*. See a participant's explanation from David Stockman, *The Triumph of Politics: Why the Reagan Revolution Failed* (New York: Harper and Row, 1986). For strategies, see William T. Gormley, Jr., *Taming the Bureaucracy: Muscles, Prayers, and Other Strategies* (Princeton, N.J.: Princeton University Press, 1989).

60. Three very useful analyses show how this whipsawing breaks down triangle-explicit responses. I. M. Destler, *Presidents, Bureaucrats, and Foreign Policy: The Politics of Organizational Reform* (Princeton, N.J.: Princeton University Press, 1972); Eugene Bardach, *The Skill Factor in Politics: Repealing the Mental Commitment Laws in California* (Berkeley and Los Angeles: University of California Press, 1972); Cathy Marie Johnson, *The Dynamics of Conflict between Bureaucrats and Legislators* (Armonk, N.Y.: M. E. Sharpe, 1992).

61. Arthur F. Bentley, *The Process of Government* (Chicago: University of Chicago Press, 1908).

62. Patrick Kenis and Volker Schneider, "Policy Networks and Policy Analy-

sis: Scrutinizing a New Analytical Toolbox," in *Policy Networks: Empirical Evidence and Theoretical Considerations*, pp. 25–59.

63. This certainly helps explain the mid-1980s rise of omnibus bills in Congress. See Alan Ehrenhalt, "Media, Power Shifts Dominate O'Neill's House," *Congressional Quarterly Weekly Report* (September 13, 1986): 2131–2138. This vehicle format essentially provides a game as a constraining system for players to coordinate their divergent strategies, which, as Michael Crozier and Erhard Friedberg note, is a precondition for networking. See their *Actors and Systems: The Politics of Collective Action* (Chicago: University of Chicago Press, 1980), p. 125.

64. Of course, the reason or the constituent may make a big substantive difference to the composite construction of the policy vehicle. But these motives need not affect the issues of the other participants as these are worked into the package.

65. Kingdon, *Congressmen's Voting Decisions*; Richard L. Hall, "Participation and Purpose in Committee Decision Making," *American Political Science Review* 81 (March 1987): 105–127.

66. This brings a minor, but important, disagreement with Fenno in *Home Style*, p. 4. Because members read and react to their districts, there are some patterns that can be seen in census data.

67. The uncertainty thesis is the basis of John Mark Hansen's work on congressional choices between interest groups and parties as sources of information, *Gaining Access: Congress and the Farm Lobby, 1919–1981* (Chicago: University of Chicago Press, 1991). As he shows, uncertainty mandates a careful search for clear choices, but that search goes on very slowly and cautiously, erring on the side of established sources until a transformation occurs.

CHAPTER 2. AGRICULTURE AS A POLICY DOMAIN

1. Gerald Schluter, *Report on Sector GNP*, data (Washington, D.C.: U.S. Department of Agriculture, Economic Research Service, 1990). The 20 percent level was maintained throughout the mid-1980s.

2. R.G.F. Spitze provided these data, using Economic Research Service files, U.S. Department of Agriculture.

3. Charles M. Hardin, *The Politics of Agriculture* (Glencoe, Ill.: Free Press, 1952); see also his *Food and Fiber in the Nation's Politics* (Washington, D.C.: GPO, 1967); his *Presidential Power and Accountability* (Chicago: University of Chicago Press, 1974), chaps. 4–6; his "Agricultural Price Policy: The Political Rule of Bureaucracy," *Policy Studies Journal* 6 (Summer 1978): 467–472. This also is the view Ross B. Talbot and Don F. Hadwiger take in their account of *The Policy Process in American Agriculture* (San Francisco: Chandler, 1968), especially pp. 184–203.

4. Grant McConnell, *Private Power and American Democracy* (New York: Alfred A. Knopf, 1966), and his *The Decline of Agrarian Democracy* (Berkeley and Los Angeles: University of California Press, 1953). Theodore J. Lowi bases

much of his analysis on McConnell in *The End of Liberalism: Ideology, Policy, and the Crisis of Public Authority* (New York: W. W. Norton, 1969), the quoted phrase is from there, p. 103; see also Lowi's "How the Farmers Get What They Want," *Reporter* (1964). May 21: 34–37.

5. Lowi, *The End of Liberalism*, p. 102. Ripley and Franklin see agriculture as the most traditional model of U.S. policymaking in Randall B. Ripley and Grace A. Franklin, *Congress, the Bureaucracy, and Public Policy*, 5th ed. (Pacific Grove, Calif.: Brooks/Cole, 1991), pp. 84–87, 93–96.

6. John Mark Hansen, *Gaining Access: Congress and the Farm Lobby, 1919–1981* (Chicago: University of Chicago Press, 1991). Curiously, given their views on labor in Ross B. Talbot and Don F. Hadwiger, *The Policy Process in Agriculture* (San Francisco: Chandler, 1968), Hadwiger and Talbot agree. Also Patrick G. O'Brien, "A Reexamination of the Senate Farm Bloc, 1921–1933," *Agriculture History* 47 (January 1973): 248–263; James T. Young, "The Origins of New Deal Agricultural Policy: Interest Groups' Role in Policy Formation," *Policy Studies Journal* 21 (Summer 1993): 190–209.

7. John P. Heinz, "The Political Impasse in Farm Support Legislation," *Yale Law Journal* 71 (April 1962): 954–970; Don F. Hadwiger and Ross B. Talbot, *Pressures and Protests: The Kennedy Farm Program and the Wheat Referendum of 1963* (San Francisco: Chandler, 1965); William P. Browne and Charles W. Wiggins, "Resolutions and Priorities: Lobbying by the General Farm Organizations," *Policy Studies Journal* 6 (Summer 1978): 493–498; William P. Browne, *Private Interests, Public Policy, and American Agriculture* (Lawrence: University Press of Kansas, 1988), pp. 89–108.

8. Don Paarlberg, "A New Agenda for Agriculture," in *The New Politics of Food*, ed. Don F. Hadwiger and William P. Browne (Lexington, Mass.: D. C. Heath, 1978), pp. 135–140; and his *Farm and Food Policy of the 1980s* (Lincoln: University of Nebraska Press, 1980), pp. 59–64.

9. Paarlberg, "A New Agenda for Agriculture," pp. 139–140.

10. Garth Youngberg, "The National Farm Coalition and the Politics of Food," paper presented at the Fourth Annual Hendricks Public Policy Symposium (Lincoln, Nebr., 1979); Browne, *Private Interests, Public Policy, and American Agriculture*, especially pp. 213–252.

11. Christiana McFadyen Campbell, *The Farm Bureau and the New Deal* (Urbana: University of Illinois Press, 1962).

12. Weldon Barton, "Coalition-Building in the U.S. House of Representatives: Agricultural Legislation in 1973," in *Cases in Public Policy*, ed. James E. Anderson (New York: Praeger, 1976), pp. 141–162; Clifford M. Hardin, "Congress is the Problem," *Choices* 1 (January 1986): 6–10; David Rapp, *How the U.S. Got Into Agriculture: And Why It Can't Get Out* (Washington, D.C.: Congressional Quarterly, 1988).

13. Neil L. Meyer and William T. Dishman, *Power Clusters: How Public Policy Originates* (Moscow: College of Agriculture, University of Idaho, 1984). Their analysis derives from Daniel M. Ogden, *How National Policy is Made* (Washington, D.C.: Office of Power Marketing Coordination, U.S. Department of Education, 1983).

14. James T. Bonnen, "Implications for Agricultural Policy," *American Jour-*

nal of Agricultural Economics 55 (August 1973): 391–398; his "U.S. Agriculture, Instability and National Political Institutions," in *United States Agricultural Policies for 1985 and Beyond* (Tucson, Ariz.: Department of Agriculture Economics, University of Arizona, 1984), pp. 53–83; William P. Browne, "The Fragmented and Meandering Politics of Agriculture," in *U.S. Agriculture in a Global Setting: An Agenda for the Future*, ed. M. Ann Tutwiler (Washington, D.C.: Resources for the Future, 1988), pp. 136–153. These are similar to Heclo's issue network complaints.

15. An example is David G. Abler's, "Vote Trading on Farm Legislation in the U.S. House," *American Journal of Agricultural Economics* 71 (August 1989): 583–591; see also Bruce L. Gardner, "Changing Economic Perspectives on the Farm Problem," *Journal of Economic Literature* 30 (March 1992): 62–101. This point is made well by Lawrence S. Rothenberg, *Linking Citizens to Government: Interest Group Politics at Common Cause* (New York: Cambridge University Press, 1992), p. 2.

16. The central theme of Hansen, *Gaining Access* is that issues rather than the emergent networks are what matter. And he does not see networks as cordial and cozy.

17. David E. Hamilton, *From New Day to New Deal: American Farm Policy from Hoover to Roosevelt, 1928–1933* (Chapel Hill: University of North Carolina Press, 1991).

18. Hansen, *Gaining Access*, p. 213.

19. Crozier and Friedberg, *Actors and Systems*.

20. Barton, "Coalition-Building in the U.S. House of Representatives," and his "Food, Agriculture, and Administrative Adaptation to Political Change," *Public Administration Review* 36 (March/April 1976): 148–154; John Ferejohn, "Logrolling in an Institutional Context: A Case Study of Food Stamp Legislation," in *Congress and Policy Change*, ed. Gerald C. Wright, Jr., Leroy N. Rieselbach, and Lawrence C. Dodd (New York: Agathon Press, 1986), pp. 223–253.

21. Barton, "Food, Agriculture, and Administrative Adaptation to Political Change," p. 199. See also Randall B. Ripley, "Legislative Bargaining and the Food Stamp Act, 1964," in *Congress and Urban Problems*, ed. Frederic N. Cleaveland and associates (Washington, D.C.: The Brookings Institution, 1969), pp. 279–310.

22. Joseph B. Kadane, "On Division of the Question," *Public Choice* 13 (Spring 1973): 47–54.

23. Ferejohn, "Logrolling in an Institutional Context," pp. 250–251.

24. Ibid., p. 251.

25. Kenneth A. Shepsle and Barry R. Weingast produced pioneering thoughts on the role of conference committees. See "The Institutional Foundations of Committee Power," *American Political Science Review* 81 (March 1987): 85–104; and "Why are Congressional Committees Powerful?" *American Political Science Review* 81(September 1987): 935–945.

26. John G. Peters, "The 1977 Farm Bill Coalitions in Congress," in *The New Politics of Food*, ed. Don F. Hadwiger and William P. Browne (Lexington, Mass.: D. C. Heath, 1978), pp. 23–35; and his "The 1981 Farm Bill," in *Food*

Policy and Farm Programs, ed. Don F. Hadwiger and Ross B. Talbot (New York: Academy of Political Science, 1982), pp. 157–170.

27. Lowi, *The End of Liberalism*, p. 103.

28. Theodore J. Schultz, *Redirecting Farm Policy* (New York: Macmillan, 1943); and his *Agriculture in an Unstable Economy* (New York: McGraw-Hill, 1945).

29. The convergence of political and administrative forces that brought forward the agricultural establishment can be seen in Leonard S. White, *The Republican Era: A Study in Administrative Management* (New York: Macmillan, 1958).

30. Several works are incorporated here. Gladys L. Baker, *The County Agent* (Chicago: University of Chicago Press, 1939); John M. Gaus and Leon O. Wolcott, *Public Administration and the United States Department of Agriculture* (Chicago: Public Service Administration, 1940); Murray R. Benedict, "Agriculture as a Commercial Industry Comparable to Other Branches of the Economy," *Journal of Farm Economics* 24 (May 1942): 476–496; and his *Farm Policies of the United States, 1790–1950* (New York: Twentieth Century Fund, 1950); Paul H. Appleby, *Policy and Administration* (University: University of Alabama Press, 1949); Gladys L. Baker, Wayne D. Rasmussen, Vivian Wiser, and Jane M. Porter, *Century of Service: The First 100 Years of the United States Department of Agriculture* (Washington, D.C.: Centennial Committee—U.S. Department of Agriculture, 1963); Ernest G. Moore, *The Agricultural Research Service* (New York: Praeger, 1967); Wayne D. Rasmussen and Gladys L. Baker, *The Department of Agriculture* (New York: Praeger, 1972).

31. Ibid.; Additional sources include Schultz, *Redirecting Farm Policy* and his *Agriculture in an Unstable Economy;* Willard W. Cochrane, *Farm Prices: Myth and Reality* (Minneapolis: University of Minnesota Press, 1958); and his *The Development of American Agriculture: A Historical Analysis* (Minneapolis: University of Minnesota Press, 1979).

32. In addition to the synthesis from the above, see James T. Bonnen's three works. "U.S. Agricultural Development: Transforming Human Capital, Technology and Institutions," in *U.S.-Mexico Relations: Agriculture and Rural Development* (Stanford, Calif.: Stanford University Press, 1987), pp. 267–300; "Institutions, Instruments, and Driving Forces Behind U.S. Agricultural Policies," in *U.S.-Canadian Agricultural Trade Challenges: Developing Common Approaches*, ed. Kristen Allen and Katie Macmillan (Washington, D.C.: Resources for the Future, 1988), pp. 21–39; "Why is There No Coherent U.S. Rural Policy?" *Policy Studies Journal* 20 (Second Quarter 1992): 190–201. On development see Glenn L. Johnson and James T. Bonnen with Darrell Fienup, C. Leroy Quance, and Neill Schaller, eds., *Social Science Agricultural Agendas and Strategies* (Lansing, Mich.: Michigan State University Press, 1991).

33. John D. Black, *Agricultural Reform in the United States* (New York: McGraw Hill, 1929); Sandra S. Osbourn, *Rural Policy in the United States: A History* (Washington, D.C.: Congressional Research Service, Library of Congress, 1988).

34. On agrarian principles, see the collected works of John M. Brewster, a philosopher in the ranks of USDA policy analysts from 1936 to 1965. J. Patrick

Madden and David J. Brewster, eds., *A Philosopher Among Economists* (Philadelphia: J. T. Murphy, 1970).

35. Hamilton, *From New Day to New Deal*, explains why in looking at the development of an "associative state" that was less immune to contemporary interest group politics and its natural divisiveness. See also Theda Skocpol and Kenneth Finegold, "State Capacity and Economic Intervention in the Early New Deal," *Political Science Quarterly* 97 (Summer 1982): 255–278. Stephen Lee Skowronek goes into greater depth as to the capacity building contributions of courts and parties in a pre-interest group era, *Building a New Administrative State: The Expansion of National Administrative Capacities, 1877–1920* (Cambridge, Mass.: Cambridge University Press, 1982). Periodic farm protest, though, also was a factor in breaking from laissez-faire government.

36. Hansen, *Gaining Access*, pp. 45–61.

37. Ibid., pp. 61–75.

38. Ibid., p. 65. The legislation at hand was the McNary-Haugen Act.

39. Although neither writes about network politics, networking can be seen in McConnell, *The Decline of Agrarian Democracy* and Benedict, *Farm Policies of the United States, 1790–1950*.

40. Richard S. Kirkendall, *Social Scientists and Farm Politics in the Age of Roosevelt* (Columbia: University of Missouri Press, 1967); see also Anthony Badger, *Prosperity Road: The New Deal, Tobacco, and North Carolina* (Chapel Hill: University of North Carolina Press, 1980).

41. Hamilton, *From New Day to New Deal;* Hansen, *Gaining Access.* Although these books have distinctly different institutional emphases, together they reveal this sharp point of departure as seen during this era. One book needs to be read in its entirety with the other.

42. David Knoke and Edward O. Laumann, "The Social Organization of National Policy Domains: An Exploration of Some Structural Hypotheses," in *Social Structure and Network Analysis*, ed. Peter V. Marsden and Nan Lin (Beverly Hills, Calif: Sage, 1982). Also see Laumann and Knoke, *The Organizational State: Social Choice in National Policy Domains* (Madison: University of Wisconsin Press, 1987).

43. Robert H. Salisbury, "Putting Interests Back into Interest Groups," in *Interest Group Politics*, 3d ed., ed. Allan J. Cigler and Burdett A. Loomis (Washington, D.C.: Congressional Quarterly Press, 1991), especially pp. 378–382. See also John P. Heinz, Edward O. Laumann, Robert H. Salisbury, and Robert L. Nelson, *The Hollow Core: Private Interests in National Policy Making* (Cambridge, Mass.: Harvard University Press, 1993). The marketplace analogy is from William P. Browne, "Organized Interests and Their Issue Niches: A Search for Pluralism in a Policy Domain," *Journal of Policy* 52 (May 1990): 500.

44. Laumann and Knoke, *The Organizational State*, pp. 387–395.

45. Salisbury, "Putting Interests Back into Interest Groups," pp. 373–377.

46. Note that the policy game of agricultural development made no progress in the conflict-ridden twenty years prior to 1862. The South, with plantation agriculture, stoutly resisted mass development for agrarians. The farm acts of 1862 were passed quickly after the Civil War began and southern members of Congress exited Washington. The policy game concept, in a later era, explains as

well why the House agriculture committee proved relatively popular as an alternative assignment for members. See Charles Stewart III, "Committee Hierarchies in the Modernizing House, 1875–1947," *American Journal of Political Science* 36 (November 1992): 835–856.

47. Osbourn, *Rural Policy in the United States: A History;* See the original *Report of the Country Life Commission.* Special Message from the President of the United States Transmitting the Report of the Country Life Commission. Senate Document 705, 60th Congress, 2d Session (Washington, D.C.: U.S. Government Printing Office, 1909).

48. Douglas E. Bowers, Wayne D. Rasmussen, and Gladys L. Baker, *History of Agricultural Price-Support and Adjustment Programs, 1933–84: Background for 1985 Farm Legislation* (Washington, D.C.: Economic Research Service, U.S. Department of Agriculture, 1987), pp. 3–15.

49. Browne, *Private Interests, Public Policy, and American Agriculture*, pp. 213–236. On economic and constituent consequences of that legislation, see R.G.F. Spitze, "The Evolution and Implications of the U.S. Food Security Act of 1985," *Agricultural Economics* 1 (June 1987): 175–190.

50. For a related critique of USDA, see *U.S. Department of Agriculture: Revitalizing Structure, Systems, and Strategies* (Washington, D.C.: General Accounting Office, 1991).

51. Office of the Secretary, U.S. Department of Agriculture, January 1993.

52. Robert H. Salisbury, John P. Heinz, Robert L. Nelson, and Edward O. Laumann, "Triangles, Networks, and Hollow Cores: The Complex Geometry of Washington Interest Representation," in *The Politics of Interests: Interest Groups Transformed*, ed. Mark P. Petracca (Boulder, Colo.: Westview, 1992), p. 143.

53. Roger H. Davidson, "The New Centralization on Capitol Hill," *Review of Politics* 50 (Summer 1988): 358–360.

54. Every respondent intuitively grasped the domain concept, recognizing it as a generally bounded set of players and issues. As I have noted in the Appendix, a domain gave them something very specific to talk about even as they remarked on its fluidity and openness.

55. Nor, it should be noted, are members acting simply by electoral calculations that link policy to majorities. See R. Douglas Arnold, *The Logic of Congressional Action* (New Haven, Conn.: Yale University Press, 1990).

56. The only evidence that previously indicated that this participation might be high was comments of lobbyists in 1985–1986 interviews. They noted, in the absence of a subcommittee member who would carry their proposals, that nearly any rank-and-file number would do. Browne, *Private Interests, Public Policy, and American Agriculture*, p. 46.

57. Laumann and Knoke, *The Organizational State*, pp. 9–18.

CHAPTER 3. MEMBERS, ISSUES, AND POLICY VEHICLES

1. Angus Campbell, Philip E. Converse, Warren E. Miller, and Donald E. Stokes provide excellent examples of unclear definition of issues in their classic work *The American Voter* (New York: John Wiley, 1960), pp. 168–176. An issue

is that to which voters respond when party and candidate images fail to motivate them. Issues in *Voter* lack any specific prescription for government action. Rather, they are generalities such as "act tough toward Russia" or "cut taxes." Until those ideas are reformulated as to how to cut taxes or to what acting tough entails, they are abstractions rather than legislative topics of policy concern.

2. David R. Mayhew, *Congress: The Electoral Connection* (New Haven, Conn.: Yale University Press, 1974), pp. 127–128.

3. Edward O. Laumann and David Knoke, *The Organizational State: Social Choice in National Policy Domains* (Madison: University of Wisconsin Press, 1987), p. 107.

4. James A. Thurber, "Budget Continuity and Change: An Assessment of the Congressional Budget Process," in *Studies in Modern American Politics*, ed. D. K. Adams (Manchester, United Kingdom: Manchester University Press, 1989), pp. 78–118; and his "The Impact of Budget Reform on Presidential and Congressional Governance," in *Divided Democracy: Cooperation and Conflict Between the President and Congress*, ed. James A. Thurber (Washington, D.C.: Congressional Quarterly Press, 1991), pp. 145–170.

5. Raymond A. Bauer, Ithiel de Sola Pool, and Lewis Anthony Dexter, *American Business and Public Policy* (New York: Atherton, 1963); Richard E. Cohen, *Washington at Work* (New York: Macmillan, 1992).

6. Case studies other than those cited at n. 5 that show this point include: Eric Redman, *The Dance of Legislation* (New York: Simon and Schuster, 1973); Jeffrey H. Birnbaum and Alan S. Murray, *Showdown at Gucci Gulch: Lawmakers, Lobbyists, and the Unlikely Triumph of Tax Reform* (New York: Random House, 1987); Paul C. Light, *Forging Legislation* (New York: W. W. Norton, 1992).

7. John Ferejohn, "Logrolling in an Institutional Context: A Case Study of Food Stamp Legislation" in *Congress and Policy Change*, ed. Gerald C. Wright, Jr., Leroy N. Rieselbach, and Lawrence C. Dodd (New York: Agathon Press, 1986), pp. 239–245.

8. Kenneth A. Shepsle, "Institutional Equilibrium and Equilibrium Institutions," in *Political Science: The Science of Politics*, ed. Herbert Weisberg (New York: Agathon, 1986), pp. 51–82; and his "The Positive Theory of Legislative Institutions: An Enrichment of Social Choice and Spatial Models," *Public Choice* 50:1–3 (1986): 135–179.

9. Ferejohn, "Logrolling in an Institutional Context, p. 245; Richard F. Fenno, Jr., *Congressmen in Committees* (Boston: Little, Brown, 1973), p. 276.

10. P.L. 101–624, S. 2830 and P.L. 101–508, H.R. 5835 passed in near immediate sequence in late October 1990 as Congress elected to pass the agreed-upon farm bill and then deal with a $11.9 billion, five-year reduction in commodity payments as authorized in the first act. P.L. 102–237 passed fifteen months later as the Food, Agriculture, Conservation, and Trade Act Amendments of 1991. For a review of the content of the 1990 legislation see R.G.F. Spitze, "A Continuing Evolution in U.S. Agricultural and Food Policy: The 1990 Act," *Agricultural Economics* 7 (July 1992): 125–139.

11. William P. Browne, "Agricultural Policy Can't Accommodate All Who Want In," *Choices* 4 (First Quarter 1989): 9–11.

12. Murray R. Benedict, *Farm Policies of the United States, 1790–1950* (New York: Twentieth Century Fund, 1950); Benedict and O. C. Stine, *The Agricultural Commodity Programs* (New York: Twentieth Century Fund, 1956); Ross B. Talbot and Don F. Hadwiger, *The Policy Process in American Agriculture* (San Francisco: Chandler, 1968), p. 267.

13. When respondents identified issues and those who provided relevant information on the issues, they also identified from where those issues were initiated and how the offices then proceeded.

14. Randall B. Ripley and Grace A. Franklin continue to employ a schema that sees agricultural price policy as essentially distributive, *Congress, the Bureaucracy and Public Policy*, 5th ed. (Pacific Grove, Calif.: Brooks/Cole, 1991). Some reconsideration of that needs be given in light of environmental and acreage reduction gains.

15. For dismantlement costs, see work on transaction cost economics as used in Chapter 10. Terry M. Moe provides an excellent survey, "The New Economics of Organization," *American Journal of Political Science* 28 (November 1984): 739–777.

16. See William P. Browne, *Private Interests, Public Policy, and American Agriculture* (Lawrence: University Press of Kansas, 1988), pp. 213–225; and his "Agricultural Policy Can't Accommodate All Who Want In."

17. These conclusions were drawn and coded on the basis of respondent assessments of what the enterprise needed to do to win on each issue.

18. Comments such as this are in keeping with Cathy Marie Johnson's four case-study findings in *The Dynamics of Conflict Between Bureaucrats and Legislators* (Armonk, N.Y.: M. E. Sharpe, 1992).

19. Although about 80 percent of the information on winning outcomes came from the interviews, as cross-referenced with public documents, fifty-eight issues were tracked to resolution in the fifteen months following the interviews. Winning means the successful attachment of an issue to a policy vehicle that succeeded either in passage, appropriating funds, securing favorable administrative action, or producing the desired information in an investigative action (i.e., a GAO report).

20. Ferejohn, "Logrolling in an Institutional Context"; Fenno, *Congressmen in Committees*.

21. Yet unspecified in the congressional staff literature is what these employees contribute to policymaking. Robert H. Salisbury and Kenneth A. Shepsle are the most suggestive as to this point in "U.S. Congressman as Enterprise," *Legislative Studies Quarterly* 6 (November 1981): 559–576. But also see John F. Manley, "Congressional Staff and Public Policy Making: The Joint Committee on Internal Revenue Taxation," *Journal of Politics* 3 (November 1968): 1046–1067; Harrison W. Fox, Jr., and Susan Webb Hammond, *Congressional Staffs: The Invisible Force in American Lawmaking* (New York: Free Press, 1977); Michael J. Malbin, *Unelected Representatives: Congressional Staff and the Future of Representation* (New York: Basic Books, 1980).

22. This suggests that enterprise staff play the entrepreneurial, policy activist role more than they do the professional role of neutral competence as identified and found to be important to policymaking by David E. Price, "Professionals and

'Entrepreneurs': Staff Orientations and Policy Making on Three Senate Committees," *Journal of Politics* 33 (May 1971): 316–336.

23. James W. Dyson and John W. Soule, "Congressional Committee Behavior on Roll Call Votes: The U.S. House of Representatives," *Midwest Journal of Political Science* 19 (November 1970): 626–647; Fenno, *Congressmen in Committees;* John D. Lees and Malcolm Shaw, eds., *Committees in Legislatures: A Comparative Analysis* (Durham, N.C.: Duke University Press, 1979); Wayne L. Francis and James W. Riddlesperger, "U.S. State Legislative Committees: Structure, Procedural Efficiency, and Party Control," *Legislative Studies Quarterly* 7 (November 1982): 453–472.

24. Donald R. Matthews, *U.S. Senators and Their World* (Chapel Hill: University of North Carolina Press, 1960), pp. 169–171; Dyson and Soule, "Congressional Committee Behavior on Roll Call Votes."

25. Matthews, *U.S. Senators and Their World*, pp. 169–170.

26. G. R. Boynton, "Telling a Good Story: Models in Argument: Models of Understanding in the Senate Agriculture Committee," in *Argument and Critical Practices*, ed. Joseph W. Wenzel (Annandale, Md.: Speech Communications Association, 1987), pp. 429–438; his "The Senate Agriculture Committee Produces a Homeostat," *Policy Science* 22 (March 1989): 50–81; his "Ideas and Action: A Cognitive Model of the Senate Agriculture Committee," *Political Behavior* 12 (June 1990): 181–213; and with Chong Lim Kim, "Legislative Representation as Parallel-Processing and Problem-Solving," *Journal of Theoretical Politics* 3 (October, 1991): 437–461.

27. The importance of causal stories and myths in interest politics can be seen in Deborah A. Stone, "Causal Stories and the Formation of Policy Agendas," *Political Science Quarterly* 104 (Summer 1989): 281–300. See also James T. Bonnen and William P. Browne, "Why Is Agricultural Policy So Difficult to Reform?" in *The Political Economy of U.S. Agriculture: Challenges for the 1990s*, ed. Carol S. Kramer (Washington, D.C.: Resources for the Future, 1989), pp. 7–55.

28. Boynton, "The Senate Agriculture Committee Produces a Homeostat," p. 77; R.G.F. Spitze shows the refinement style of these and later farm bills in four of his fine works: "Economic Redirection in Recent U.S. Agricultural Policy," *Journal of Agricultural Economics* 19 (September 1968): 327–338; "Policy Direction and Economic Interpretations of the U.S. Agricultural Act of 1970," *Journal of Agricultural Economics* 23 (June 1972): 99–108; "The Food and Agriculture Act of 1977: Issues and Decisions," *American Journal of Agricultural Economics* 60 (May 1978): 225–235; "The Agriculture and Food Act of 1981: Continued Policy Evolution," *North Central Journal of Agricultural Economics* 5 (July 1983): 65–75.

29. Charles O. Jones, "Representation in Congress: The Case of the House Agriculture Committee," *American Political Science Association* 55 (June 1961): 358–367; Michael S. Lyons and Marcia Whicker Taylor, "Farm Politics in Transition: The House Agriculture Committee," *Agricultural History* 55 (January 1981): 128–146.

30. Browne, *Private Interests, Public Policy, and American Agriculture*, p. 96.

31. The narrowness and conflict-avoidance in the demands correspond greatly

to the issue-niche behavior of interest groups. Yet they are different as well in that the group retains a core issue-identity whereas the congressional enterprise cannot do so and succeed with its multiple tasks. See William P. Browne, "Organized Interests and Their Issue Niches: A Search for Pluralism in a Policy Domain," *Journal of Politics* 52 (May 1990: 477–509).

CHAPTER 4. PEAK INTERESTS

1. Richard Fenno, Jr., *Home Style* (Boston: Little, Brown, 1978).

2. As Fenno notes, members have three sets of personal goals that embroil them in both Washington and district politics. They are: getting reelected, accumulating Washington influence, and making good policy (*Home Style*, p. 137). Morris Fiorina's emphasis on the effects of a reelection concern underscore the same point. See his *Congress: Keystone of the Washington Establishment*, 2d ed. (New Haven, Conn.: Yale University Press, 1989).

3. Jeffrey M. Berry, "Subgovernments, Issue Networks, and Political Conflict," in *Remaking American Politics,* ed. Richard Harris and Sidney Milkus (Boulder, Colo.: Westview, 1989), p. 248.

4. Steven S. Smith and Christopher J. Deering, *Committees in Congress,* 2d ed. (Washington, D.C.: Congressional Quarterly Press, 1990).

5. Ibid., pp. 61–117.

6. Ibid., pp. 153–154.

7. The openness and frequency of member appeals to the agriculture committees is noted by Smith and Deering, *Committees in Congress,* p. 77.

8. For typing of issues, see William P. Browne, *Private Interests, Public Policy, and American Agriculture* (Lawrence: University Press of Kansas, 1988).

9. A set of rigid decisional rules for mutually exclusive categorization were applied for the analysis here. Farm-benefit issues were those where the issue: (1) was intended to provide economic gain to farmers, either through direct payments, indirect cost savings, or increased commodity sales; (2) was advocated by one or more farmers or their representatives as being in farmers' interests; (3) and was not advanced or sold to others as serving other specified agricultural goals such as those from other categories (excluding the generic idea of a public good in all issues). Issues for other purposes were assigned the appropriate category: (1) if they served that specific end; (2) even though farmers may have received assignable benefits from them as well; and (3) even if farm groups and farmers were coadvocates for them along with nonfarm-interest representatives. This method meant that 36 (28 percent) of these benefits for nonfarm purposes also served a farm purpose as well.

10. Representative Armey's quote is from his interview as a survey respondent, a quote he encouraged me to attribute to him publicly.

11. Most agricultural economists would argue that price-supports distort the market and, in effect, retard development. See William P. Browne, Jerry R. Skees, Louis E. Swanson, Paul B. Thompson, and Laurian J. Unnevehr, *Sacred Cows and Hot Potatoes: Agrarian Myths in Agricultural Policy* (Boulder, Colo.: Westview, 1992), pp. 61–74.

12. For Carlisle Ford Runge's finding of the extensive decline of this type of producer, see "Inefficiency and Structural Adjustment in American Agriculture: Who Will Quit and Why?" in *Public Policy and Agricultural Technology: Adversity Despite Achievement,* ed. Don F. Hadwiger and William P. Browne (New York: St. Martin's Press, 1987), pp. 33–51.

13. Keith Krehbiel, *Information and Legislative Organization* (Ann Arbor: University of Michigan Press, 1991).

14. Jess Gilbert and Carolyn Howe, "Beyond 'State vs. Society': Theories of the State and New Deal Agricultural Policies," *American Sociological Review* 56 (April 1991): 204–220.

15. For an example of deals made on this topic in the Senate, see Smith and Deering, p. 106. As excerpted from David S. Cloud, "All Things to All Senators," *Congressional Quarterly Weekly Report* (August 12, 1989): 2119.

16. Ibid., for a list of some issues dealt with by Leahy.

17. Ibid.

18. John Ferejohn, "Logrolling in an Institutional Context: A Case Study of Food Stamp Legislation," in *Congress and Policy Change,* ed. Gerald C. Wright, Jr., Leroy N. Rieselbach, and Lawrence C. Dodd (New York: Agathon Press, 1986).

19. Lewrene K. Glaser, *Provisions of the Food Security Act of 1985* (Washington, D.C.: National Economics Division, Economic Research Service, U.S. Department of Agriculture, 1985); R.G.F. Spitze, "The Evolution and Implications of the U.S. Food Security Act of 1985;" and Browne, *Private Interests, Public Policy, and American Agriculture,* pp. 213–236.

20. After the pretest and about fifteen interviews in the Senate, it became evident that these two types of issues, along with farm-benefit ones, were especially popular. As a consequence, the interviews followed up on these two types of issue responses by asking about enterprise initiatives in the Food Security Act of 1985.

21. It is interesting to note that the policy process stirs similar metaphors in both theorists and politicians. See Michael D. Cohen, James D. March, and Johan P. Olsen, "A Garbage Can Model of Organizational Choice," *Administrative Science Quarterly* 17 (March 1972): 1–25.

22. The chi-square for differences in these three reaggregated categories was 5.99, which was not statistically significant.

23. Willard J. Cochrane, *Farm Prices: Myth and Reality* (Minneapolis: University of Minnesota Press, 1958); Dale E. Hathaway, "The Implications of Changing Political Power in Agriculture," in *Agricultural Policy in an Affluent Society,* ed. Vernon W. Ruttan et al. (New York: Norton, 1969).

24. James T. Bonnen and William P. Browne, "Why Is Agricultural Policy So Difficult to Reform?" in *The Political Economy of U.S. Agriculture: Challenges for the 1990s,* ed. Carol S. Kramer (Washington, D.C.: Resources for the Future, 1989), p. 10. Four other especially good critiques of the agrarian myth and their policy impact are by Joseph S. Davis, "Agricultural Fundamentalism," in *Economics, Sociology and the Modern World,* ed. Norman E. Himes (Cambridge, Mass.: Harvard University Press, 1935), pp. 3–22; Whitney A. Griswold, *Farming and Democracy* (New York: Harcourt, Brace, 1948); John M. Brewster, "The

Relevance of the Jeffersonian Dream Today," in *Land Use Policy and Problems in the United States,* ed. H. W. Ottoson (Lincoln: University of Nebraska Press, 1963), pp. 86–136; Luther Tweeten, "Sector as Personality: The Case of Farm Protest Movements," *Agriculture and Human Values* 4 (Winter 1987): 66–74.

25. John Kingdon, *Congressmen's Voting Decisions* (New York: Harper and Row, 1973).

26. For an analysis of the 1985 Act's new policies as they impact on pending 1990 legislation, see Kristen Allen, "Reflections on the Past, Challenges for the Future: An Examination of U.S. Agricultural Policy Goals," in *Agricultural Policies in a New Decade,* ed. Kristen Allen (Washington, D.C.: Resources for the Future and National Planning Association, 1990), pp. 3–23. For the importance of such media attention to reform, see Frank R. Baumgartner and Bryan D. Jones, *Agendas and Instability in American Politics* (Chicago: University of Chicago Press, 1993).

CHAPTER 5. DISTRICT EFFECTS

1. Charles L. Clapp, *The Congressman: His Work as He Sees It* (Washington, D.C.: The Brookings Institution, 1963), pp. 373–443.

2. R. Douglas Arnold, *The Logic of Congressional Action* (New Haven, Conn.: Yale University Press, 1990), p. 15.

3. Richard F. Fenno, Jr., *Home Style* (Boston: Little, Brown, 1978).

4. Arnold, *The Logic of Congressional Action.*

5. Steven S. Smith, *Call to Order: Floor Politics in the House and Senate* (Washington, D.C.: Brookings, 1989), pp. 250–252.

6. John Mark Hansen, *Gaining Access: Congress and the Farm Lobby, 1919–1981* (Chicago: University of Chicago Press, 1991), pp. 2–77.

7. James T. Bonnen, "Institutions, Instruments, and Driving Forces Behind U.S. Agricultural Policies," in *U.S.-Canadian Agricultural Trade Challenges: Developing Common Approaches,* ed. Kristen Allen and Katie Macmillan (Washington, D.C.: Resources for the Future, 1988).

8. David G. Abler, "Vote Trading on Farm Legislation in the U.S. House," *American Journal of Agricultural Economics* 71 (August 1989).

9. Willard J. Cochrane, *Farm Prices: Myth and Reality* (Minneapolis: University of Minnesota Press, 1958); Dale E. Hathaway, "The Implications of Changing Political Power in Agriculture," in *Agricultural Policy in an Affluent Society,* ed. Vernon W. Ruttan et al. (New York: Norton, 1969).

10. Hansen, in *Gaining Access,* develops those key points, and he notes that members of Congress turned to interest groups and away from parties for the electoral support they provided. Yet he never contends that farm numbers gave farm groups power. On the contrary, their more reliable information and the way that translated to electoral support back home were responsible. Members who refused to listen to farm group pleas, even then, were likely to be losing more than the votes of farmers in the districts.

11. John G. Peters, "The 1977 Farm Bill Coalitions in Congress," in *The New Politics of Food,* ed. Don F. Hadwiger and William P. Browne (Lexington,

Mass.: D. C. Heath, 1978), pp. 23–35; and "The 1981 Farm Bill," in *Food Policy and Farm Programs,* ed. Don F. Hadwiger and Ross B. Talbot (New York: Academy of Political Science, 1982), pp. 157–170.

12. Cornelia Butler Flora, Jan L. Flora, Jacqueline D. Spears, Louis E. Swanson with Mark B. Lapping and Mark L. Weinberg, *Rural Communities: Legacy and Change* (Boulder, Colo.: Westview, 1992), pp. 29–55. The rise and fall of employment levels by type (agriculture, manufacturing, etc.) can be seen in David W. Sears, John M. Redman, Lorin D. Kusmin, and Molly S. Killian, *Growth and Stability of Rural Economies in the 1980s: Differences Among Counties* (Washington, D.C.: Agriculture and Rural Economy Division, Economic Research Service, U.S. Department of Agriculture, 1992).

13. John A. Crampton, *The National Farmers Union: Ideology of a Pressure Group* (Lincoln: University of Nebraska Press, 1965); Allen J. Matusow, *Farm Policies and Politics in the Truman Years* (Cambridge, Mass.: Harvard University Press, 1967). See also Graham K. Wilson, *Special Interests and Policymaking: Agriculture Politics and Policies in Britain and the United States* (London: Wiley, 1977); and his *Unions in American National Politics* (London: Macmillan, 1979).

14. The data on congressional district size was the most difficult to find. It came from David C. Huckabee, *Land Area of 101st Congress Districts in Square Miles and Acres* (Washington, D.C.: Library of Congress, Congressional Research Service, 1989). All other demographic information on state land mass size, population density, and employment characteristics were extracted from *Census Bureau Summary Tapes* for the 1980 census, updated estimates when possible (Washington, D.C.: U.S. Census Bureau, 1982, 1987).

15. And that enterprise also selected a consumer safety issue about food labeling standards.

16. Katherine Reichelderfer, "Environmental Protection and Agricultural Support," in *Agricultural Policies in a New Decade,* ed. Kristen Allen (Washington, D.C.: Resources for the Future and National Planning Association, 1990); and her article with Maureen Kuwano Hinkle, "The Evolution of Pesticide Policy: Environmental Interests and Agriculture," in *The Political Economy of U.S. Agriculture,* ed. Carol S. Kramer (Washington, D.C.: Resources for the Future, 1989), pp. 147–173. Earlier Lester W. Milbrath addressed the middle-class bias of environmentalism. See *Environmentalists: Vanguard for a New Society* (Albany: State University of New York Press, 1984).

17. Logit analysis was chosen over OLS because the latter assumes a linear relationship. If the dependent variable measures a probability that an individual will display one or the other value, it makes no sense to assume that a unit change in Xs will always have the same effect on Y. In addition, for the dichotomous dependent variable, which takes the values of 0 and 1, there are two possible error terms for each case. It is most likely that error terms are heteroskedastic, which would produce biased coefficient variances. See Eric A. Hanushek and John E. Jackson, *Statistical Methods for Social Scientists* (New York: Academic Press, 1977), pp. 179–216.

To analyze each legislator's domain activity, the logit model took the following form:

$$L_1 = {}^{\log} \frac{\text{prob (issue type)}}{1 - \text{prob (issue type)}} = B_0 + B_1M_1 + B_2M_2 + B_3M_3$$

In that model, L_1 was the logit or the log of the odd ratio for each legislator, and "Prob (issue type)" represented the probability of initiating (in five separate operations) farm-benefit issues, rural issues, environmental issues, food/nutrition issues, and finally, trade issues. The percent of farm employment was represented by M_1, the population density index by M_2, and the percent of white-collar employment by M_3. Since blue-collar plus white-collar employees do not quite equal 100 percent of total employment in any congressional district, we ran only the single white-collar variable ranked high to low as our indicator.

18. Time-consuming issues were used to examine the broadest range of issues and the widest range of district effects. The accuracy of the logit model's predictions can be seen in the two-by-two frequency cells for farm benefits, rural issues, environmental issues, food/nutrition issues, and trade:

	Predicted				Predicted				Predicted				Predicted	
Observed	*No*	*Yes*		*Observed*	*No*	*Yes*		*Observed*	*No*	*Yes*		*Observed*	*No*	*Yes*
No	0	29		No	102	0		No	82	0		No	105	1
Yes	0	84		Yes	11	0		Yes	31	0		Yes	6	1

	Predicted	
Observed	*No*	*Yes*
No	83	0
Yes	30	0

19. As expected, the logit and the correlations of the determinate variables for miscellaneous issues were all insignificant. The chi-square for the model on these issues was 3.7.

20. The pods were plotted as a best-fit regression line would be, only using three dimensional representation.

21. J. Norman Reid, *Rural America: Economic Performance 1989* (Washington, D.C.: Agriculture and Rural Economy Division, Economic Research Service, U.S. Department of Agriculture, 1989). For a brief recapturing, see William P. Browne, Jerry R. Skees, Louis E. Swanson, Paul B. Thompson, and Laurian J. Unnevehr, *Sacred Cows and Hot Potatoes: Agrarian Myths in Agricultural Policy* (Boulder, Colo.: Westview, 1992), pp. 17–36, 18.

22. For a set of readings that makes use of games at different levels in international agricultural policy see *World Agriculture and the GATT*, ed. William P. Avery (Boulder, Colo.: Lynne Rienner, 1993). Especially see Robert L. Paarlberg, "Why Agriculture Blocked the Uruguay Round: Evolving Strategies in a Two-Level Game," in Avery, *World Agriculture and the GATT*, pp. 39–54.

23. Logit coefficients and standard error were .54 (.36) for farm, .35 (.51) for rural, .12 (.38) for environmental, .86 (.87) for nutrition, and .02 (.34) for trade issues for committee assignment (agriculture, ag-related, and other). For leadership, they were .08 (.55), .1 (1.1), .09 (.56), .95 (1.1), and .55 (.53). Leadership positions included all caucus leaders plus committee chairs and ranking members plus those of appropriations subcommittees.

24. The best fit was for committee and leadership run with district characteristics. Chi-square and levels of significance and correct predictions were for farm, 1.4 (.1, .73); rural, 9.4 (.1, .89); environmental, 15.5 (.1, .76); nutrition, 11.6 (.05, .95); and trade, 10.7 (.1, .73).

25. David G. Abler, in "Campaign Contributions and House Voting on Sugar and Dairy Legislation," *American Journal of Agricultural Economics* 73 (Feb. 1991): 11–17, shows the effects of the major commodity PACs. He notes that contributions, when broken down by region, do little good in places where legislators have no constituency-based reasons to vote for these programs.

26. This estimate of district production costs was made from an evolving and massive data set administered by James D. Johnson, Farm Sector Financial Analysis Branch, Economic Research Service, U.S. Department of Agriculture. Since the data are not broken down by district, the estimates are made from regional breakdowns that encompass districts in near perfect detail. Data were first obtained from the Office of the Administrator, Economic Research Service, U.S. Department of Agriculture. See "Production Cost Data by Region" (Washington, D.C.: 1991). See also Economic Research Service, *Economic Indicators of the Farm Sector: Production and Efficiency Statistics, 1990* (Washington, D.C.: Economic Research Service, U.S. Department of Agriculture, 1992).

27. Two-by-two cells for market issues and for production-control issues were, respectively:

	Predicted				Predicted	
Observed	*No*	*Yes*	*and*	*Observed*	*No*	*Yes*
No	89	0		No	104	0
Yes	24	0		Yes	9	0

28. Don F. Hadwiger and Ross B. Talbot, *Pressures and Protests: The Kennedy Farm Program and the Wheat Referendum of 1963* (San Francisco: Chandler, 1965); David E. Hamilton, *From New Day to New Deal: American Farm Policy from Hoover to Roosevelt, 1928–1933* (Chapel Hill: University of North Carolina Press, 1991); John A. Crampton, *The National Farmers Union: Ideology of a Pressure Group* (Lincoln: University of Nebraska Press, 1965).

29. When production costs and partisanship were analyzed together, the logit model had the goodness of fit 15.8, significant at the .005 level. For the individual coefficients, however, production cost was significant at .01, but partisanship was not significant. Thus, the effects of partisanship were questionable. The high standard error (five times the slope) revealed the same thing.

30. Strong constituency influences on a not dissimilar probit analysis of Senate voting can be seen in Keith Krehbiel and Douglas Rivers, "The Analysis of Committee Power: An Application to Senate Voting on the Minimum Wage," *American Journal of Political Science* 32 (November 1988): 1151–1174.

31. Richard L. Hall, "Participation and Purpose in Committee Decision Making," *American Political Science Review* 81 (March 1987): 105–127; Eileen Burgin, "Representatives' Decisions on Participation in Foreign Policy Issues," *Legislative Studies Quarterly* 16 (November 1991): 521–546.

CHAPTER 6. WHO LISTENS TO WHOM

1. Also see Steven S. Smith, *Call to Order: Floor Politics in the House and Senate* (Washington, D.C.: Brookings, 1989), pp. 250–252.

2. Barbara Sinclair, *The Transformation of the U.S. Senate* (Baltimore: Johns Hopkins University Press, 1989), pp. 51–70.

3. William P. Browne, *Private Interests, Public Policy, and American Agriculture* (Lawrence: University Press of Kansas, 1988), pp. 44–55. Alan Rosenthal also notes this in *The Third House: Lobbyists and Lobbying in the States* (Washington, D.C.: Congressional Quarterly Press, 1993), pp. 155–157.

4. Lester W. Milbrath first made this point. *The Washington Lobbyists* (Chicago: Rand McNally, 1963), pp. 140–141. Rosenthal expands in *The Third House*, especially pp. 82–111. There are numerous other studies that point out this feature.

5. Richard F. Fenno, Jr., *Home Style* (Boston: Little, Brown, 1978), pp. 1–8.

6. Ibid, pp. 18–24.

7. Ibid, p. 24. These are not all what Fenno calls "intimates."

8. Burdett A. Loomis, a great idea guy who also helped with the title, provided the astroturf analogy.

9. See Fenno, *Home Style,* p. 4.

10. Jerry R. Skees, *U.S. Farm Structure* (Lexington: Department of Agricultural Economics, University of Kentucky, 1993), p. 1. Derived from U.S. Department of Agriculture data.

11. Ibid.; Fumiaki Kubo raises the point that U.S. public policymakers only rarely felt comfortable advocating for small farmers. "Henry A. Wallace and Radical Politics in the New Deal: Farm Programs and a Vision of the New American Political Economy," *Japanese Journal of American Studies* 4, no. 1 (1991): 37–76.

12. This point on sector bifurcation is made elsewhere, in William P. Browne, "Challenging Industrialization: The Rekindling of Agrarian Protest, 1977–1987," *Studies in American Political Development* 7 (Spring 1993): 27–60.

13. As "Challenging Industrialization" indicates, these producers gradually had moved from identification with traditional farm policies and politics to an interest in broader coalitions with liberal groups as a result of their involvement in farm-protest movements of the 1977–1987 era.

14. Kenneth A. Shepsle, "The Changing Textbook Congress," in *Can the Government Govern?* ed. John E. Chubb and Paul E. Peterson (Washington, D.C.: Brookings, 1989), p. 239.

15. Christopher J. Bosso, *Pesticides and Politics: The Life Cycle of a Public Issue* (Pittsburg, Penn.: University of Pittsburg Press, 1987), pp. 246–255. This is a very different type of constituent networking than that described by Charles O. Jones for agriculture in "Representation in Congress: The Case of the House Agriculture Committee," *American Political Science Association* 55 (June 1961): 358–367.

16. Shepsle, "The Changing Textbook Congress," pp. 240–242. Because issue work is so labor-intensive, staff get more credit for it than John Kingdon found they received in voting decisions, *Congressmen's Voting Decisions* (New York: Harper and Row, 1973), pp. 201–208.

17. Richard F. Fenno, Jr., *Congressmen in Committees* (Boston: Little, Brown, 1973).

18. Arthur F. Bentley, *The Process of Government* (Chicago: University of Chicago Press, 1908).

19. Fenno, *Congressmen in Committees*, p. 276.

20. In fact, by breaking these two farm-beneficiaries down by type and reducing the number of each per category in the model, the chi-square for each dropped below 5 and the level of significance was lost.

21. The electoral margins of our member sample were quite close to those for all members as these data are available at the 60 percent level. See Norman J. Ornstein, Thomas E. Mann, and Michael J. Malbin, *Vital Statistics on Congress, 1991–1992* (Washington, D.C.: Congressional Quarterly Inc., 1992), pp. 61–62.

22. John Mark Hansen, *Gaining Access: Congress and the Farm Lobby, 1919–1981* (Chicago: University of Chicago Press, 1991).

23. J. Leiper Freeman, *The Political Process: Executive Bureau-Legislative Committee Relations,* revised edition (New York: Random House, 1965, original edition 1955); Robert H. Salisbury, John P. Heinz, Robert L. Nelson, and Edward O. Laumann, "Triangles, Networks, and Hollow Cores: The Complex Geometry of Washington Interest Representation," in *The Politics of Interests: Interest Groups Transformed,* ed. Mark P. Petracca (Boulder, Colo.: Westview, 1992), p. 131.

24. Shepsle, "The Changing Textbook Congress"; Smith, *Call to Order;* David W. Rohde, *Parties and Leaders in The Postreform House* (Chicago: University of Chicago Press, 1991); *The Postreform Congress,* ed. Roger H. Davidson (New York: St. Martins Press, 1992).

25. Sinclair, *The Transformation of the U.S. Senate.*

26. Kingdon, *Congressmen's Voting Decisions*, pp. 72–109.

27. Hansen, *Gaining Access*, pp. 26–77.

CHAPTER 7. GROUPS AND AGENCIES

1. This seems to have gone on in two stages: first, the creation of establishment organizations and, second, the formation of price policy. See Rural Sociological Society Task Force, ed., *Persistent Poverty in Rural America* (Boulder, Colo.: Westview, 1993), chap. 10.

2. John Mark Hansen, *Gaining Access: Congress and the Farm Lobby, 1919–1981* (Chicago: University of Chicago Press, 1991), stands alone in explaining that changing relationship.

3. Jess Gilbert and Carolyn Howe appear to be the only scholars who predict, in "Beyond 'State vs. Society': Theories of the State and New Deal Agricultural Policies," *American Sociological Review* 56 (April 1991): 204–220, that grassroots forces might effectively challenge Washington interests.

4. Robert H. Salisbury, John P. Heinz, Robert L. Nelson, and Edward O. Laumann, "Triangles, Networks, and Hollow Cores: The Complex Geometry of Washington Interest Representation," in *The Politics of Interests: Interest Groups Transformed,* ed. Mark P. Petracca (Boulder, Colo.: Westview, 1992), p. 131.

5. Keith Krehbiel, *Information and Legislative Organization* (Ann Arbor: University of Michigan Press, 1991), p. 227.

6. Arthur F. Bentley, *The Process of Government* (Chicago: University of Chicago Press, 1908).

7. Kevin W. Hula shows this problem and notes serious skepticism about coalition politics as a result in "Rounding Up the Usual Suspects: Forging Interest Group Coalitions in Washington" (Paper presented at the annual meeting of the Midwest Political Science Association, Chicago, April 1993).

8. Mancur Olson, Jr., *The Logic of Collective Action: Public Goods and the Theory of Groups* (Cambridge, Mass.: Harvard University Press, 1965); quote from Robert H. Salisbury, "Putting Interests Back into Interest Groups," in *Interest Group Politics*, 3d ed., ed. Allan J. Cigler and Burdett A. Loomis, (Washington, D.C.: Congressional Quarterly Press, 1991), p. 372.

9. Robert H. Salisbury, "An Exchange Theory of Interest Groups," *Midwest Journal of Political Science* 13 (February 1969): 1–32.

10. Olson, *The Logic of Collective Action;* Salisbury, "An Exchange Theory of Interest Groups." But policy is important as well to sizable numbers of the members; see William P. Browne, "Benefits and Memberships; A Reappraisal of Interest Group Activity," *Western Political Quarterly* 24 (June 1976): 258–273; Terry M. Moe, *The Organization of Interests: Incentives and the Internal Dynamics of Political Interest Groups* (Chicago: University of Chicago Press, 1980).

11. On group maintenance, see William P. Browne, "Organizational Maintenance: The Internal Operation of Interest Groups," *Public Administration Review* 37 (January/February 1977): 48–57; Jack L. Walker, "The Origins and Maintenance of Interest Groups in America," *American Political Science Review* 77 (June 1983): 390–406; Allan J. Cigler, "Organizational Maintenance and Political Activity on the Cheap: The American Agriculture Movement," in *Interest Group Politics*, 3d ed., pp. 81–107.

12. Sam Peltzman models the advantages of smaller group size in "Constituent Interests and Congressional Voting," *Journal of Law and Economics* 27 (April 1984): 181–200.

13. Those criticisms and evidence of conflict were volunteered responses and, accordingly, do not reflect all the negative views of groups and lobbyists. They do, however, reflect most conflicts. The probe question on value of information always followed questions on information sources. Criticisms and conflicts were raised in that context. When contradictions appeared evident to the interviewer, respondents were asked about how they resolved what seemed to be competing demands.

14. See note 13 for conflict responses.

15. Bosso helps explain the conflict within environmental interests by noting the third wave of the organizations emerging at the grassroots. See Christopher J. Bosso, "Adaptation and Change in the Environmental Movement," in *Interest Group Politics*, 3d ed., pp. 151–176.

16. Conflict avoidance among interest groups makes this an expected finding when constituent conflicts are intense; see William P. Browne, "Organized Interests and Their Issue Niches: A Search for Pluralism in a Policy Domain," *Journal of Politics* 52 (May 1990): 477–509.

17. Interest-group and lobbyist honesty is a point made since Lester W. Milbrath, *The Washington Lobbyists* (Chicago: Rand McNally, 1963). Respondents still contended that lobbyists seldom lied to them and never got a second chance to do so.

18. Lawrence S. Rothenberg, *Linking Citizens to Government: Interest Group Politics at Common Cause* (New York: Cambridge University Press, 1992).

19. Krehbiel, *Information and Legislative Organization;* For reasons why more interests are in demand given this response, see Valerie Heitshusen, "Strategic Lobbying by Interest Groups: The Role of Information and Institutional Change" (Paper presented at the annual meeting of the Midwest Political Science Association, Chicago, April 1993).

20. The importance of this decline can be seen in Edward V. Schneier and Bertram Gross, *Legislative Strategy: Shaping Public Policy* (New York: St. Martins, 1993), pp. 29–31. Although David B. Truman emphasizes member resources in *The Governmental Process: Political Interests and Public Opinion* (New York: Alfred A. Knopf, 1951), pp. 156–187, Schneier and Gross note his preoccupation with circumstances that minimize rather than enhance cohesion.

21. Hansen, *Gaining Access,* pp. 112–163.

22. E. E. Schattschneider, *Politics, Pressures, and the Tariff: A Study of Free Enterprise in Pressure Politics as Shown in the 1929–1930 Revision of the Tariff* (New York: Prentice-Hall, 1935); his *The Semi-Sovereign People: A Realist's View of Democracy in America* (New York: Holt, Rinehart and Winston, 1960); Earl Latham, *The Group Basis of Politics: A Study of Basing-Point Legislation* (Ithaca, N.Y.: Cornell University Press, 1952). Other works of this period tend to take the pressure view as well. See, in agriculture, Grant McConnell, *The Decline of Agrarian Democracy* (Berkeley: University of California Press, 1953).

23. Raymond A. Bauer, Ithiel de Sola Pool, and Lewis Anthony Dexter, *American Business and Public Policy: The Politics of Foreign Trade* (New York: Atherton, 1963), pp. 485–490.

24. Michael T. Hayes, *Lobbyists and Legislators: A Theory of Political Markets* (New Brunswick, N.J.: Rutgers University Press, 1981). For the market economy of agricultural interests, see Browne, "Organized Interests and Their Issue Niches," pp. 499–504.

25. Fenno's goals seem to matter. See his *Congressmen in Committees* (Boston: Little, Brown, 1973), pp. 1–14. As Stephen S. Smith and Christopher J. Deering conclude, in *Committees in Congress,* 2d ed. (Washington, D.C.: Congressional Quarterly Press, 1990), agriculture and the interior committees are election rather than policy focused.

26. Two works show this best for modern bureaucracies. Laurence E. Lynn, Jr., *Managing the Public's Business: The Job of the Government Executive* (New York: Basic Books, 1981); James Q. Wilson, *Bureaucracy: What Government Agencies Do and Why They Do It* (New York: Basic Books, 1989).

27. The several chapters in *Policy Networks: Empirical Evidence and Theoretical Considerations,* ed. Bernd Marin and Renate Maynatz (Frankfurt, Germany, and Boulder, Colo.: Campus Verlug and Westview Press, 1991), make this point, as do the earlier cited classics of iron-triangle theory. See also comments on agencies in Edward O. Laumann and David Knoke, *The Organizational State: Social Choice in National Policy Domains* (Madison: University of Wisconsin Press, 1987).

28. Salisbury, "Triangles, Networks, and Hollow Cores," p. 131.

29. William P. Browne, *Private Interests, Public Policy, and American Agriculture* (Lawrence: University Press of Kansas, 1988), pp. 150–166.

30. John R. Johannes, *To Serve the People: Congress and Constituency Service* (Lincoln: University of Nebraska Press, 1984).

31. As does David J. Webber, this section argues that legislators' goals affect their use of policy information. Members of Congress did not gravitate to other-than-agency sources of information only because analysts and politicians live in two communities with competing belief systems. See his "Political Conditions Motivating Use of Policy Information," *Policy Studies Review* 4 (August 1984): 110–118; his "State Legislators' Use of Policy Information: The Importance of Legislative Goals," *State and Local Government Review* 17 (Spring 1985): 213–218; his "Explaining Policymakers' Use of Policy Information: The Relative Importance of the Two-Community Theory Versus Decision-Maker Orientation," *Knowledge: Creation, Diffusion, Utilization* 7 (March 1986): 249–290; and his "Legislators Use of Policy Information," *American Behavioral Scientist* 30 (August 1987): 612–631.

32. Paul H. Appleby, *Policy and Administration* (University: University of Alabama Press, 1949), p. 41. For a look at careerists and political appointee conflict in the 1980s, see Robert Maranto, "Still Clashing After All These Years: Ideological Conflict in the Reagan Executive," *American Journal of Political Science* 37 (August 1993): 681–698.

33. Harold Seidman's most recent edition of his classic work is now coauthored by Robert Gilmour, *Politics, Position, and Power: From the Positive to the Regulatory State*, 4th ed. (New York: Oxford University Press, 1986), pp. 46–47, 186–188.

34. Hugh Heclo, *A Government of Strangers: Executive Politics in Washington* (Washington, D.C.: Brookings, 1977), pp. 44–45.

35. Robert A. Heineman, William T. Bluhm, Steven A. Peterson, and Edward N. Kearny, *The World of the Policy Analyst: Rationality, Values, and Politics* (Chatham, N.J.: Chatham House, 1990), pp. 118–126.

36. Lawrence C. Dodd and Richard L. Schott, *Congress and the Administrative State* (New York: Wiley, 1979). But oversight in USDA programs was never a strong suit of the administrations of the 1970s and 1980s either. See George C. Edwards III and Stephen J. Wayne, *Presidential Leadership: Politics and Policy Making*, 2d ed. (New York: St. Martins, 1990), pp. 250–252.

37. Burton I. Kaufman, *The Presidency of James Earl Carter* (Lawrence: University Press of Kansas, 1993), pp. 55–57. For an analysis of these problems, see William P. Browne, "Mobilizing and Activating Group Demands: The American Agriculture Movement," *Social Science Quarterly* 64 (March 1983): 19–34.

38. Richard P. Nathan, *The Plot that Failed: Nixon and the Administrative Presidency* (New York: Wiley, 1975); Larry Berman, *The Office of Management and Budget and the Presidency, 1921–1979* (Princeton, N.J.: Princeton University Press, 1979), pp. 105–130; Nathan, *The Administrative Presidency* (New York: Wiley, 1983).

39. Walter Williams, *Mismanaging America: The Rise of the Anti-Analytic Presidency* (Lawrence: University Press of Kansas, 1990); Peter M. Benda and Charles H. Levine, "Reagan and the Bureaucracy: The Bequest, the Promise, and the Legacy," in *The Reagan Legacy: Promise and Performance*, ed. Charles O.

Jones (Chatham, N.J.: Chatham House, 1988), pp. 102–142; Joel D. Aberbach, "The President and the Executive Branch, " in *The Bush Presidency: First Appraisals,* ed. Colin Campbell, S.J., and Bert A. Rockman (Chatham, N.J.: Chatham House, 1991), pp. 223–247. For a good analysis in defense of extreme controls, see Terry M. Moe, "The Politics of Bureaucratic Structure," in *Can the Government Govern?* ed. John E. Chubb and Paul E. Peterson (Washington, D.C.: Brookings, 1989), pp. 267–329.

40. And they complained of unexpected conflict. Cathy Marie Johnson, *The Dynamics of Conflict between Bureaucrats and Legislators* (Armonk, N.Y.: M. E. Sharpe, 1992).

41. Their importance is noted by Arnold J. Meltsner, *Policy Analysts in the Bureaucracy* (Berkeley and Los Angeles: University of California Press, 1976), pp. 36–48.

42. Scientists could well be expected as supplemental informants, given the size and scope of research in the agricultural establishment. On scientists' policy roles, see Bruce L. R. Smith, *The Advisors: Scientists in the Policy Process* (Washington, D.C.: Brookings, 1992). Agriculture's mention in the book is bleak, pp. 24, 72, and 81.

43. The primary theme of Browne, *Private Interests, Public Policy, and American Agriculture* is that there are more groups who more frequently are interacting but doing so with greater distinctiveness in their goals.

44. Hansen, *Gaining Access.* For analysis premised on a stream of time, see Richard E. Nuestadt and Ernest R. May, *Thinking in Time: The Uses of History for Decision Makers* (New York: Free Press, 1990).

45. As R. Douglas Arnold notes, local legislative ties have always mattered; see "The Local Roots of Domestic Policy," in *The New Congress,* ed. Thomas Mann and Norman J. Ornstein (Washington, D.C.: American Enterprise Institute, 1981), pp. 250–287. Earlier, see Warren E. Miller and Donald E. Stokes, "Constituency Influence in Congress," *American Political Science Review* 57 (March 1963): 45–56.

46. Hansen, *Gaining Access.*

47. Krehbiel, *Information and Legislative Organization,* p. 227.

CHAPTER 8. THE NEW COMMITTEES?

1. Clifford M. Hardin, "Congress Is the Problem," *Choices* 1 (Premier Edition 1986): 6–10; Nicholas A. Masters, "Committee Assignments in the House of Representatives," *American Political Science Review* 55 (June 1961), see p. 354; James E. Anderson, David W. Brady, and Charles Bullock III, *Public Policy and Politics in America* (North Scituate, Mass.: Duxbury Press, 1978), pp. 368–371.

2. See David R. Mayhew, *Congress: The Electoral Connection* (New Haven, Conn.: Yale University Press, 1974), pp. 81–82. He notes how well Congress is organized to meet members' electoral needs in nonzero-sum fashion.

3. Several studies find that unidimensional explanations best explain congressional behavior. Jerrold E. Schneider, *Ideological Coalitions in Congress* (Westport, Conn.: Greenwood Press, 1979); Keith Poole, "Dimensions of Interest

Group Evaluation of the U.S. Senate, 1969–1978," *American Political Science Review* 25 (March 1981): 149–163; Keith Poole and R. Steven Daniels, "Ideology, Party, and Voting in the U.S. Congress, 1959–1980," *American Political Science Review* 79 (June 1985): 323–399; Keith Poole and Howard Rosenthal, "A Spatial Model for Legislative Roll Call Analysis," *American Journal of Political Science* 29 (May 1985): 357–384; James M. Snyder, "Committee Power, Structure-Induced Equilibria, and Roll Call Votes," *American Journal of Political Science* 36 (February 1992): 1–30.

4. Stephen S. Smith and Christopher J. Deering, *Committees in Congress*, 2d ed. (Washington, D.C.: Congressional Quarterly Press, 1990), pp. 10–12; Keith Krehbiel, *Information and Legislative Organization* (Ann Arbor: University of Michigan Press, 1991). On ex post vetoes, see Kenneth A. Shepsle and Barry R. Weingast, "The Institutional Foundations of Committee Power," *American Political Science Review* 81 (March 1987): 85–104; and Keith Krehbiel, Kenneth A. Shepsle, and Barry R. Weingast, "Why are Congressional Committees Powerful?" *American Political Science Review* (September 1987): 929–945.

5. Keith Krehbiel and Douglas Rivers, "The Analysis of Committee Power: An Application to Senate Voting on the Minimum Wage," *American Journal of Political Science* 32 (November 1988): 1151–1174; John Wilkerson, "Analyzing Committee Power: A Critique," *American Journal of Political Science* 35 (August 1991): 613–623.

6. Krehbiel and Rivers, "The Analysis of Committee Power," 1163–1164.

7. Richard L. Hall, "Participation and Purpose in Committee Decision Making," *American Political Science Review* 81 (March 1987): 105–127.

8. Ibid., p. 121.

9. John R. Wright argues that contacts and their increasing frequency, as opposed to campaign contributions, are the most effective explanations of influence. That argument seems consistent with member-to-member contacts in this study, where interaction strongly influences issue choices in ways that committee position and leadership do not. See Wright's "Contributions, Lobbying, and Committee Voting in the U.S. House of Representatives," *American Political Science Review* 84 (June 1990): 417–438.

10. Respondents agreed with Fenno that a successfully integrated committee could move legislation more successfully than one that lacked cohesion. See Richard F. Fenno, Jr., *Congressmen in Committees* (Boston: Little, Brown, 1973), pp. 81–138.

11. That is, contrary to what Krehbiel argues, the committees are to an important degree composed of preference outliers, even as extreme positions, are noted in the last chapter, are avoided. Keith Krehbiel, "Are Congressional Committees Composed of Preference Outliers?" *American Political Science Review* 84 (March 1990): 149–163.

12. These reasons are similar to the most frequent reasons given for assignments to all committees. Smith and Deering, *Committees in Congress*, p. 74. Robert P. Weber shares that view, "Home Style and Committee Behavior: The Case of Richard Nolan," in *Home Style and Washington Work: Studies of Congressional Politics*, ed. Morris P. Fiorina and David W. Rohde (Ann Arbor: University of Michigan Press, 1989), pp. 81–83.

13. Stewart found more, not less, attractiveness in serving on the House agriculture committee as the nation urbanized. It was the third most attractive committee in the chamber in the 1930s and 1940s. Charles Stewart III, "Committee Hierarchies in the Modernizing House, 1875–1947," *American Journal of Political Science* 36 (November 1992): 835–856.

14. Which squares with Smith and Deering's observation of the purpose of the agriculture committees in *Committees in Congress*.

15. Membership on the four agriculture committees, both present and former, was associated quite strongly (.01) with the low end of the population index and the high end of the farm and farm-dependent employment index.

16. John Berg, "Reforming Seniority in the House of Representatives: Did it Make a Difference?" *Policy Studies Journal* 5 (Summer 1977): 437–443.

17. Joel Solkoff, *The Politics of Food: The Decline of Agriculture and the Rise of Agribusiness in America* (San Francisco: Sierra Club, 1985), pp. 195–205.

18. Boynton can predict this particular outcome because members' state constituency problems mandate that they address very specific issues. See G. R. Boynton, "Telling a Good Story: Models in Argument: Models of Understanding in the Senate Agriculture Committee," in *Argument and Critical Practices*, ed. Joseph W. Wenzel (Annandale, Md.: Speech Communications Association, 1987), pp. 429–438, and his "The Senate Agriculture Committee Produces a Homeostat," *Policy Science* 22 (March 1989): 50–81.

19. Smith and Deering, *Committees in Congress*, pp. 10–12.

20. For recent analyses of public lands politics, see C. Brant Short, *Ronald Reagan and the Public Lands: America's Conservation Debate, 1979–1984* (College Station: Texas A & M University Press, 1989); Daniel McCool, *Command of the Waters: Iron Triangles, Federal Water Development, and Indian Water* (Berkeley and Los Angeles: University of California Press, 1987).

21. William P. Browne, "Agricultural Policy Can't Accommodate All Who Want In," *Choices* 4 (First Quarter 1989): 9.

22. John G. Peters, "The 1981 Farm Bill," in *Food Policy and Farm Programs*, ed. Don F. Hadwiger and Ross B. Talbot (New York: Academy of Political Science, 1982), pp. 157–170.

23. Albert D. Cover, "Contacting Congressional Constituents: Some Patterns of Perquisite Use," *American Journal of Political Science* 24 (February 1980): 125–135; Steven J. Rosenstone and John Mark Hansen, *Mobilization, Participation, and Democracy in America* (New York: Macmillan, 1993).

24. Peters, "The 1981 Farm Bill," p. 169.

25. William P. Browne, *Private Interests, Public Policy, and American Agriculture* (Lawrence: University Press of Kansas, 1988), pp. 220–223.

26. Kenneth A. Shepsle, "The Changing Textbook Congress," in *Can the Government Govern?* ed. John E. Chubb and Paul E. Peterson (Washington, D.C.: Brookings, 1989), pp. 240–243.

27. This number would have been higher but for the tendency of agriculture staffers to sign on with a member early in the farm-bill cycle and move on to a better job after the bill's completion.

28. Charles H. Riemenschneider and Robert E. Young II, "Agriculture and the Failure of the Budget Process," in *The Political Economy of U.S. Agriculture:*

Challenges for the 1990s, ed. Carol S. Kramer (Washington, D.C.: Resources for the Future, 1989), pp. 87–102. They were, respectively, majority staff director and chief economist of the Senate agriculture committee.

29. The Senate practices multiple referral less, anyway. On average, 10 percent of Senate bills and 25 percent of House bills gain multiple referrals. Roger H. Davidson and Walter J. Oleszek, "From Monopoly to Management: Changing Patterns of Committee Deliberation," in *The Postreform Congress,* ed. Roger H. Davidson (New York: St. Martin's Press, 1992), p. 129.

30. Former agriculture-committee members reflected the views of current members: five agreed with reservations and seven disagreed with reservations. The only point these members added concerned the difficulty of making a knowledgeable policy request without having routine access to committee information. As one said, "You operate more in the dark, just politic your way in and hope. Obstacles are better understood when you're on the committee."

31. William P. Browne, "The Fragmented and Meandering Politics of Agriculture," in *U.S. Agriculture in A Global Setting: An Agenda for the Future,* ed. M. Ann Tutwiler (Washington, D.C.: Resources for the Future, 1988).

32. Fenno, *Congressmen in Committees,* chap. 1; his *Home Style* (Boston: Little, Brown, 1978), chap. 5; Hall, "Participation and Purpose in Committee Decision Making," p. 112.

33. David W. Rohde, *Parties and Leaders in the Postreform House* (Chicago: University of Chicago Press, 1991); D. Roderick Kiewiet and Mathew D. McCubbins, *The Logic of Delegation: Congressional Parties and the Appropriations Process* (Chicago: University of Chicago Press, 1991).

34. It was difficult for the committee when reapportionment tossed two of its members, David Nagle and Jim Nussel, into the Second Iowa District. Most members avoided comment on this bitterly contested race.

35. John G. Peters, "The 1977 Farm Bill Coalitions in Congress," in *The New Politics of Food,* ed. Don F. Hadwiger and William P. Browne (Lexington, Mass.: D.C. Heath, 1978), pp. 23–35; his "The 1981 Farm Bill," in *Food Policy and Farm Programs,* ed. Don F. Hadwiger and Ross B. Talbot (New York: Academy of Political Science, 1982), pp. 157–170; and William P. Browne and Mark H. Lundgren, "Farmers Helping Farmers: Constituent Services and the Development of a Grassroots Farm Lobby," *Agriculture and Human Values* 4 (Spring-Summer 1987): 11–28.

36. That probably explains why this agenda variable was found important by Hall, "Participation and Purpose in Committee Decision Making."

37. Given patterns of legislative-executive interaction, this one suggests that presidents have not set their legislative programs with agriculture in mind. See Mark A. Peterson, *Legislating Together: The White House and Capitol Hill from Eisenhower to Reagan* (Cambridge, Mass.: Harvard University Press, 1990). Nonetheless, there exists consistent evidence that since 1925 farm supports are moderately good indicators for predicting congressional votes by party. Thus, a Republican White House could be seen as likely to galvanize some partisan support for limiting agricultural expenditures. This seems to explain what happened in 1981 with a low-cost farm bill. See Aage R. Clausen, *How Congressmen*

Decide: A Policy Focus (New York: St. Martins, 1973); Barbara Sinclair, *Congressional Realignment, 1925–1978* (Austin: University of Texas Press, 1982).

38. Daniel J. Palazzolo speaks of party leaders as process managers. That is much what they appear here. See *The Speaker and the Budget: Leadership in the Post-Reform House of Representatives* (Pittsburgh: University of Pittsburgh Press, 1992). See also John J. Kornacki, ed., *Leading Congress: New Styles, New Strategies* (Washington, D.C.: Congressional Quarterly, 1990).

39. The lack of perceived national public interest in agriculture probably explains the White House's lack of interest in an agricultural legislative program. See Samuel Kernell, *Going Public: New Strategies of Presidential Leadership,* 2d ed. (Washington, D.C.: Congressional Quarterly Press, 1993).

40. Hall, "Participation and Purpose in Committee Decision Making."

41. Boynton, "Telling a Good Story," and "Ideas and Action: A Cognitive Model of the Senate Agriculture Committee," *Political Behavior* 12 (June 1990): 181–213.

42. On private-sector research and limited information as to its scope, see Vernon W. Ruttan, *Agricultural Research Policy* (Minneapolis: University of Minnesota Press, 1982), pp. 181–214; Lawrence Busch and William B. Lacy, *Science, Agriculture, and the Politics of Research* (Boulder, Colo.: Westview, 1983).

43. Information that these were the farmers most troubled by economic problems of the farm-debt crisis of the 1980s was particularly troubling to the committee, as were the demographics of an aging, over-fifty farm population that raised most crops. On exit, see Carlisle Ford Runge, "Inefficiency and Structural Adjustment in American Agriculture: Who Will Quit and Why?" In *Public Policy and Agricultural Technology: Adversity Despite Achievement,* ed. Don F. Hadwiger and William P. Browne (New York: St. Martins, 1987), pp. 33–51.

44. Shepsle, "The Changing Textbook Congress," pp. 240–243.

45. Don F. Hadwiger, *The Politics of Agricultural Research* (Lincoln: University of Nebraska Press, 1982), p. 25.

46. Wright, "Contributions, Lobbying, and Committee Voting in the U.S. House of Representatives."

47. Given the politics of research in the past two decades, there were good reasons for worry. As old and new clientele clamored for support, service providers were left politically vulnerable. Hadwiger, *The Politics of Agricultural Research.*

48. Fenno sees goals as more inseparably met in policymaking, perhaps because he focuses more on bills than on issues. See *Congressmen in Committees.*

49. Although most members disliked the agriculture committees for limiting their respect among colleagues, six members disagreed and were using the committees to emulate Foley and Dole.

50. Shepsle, "The Changing Textbook Congress."

51. Christiana McFadyen Campbell, *The Farm Bureau and the New Deal* (Urbana: University of Illinois Press, 1962). For modern comparisons and contracts with agriculture committee leadership, see C. Lawrence Evans, *Leadership*

in Committee: A Comparative Analysis of Leadership Behavior in the U.S. Senate (Ann Arbor: University of Michigan Press, 1991).

52. This can also be seen in Weber, "Home Style and Committee Behavior."

53. Hansen, *Gaining Access,* and David E. Hamilton, *From New Day to New Deal: American Farm Policy from Hoover to Roosevelt, 1928–1933* (Chapel Hill: University of North Carolina Press, 1991), argue that interest groups and agencies performed this function in the 1920s and 1930s. It seems for a modern Congress, with greater demands, that its members have been their own sources of greatest influence. See John W. Kingdon, *Congressmen's Voting Decisions,* 3d ed. (Ann Arbor: University of Michigan Press, 1989).

54. R. Douglas Arnold, *The Logic of Congressional Action* (New Haven, Conn.: Yale University Press, 1990).

55. This lack of conceptual sweep should not be surprising since, as Davidson explains, the entire move to a postreform Congress has been one of a series of gradual institutional innovations. Members are not inclined to be introspective critics of their institutions; see "The Emergence of the Postreform Congress," in *The Postreform Congress,* p. 23.

CHAPTER 9. CHANGE AND STABILITY IN AGRICULTURAL POLICY

1. Majoritarian response was a view articulated especially well by Willard J. Cochrane, *Farm Prices: Myth and Reality* (Minneapolis: University of Minnesota Press, 1958); and Dale E. Hathaway, "The Implications of Changing Political Power in Agriculture," in *Agricultural Policy in an Affluent Society,* ed. Vernon W. Ruttan et al. (New York: Norton, 1969).

2. Richard L. Hall and Frank W. Wayman, "Buying Time: Moneyed Interests and the Mobilization of Bias in Congressional Committees," *American Political Science Review* 84 (September 1990): 797–820.

3. Lawrence S. Rothenberg, *Linking Citizens to Government: Interest Group Politics at Common Cause* (New York: Cambridge University Press, 1992).

4. Allan J. Cigler, "From Protest Group to Interest Group," in *Interest Group Politics,* 2d ed., ed. Allan J. Cigler and Burdett A. Loomis (Washington, D.C.: Congressional Quarterly, 1986), pp. 55–57; William P. Browne, "Challenging Industrialization: The Rekindling of Agrarian Protest, 1977–1987," *Studies in American Political Development* 7 (Spring 1993): 14.

5. Respondents felt this went on despite convincing evidence that agricultural dependency was a condition of few congressional districts. See *U.S. Agriculture: Myth, Reality and National Policy* (Washington, D.C.: Center for National Policy, n.d.).

6. See, for an overview of farm protest, William P. Browne, "Mobilizing and Activating Group Demands: The American Agriculture Movement," *Social Science Quarterly* 64 (March 1983): 19–34; and his "Challenging Industrialization."

7. John Mark Hansen, *Gaining Access: Congress and the Farm Lobby, 1919– 1981* (Chicago: University of Chicago Press, 1991).

8. This farm influence exists despite the four-fifths of USDA budgets and personnel that are not directly allocated to farm programs. Those resources,

however, are stretched over multiple beneficiaries and policy claimants as well as to programs that indirectly benefit farmers and can be directed to farm ends.

9. John P. Heinz, Edward O. Laumann, Robert L. Nelson, and Robert H. Salisbury, *The Hollow Core: Private Interests in National Policy Making* (Cambridge: Harvard University Press, 1993), pp. 358–360; for an alternative set of policy results, see Willard W. Cochrane and C. Ford Runge, *Reforming Farm Policy: Toward a National Agenda* (Ames: Iowa State University Press, 1992).

10. Murray R. Benedict, *Farm Policies of the United States, 1790–1950* (New York: Twentieth Century Fund, 1950); Don Paarlberg, *Farm and Food Policy of the 1980s* (Lincoln: University of Nebraska Press, 1980), pp. 20–58; Kenneth L. Robinson, *Farm and Food Policies and Their Consequences* (Englewood Cliffs, N.J.: Prentice-Hall, 1989), pp. 48–68.

11. Garth Youngberg, "U.S. Agriculture Policy in the 1970's: Continuity and Change in an Uncertain World," *Policy Studies Journal* 4 (Autumn 1975): 25–31.

12. Heinz, Laumann, Nelson, and Salisbury, *The Hollow Core*, p. 338.

13. Glenn R. Parker and Roger H. Davidson, "Why Do Americans Love Their Congressmen So Much More Than Their Congress," *Legislative Studies Quarterly* 4 (February 1979): 52–61; Glenn R. Parker, "Can Congress Ever Be a Popular Institution?" in *The House at Work*, ed. Joseph Cooper and G. Calvin Mackenzie (Austin: University of Texas Press, 1981), pp. 31–55.

14. *Economic Indicators of the Farm Sector, 1991* (Washington, D.C.: Agriculture and Rural Economy Division, Economic Research Service, U.S. Department of Agriculture, 1993), pp. 65–74.

15. This division can be seen in *U.S. Agriculture* (Center for National Policy).

16. John G. Peters, "The 1977 Farm Bill Coalitions in Congress," in *The New Politics of Food*, ed. Don F. Hadwiger and William P. Browne (Lexington, Mass.: D. C. Heath, 1978), pp. 23–35; and his "The 1981 Farm Bill," in *Food Policy and Farm Programs*, ed. Don F. Hadwiger and Ross B. Talbot (New York: Academy of Political Science, 1982), pp. 157–170.

17. For an explanation of this conflict and a concurring view, see R. McGregor Cawley, *Federal Land, Western Anger: The Sagebrush Rebellion and Environmental Politics* (Lawrence: University Press of Kansas, 1993), p. 162.

18. Louis E. Swanson and Jerry R. Skees, "Issues Facing Agricultural Policy," in *Rural Policies for the 1990s*, ed. Cornelia B. Flora and James A. Christenson (Boulder, Colo.: Westview, 1991), pp. 60–75.

19. Christopher J. Bosso, "After the Movement: Environmental Activism in The 1990s," in *Environmental Policy in the 1990s*, 2d ed., ed. Norman J. Vig and Michael E. Kraft (Washington, D.C.: Congressional Quarterly Press, 1994), pp. 31–50.

20. Ibid.

21. Daniel A. Mazmanian and David Morell, "The 'NIMBY' Syndrome: Facility Siting and the Failure of Democratic Discourse," in *Environmental Policy in the 1990s*, pp. 233–249.

22. Bosso, "After the Movement," Robert Mitchell, "Public Opinion and the Green Lobby: Poised for the 1990s," in *Environmental Policy in the 1990s*, ed. Norman J. Vig and Michael E. Kraft (Washington, D.C.: Congressional Quarterly Press, 1990), p.84.

23. Jeffrey M. Berry, *Lobbying for the People* (Princeton, N.J.: Princeton University Press, 1977); Christopher J. Bosso, "Adptation and Change in the Environmental Movement," in *Interest Group Politics,* 3d ed., pp. 151–176.

24. Michael S. Greve and Fred L. Smith, Jr., eds., *Environmental Politics: Public Costs, Private Rewards* (New York: Praeger, 1992).

25. Jerry W. Calvert, "Party Politics and Environmental Policy," in *Environmental Politics and Policy: Theories and Evidence*, ed. James P. Lester (Durham, N.C.: Duke University Press, 1989), pp. 158–173.

26. Richard E. Cohen, *Washington At Work: Back Rooms and Clean Air* (New York: Macmillan, 1992).

27. Kent E. Portney, *Controversial Issues in Environmental Policy: Science vs. Economics vs. Politics* (Thousand Oaks, Calif.: Sage, 1992).

28. Michael E. Kraft, "Environmental Gridlock: Searching for Consensus in Congress," in *Environmental Policy in the 1990s,* 2d ed., pp. 97–119. Either the response is slow or the response is to reject environmental initiatives that seem suspect to the public. The failure to immediately ban saccharine (but still not to lift later the Delaney Clause, with its ban on all carcinogenic additives) in the face of a massive ad campaign featuring mad scientists as environmentalists is a case in point. See John T. Tierney and Kay Lehman Schlozman, "Congress and Organized Interests," in *Congressional Politics*, ed. Christopher J. Deering (Chicago: Dorsey, 1989), p. 221.

29. William P. Browne, *Private Interests, Public Policy, and American Agriculture* (Lawrence: University Press of Kansas, 1988); Hansen, *Gaining Access.*

30. Mark Allen Eisner, *Regulatory Politics in Transition* (Baltimore: Johns Hopkins University Press, 1993).

31. David Vogel, *Fluctuating Fortunes: The Political Power of Business in America* (New York: Basic Books, 1989), pp. 38–42; see also Alan I Marcus, *Cancer from Beef: DES, Federal Food Regulation, and Consumer Confidence* (Baltimore: Johns Hopkins University Press, 1994).

32. Richard A. Harris and Sidney M. Milkis, *The Politics of Regulatory Change: A Tale of Two Agencies* (New York: Oxford University Press, 1989); Eisner, *Regulatory Politics in Transition*, pp. 170–201.

33. The 1993 Jack In The Box fast-food chain scare is an insufficient example. That tainted hamburger episode was shortlived, localized, and never created a public interest intense enough to overcome the widespread belief that the U.S. food supply is generally safe.

34. Loree Bykerk and Ardith Maney, "Where Have All the Consumers Gone?" *Political Science Quarterly* 106 (Winter 1991–1992): 677–693.

35. Daniel W. Bromley, *Environment and Economy: Property Rights and Public Policy* (Cambridge, Mass.: Basil Blackwell, 1991), pp. 218–222.

36. James T. Bonnen and William P. Browne, "Why Is Agricultural Policy So Difficult to Reform?" in *The Political Economy of U.S. Agriculture: Challenges for the 1990s*, ed. Carol S. Kramer (Washington, D.C.: Resources for the Future, 1989), pp. 15–16.

37. Vernon W. Ruttan, *Agricultural Research Policy* (Minneapolis: University of Minnesota Press, 1982), p. 351.

38. *Report of the Country Life Commission.* Special Message from the Presi-

dent of the United States Transmitting the Report of the Country Life Commission. Senate Document 705, 60th Congress, 2nd Session (Washington, D.C.: U.S. Government Printing Office, 1909); for a review analysis, see James T. Bonnen, "Why Is There No Coherent U.S. Rural Policy?" *Policy Studies Journal* 20 (Second Quarter 1992): 190–201.

39. John D. Black, *Agricultural Reform in the United States* (New York: McGraw Hill, 1929); M. L. Wilson, "Problem of Poverty in Agriculture," *Journal of Farm Economics* 22 (February 1940): 10–33.

40. For a more detailed analysis of the following synopsis, see Rural Sociological Society Task Force, ed., *Persistent Poverty in Rural America* (Boulder, Colo.: Westview, 1993), chap. 10; and for a still more extensive review, William P. Browne, *Form over Substance, Past over Present: The Institutional Failure of National U.S. Rural Policy* (Washington, D.C.: Ford Foundation and the Aspen Institute, Rural Economic Policy Program, 1992).

41. Willard W. Cochrane, *The Development of American Agriculture: A Historical Analysis* (Minneapolis: University of Minnesota Press, 1979), pp. 378–395.

42. David E. Hamilton, *From New Day to New Deal: American Farm Policy from Hoover to Roosevelt, 1928–1933* (Chapel Hill: University of North Carolina Press, 1991), p. 88.

43. Bonnen, "Why Is There No Coherent U.S. Rural Policy?"

44. G. R. Boynton, "Telling a Good Story: Models in Argument: Models of Understanding in the Senate Agriculture Committee," in *Argument and Critical Practices,* ed. Joseph W. Wenzel (Annandale, Md.: Speech Communications Association, 1987), pp. 429–438. For the major stories within the central development story, see William P. Browne, Jerry R. Skees, Louis E. Swanson, Paul B. Thompson, and Laurian J. Unnevehr, *Sacred Cows and Hot Potatoes: Agrarian Myths in Agricultural Policy* (Boulder, Colo.: Westview, 1992).

45. Bonnen and Browne, "Why Is Agricultural Policy So Difficult to Reform?" p. 15.

46. Glenn L. Johnson and James T. Bonnen with Darrell Fienup, C. Leroy Quance, and Neill Schaller, ed., *Social Science Agricultural Agendas and Strategies* (Lansing, Mich.: Michigan State University Press, 1991), pt. III, pp. 52–53, especially on the creation of income streams.

47. Lloyd D. Bender, Bernal L. Green, Thomas F. Hady, John A. Kuehn, Marlys K. Nelson, Lem B. Perkinson, and Peggy Ross, *The Diverse Social and Economic Structure of Nonmetropolitan America* (Washington, D.C.: Agricultural and Rural Economy Division, Economic Research Service, U.S. Department of Agriculture, 1985); J. Norman Reid, *Rural America: Economic Performance 1989* (Washington, D.C.: Agriculture and Rural Economy Division, Economic Research Service, U.S. Department of Agriculture, 1989); David W. Sears, John M. Redman, Lorin D. Kusmin, and Molly S. Killian, *Growth and Stability of Rural Economies in the 1980s: Differences Among Counties* (Washington, D.C.: Agriculture and Rural Economy Division, Economic Research Service, U.S. Department of Agriculture, 1992); *U.S. Agriculture* (Center for National Policy).

48. Lynn M. Daft, "The Rural Poor," *Policy Studies Review* 2 (August 1982):

65–71; Kenneth L. Deavers, Robert A. Hoppe, and Peggy Ross, "Public Policy and Rural Poverty: A View from the 1980s," *Policy Studies Journal* 15 (December 1986): 291–309.

49. William P. Browne and J. Norman Reid, "Misconceptions, Institutional Impediments, and the Problems of Rural Governments," *Public Administration Quarterly* 14 (Fall 1990): 265–284.

50. William J. Nagle, "Federal Organization for Rural Policy," in *Towards Rural Development for the 1990's: Enhancing Income and Employment Opportunities*. Symposium Proceedings of the Congressional Research and Joint Economic Committee of Congress, Washington, D.C., 101st Congress, 1st session, Senate Print 101–150, 1990; see also Browne, *Private Interests, Public Policy, and American Agriculture*, pp. 134–137; Dennis U. Fisher and Ronald D. Knutson, "Politics of Rural Development," in *Increasing Understanding of Public Programs and Policies, 1989* (Oak Brook, Ill.: Farm Foundation, 1989), pp. 62–72.

51. Bonnen, "Why Is There No Coherent U.S. Rural Policy?" pp. 198–199; Steven J. Rosenstone and John Mark Hansen, *Mobilization, Participation, and Democracy in America* (New York: Macmillan, 1993), pp. 211–227.

52. Avery, *World Agriculture and the GATT*. However, member consideration of the effects of GATT was extensive. Twenty-six members reacted to GATT in their issue initiatives, with twelve of them attempting measures addressing conditions perceived as reflecting district inequities facing their constituents: "The GATT was still subject to domestic political concerns." Also, Kevin C. Kennedy, "The International Law and Politics of Agricultural Trade," *Journal of International Law and Practice* 2 (Winter 1993): 307–319.

53. Laumann and Knoke, *The Organizational State*, pp. 9–18.

54. Kenneth A. Shepsle, "Studying Institutions: Some Lessons from the Rational Choice Approach," *Journal of Theoretical Politics* 1, no. 2: 131–147.

55. Heinz, Laumann, Nelson, and Salisbury, *The Hollow Core*, pp. 24–58.

56. William P. Browne, "Organized Interests and Their Issue Niches: A Search for Pluralism in a Policy Domain," *Journal of Politics* 52 (May 1990): 477–509.

57. Grant McConnell, *The Decline of Agrarian Democracy* (Berkeley: University of California Press, 1953); Theodore J. Lowi, *The End of Liberalism: Ideology, Policy, and the Crisis of Public Authority* (New York: W. W. Norton, 1969).

CHAPTER 10. UNDERSTANDING THE DYNAMICS OF
CONGRESSIONAL NETWORKING

1. Roger H. Davidson, "The Emergence of the Postreform Congress," in *The Postreform Congress*, ed. Roger H. Davidson (New York: St. Martins Press, 1992), p. vii.

2. Ibid.

3. Kenneth A. Shepsle, "The Changing Textbook Congress," in *Can the Government Govern?* ed. John E. Chubb and Paul E. Peterson (Washington, D.C.: Brookings, 1989).

4. Richard F. Fenno, Jr., *Home Style* (Boston: Little, Brown, 1978); Morris P. Fiorina and David W. Rohde, eds., *Home Style and Washington Work: Studies of Congressional Politics* (Ann Arbor: University of Michigan Press, 1989).

5. Arthur F. Bentley, *The Process of Government* (Chicago: University of Chicago Press, 1908).

6. This persistence suggests a congressional self-policing effect much like that postulated by Rick K. Wilson, "An Empirical Test of Preferences for the Political Pork Barrel: District Level Appropriations for River and Harbor Legislation, 1889–1913," *American Journal of Political Science* 30 (November 1986): 729–754.

7. Charles O. Jones, "Representation in Congress: The Case of the House Agriculture Committee," *American Political Science Association* 55 (June 1961); Patrick G. O'Brien, "A Reexamination of the Senate Farm Bloc, 1921–1933," *Agriculture History* 47 (January 1973); John Mark Hansen, *Gaining Access: Congress and the Farm Lobby, 1919–1981* (Chicago: University of Chicago Press, 1991).

8. William P. Browne, *Private Interests, Public Policy, and American Agriculture* (Lawrence: University Press of Kansas, 1988), pp. 64–88.

9. As Hansen emphasizes, interest groups replaced parties as primary information sources in agriculture because they maintained a competitive advantage in knowledge of farm wants. *Gaining Access*, pp. 26–77.

10. Robert H. Salisbury, "Must All Politics Be Local: Spatial Attachments and the Politics of Place" (Paper presented at the annual meeting of the American Political Science Association, Washington, D.C., August 1993).

11. John Ferejohn, "Logrolling in an Institutional Context: A Case Study of Food Stamp Legislation," in *Congress and Policy Change*, ed. Gerald C. Wright, Jr., Leroy N. Rieselbach, and Lawrence C. Dodd (New York: Agathon Press, 1986).

12. They become another form of what Patricia A. Hurley called "issue-based voting alliances" in "Parties and Coalitions in Congress," in *Congressional Politics*, ed. Christopher J. Deering (Chicago: Dorsey, 1989), pp. 113–154.

13. Robert H. Salisbury, "Interest Structures and Policy Domains: A Focus for Research," in *Representing Interests and Interest Group Representation*, ed. William Crotty, Mildred A. Schwartz, and John C. Green (Washington, D.C.: University Press of America, 1994), p. 17.

14. Browne, *Private Interests, Public Policy, and American Agriculture*, p. 243.

15. Stephanie Greco Larson finds supportive evidence for this response. See "Information and Learning in a Congressional District: A Social Experiment," *American Journal of Political Science* 34 (November 1990): 1102–1118.

16. John R. Johannes, "Individual Outputs: Legislators and Constituency Service," in *Congressional Politics*, p. 107.

17. Steven J. Rosenstone and John Mark Hansen, *Mobilization, Participation, and Democracy in America* (New York: Macmillan, 1993), p. 226–227.

18. Steven S. Smith and Christopher J. Deering, *Committees in Congress*, 2d ed. (Washington, D.C.: Congressional Quarterly Press, 1990).

19. John P. Heinz, Edward O. Laumann, Robert L. Nelson, and Robert H. Salisbury, *The Hollow Core: Private Interests in National Policy Making* (Cambridge, Mass.: Harvard University Press, 1993).

20. Michael S. Lewis-Beck, "Agrarian Political Behavior in the United States," *American Journal of Political Science* 21 (August 1977): 543–565. Farmer behavior, as he points out, is not well studied. Evidence of marginality is from Angus Campbell, Philip E. Converse, Warren E. Miller, and Donald E. Stokes, *The American Voter* (New York: John Wiley, 1960).

21. Kenneth R. Mayer, *The Political Economy of Defense Contracting* (New Haven, Conn.: Yale University Press, 1991).

22. Interestingly, Bonier was sharply critical of Boren for breaking party ranks.

23. Edward O. Laumann and David Knoke, *The Organizational State: Social Choice in National Policy Domains* (Madison: University of Wisconsin Press, 1987), pp. 107–108.

24. Heinz, Laumann, Nelson, and Salisbury, *The Hollow Core*, p. 42.

25. Rosenstone and Hansen, *Mobilization, Participation, and Democracy in America*, p. 96. See also Jeffrey S. Hill and Kenneth C. Williams, "The Decline of Private Bills: Resource Allocation, Credit Claiming, and the Decision to Delegate," *American Journal of Political Science* 37 (November 1993): 1008–1031.

26. Steven S. Smith, *Call to Order: Floor Politics in the House and Senate* (Washington, D.C.: Brookings, 1989), pp. 55–59.

27. Ibid.

28. Jeffrey M. Berry, "An Agenda for Research on Interest Groups," in *Representing Interests and Interest Group Representation*, p. 25.

29. William P. Browne, "Organized Interests and Their Issue Niches: A Search for Pluralism in a Policy Domain," *Journal of Politics* 52 (May 1990), p. 505.

30. Berry identifies the need to clarify the domain concept in "An Agenda for Research on Interest Groups," pp. 25–26.

31. Stephen Lee Skowronek, *Building a New Administrative State: The Expansion of National Administrative Capacities, 1877–1920* (Cambridge, Mass.: Cambridge University Press, 1982).

32. Richard Rose, "Inheritance Before Choice in Public Policy," *Journal of Theoretical Politics* 2 (July 1990): 263–291.

33. Douglass C. North, "A Transaction Cost Theory of Politics," *Journal of Theoretical Politics* 2 (October 1990): 362; see also his *Institutions, Institutional Change, and Economic Performance* (Cambridge: Cambridge University Press, 1990).

34. Johnson et al. help provide this synthesis of factors. See Glenn L. Johnson and James T. Bonnen with Darrell Fienup, C. Leroy Quance, and Neill Schaller, eds., *Social Science Agricultural Agendas and Strategies* (Lansing, Mich.: Michigan State University Press, 1991).

35. Browne, "Organized Interests and Their Issue Niches," pp. 499–503.

36. William P. Browne, "Challenging Industrialization: The Rekindling of Agrarian Protest, 1977–1987," *Studies in American Political Development* 7 (Spring 1993): 25–29; see also Virginia Gray and David Lowery, "Competition,

Niches, and Organized Interests in the American States" (Paper presented at the annual meeting of the Midwest Political Science Association, Chicago, 1994).

37. This is a point made in William P. Browne, "Issue Niches and the Limits of Interest Group Influence," in *Interest Group Politics,* 3d ed., ed. Allan J. Cigler and Burdett A. Loomis (Washington, D.C.: Congressional Quarterly Press, 1991), pp. 362–366.

38. Glenn L. Johnson deserves credit for posing questions about dismantlement costs for which this answer is provided.

39. Browne, "Challenging Industrialization," pp. 11–18.

40. To understand this better, see the numerous examples in Paul A. Sabatier and Hank C. Jenkins-Smith, eds., *Policy Change and Learning: An Advocacy Coalition Approach* (Boulder, Colo.: Westview, 1993).

41. This raises a critical research question, are we, as it seems, seeing the decline of Skowronek's administrative state and all that it did?

42. For a supportive case analysis, see Andrew S. McFarland, *Cooperative Pluralism: The National Coal Policy Experiment* (Lawrence: University Press of Kansas, 1993).

APPENDIX

1. For a review of the characteristics considered to be important, see John R. Hibbing, *Congressional Careers: Contours of Life in the U.S. House of Representatives* (Chapel Hill: University of North Carolina Press, 1991), and his "Contours of the Modern Congressional Career," *American Political Science Review* 85 (June 1991): 405–428.

2. Robert H. Salisbury spent long hours helping, and James T. Bonnen and David W. Rohde also deserve special thanks for assisting after the pretests.

3. This entailed considerable prodding, and naming of members was the only item on the questionnaire where respondents hesitated. Many preferred instead to describe the characteristics of those in Congress on whom they relied.

4. No less a challenge was figuring out incentives that possible funding sources would find attractive. What would they consider sufficiently worthy of discussing that would give the principal investigator the large sums of money needed for completing the project? The answer, for our patrons, was always one of specific substantive policy information and problems. None suggested that the pursuit of disciplinary knowledge was, by itself, a worthy and fundable end.

5. The high rate of response can be attributed to superior help in securing access to members of Congress (see Acknowledgments) and to a flexible scheduler. David Hadwiger worked full-time for many weeks to play telephone tag, to schedule and reschedule meetings, and to get the principal investigator to the right place at the right time.

6. These were in the background interviews and take into account opinions of over fifty individuals.

7. Robert H. Salisbury and Kenneth A. Shepsle, "U.S. Congressman as Enterprise," *Legislative Studies Quarterly* 6 (November 1981): 559–576.

INDEX